Choral Connections...

Enhancing the Choral Experience

Glencoe McGraw-Hill

CHORAL CONNECTIONS...

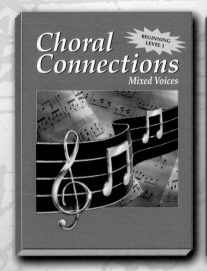
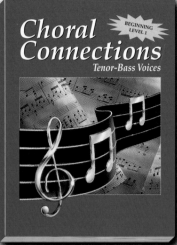
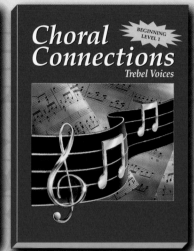
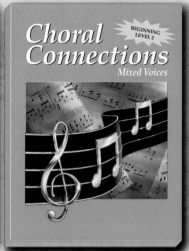

Sets a new standard for choral music

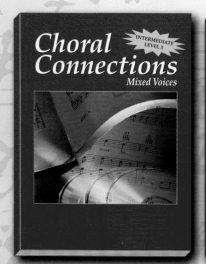
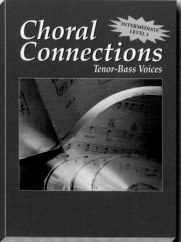
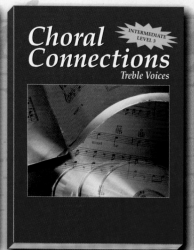
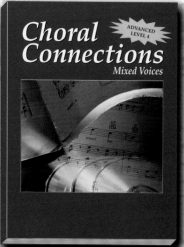

- **Provides High Quality Literature**
- **Develops Skills and Concepts**
- **Meets the National Standards**
- **Promotes Music Literacy**
- **Systematic, Objective, Authentic Assessment**
- **Organization Provides Maximum Flexibility**
- **Connects Music to the Arts and Other Academic Subject Areas**

STUDENT MATERIALS
STUDENTS SUCCEED WITH RICH MATERIALS, APPROPRIATE ACTIVITIES, AND VARIED LEARNING OPPORTUNITIES

A *four-level series of eight books:*
Beginning Level 1 - Mixed, Tenor-Bass, or Treble Voices
Beginning Level 2 - Mixed Voices
Intermediate Level 3 - Mixed, Tenor-Bass, or Treble Voices
Advanced Level 4 - Mixed Voices

El Progreso Honduras

Dindirin, Dindirindaña
Anonymous Spanish (c. 1...)
Arranged by Francis L. Guentner

South African Suite
I. Tshotsholoza

Stormy Weather
Music by Harold Arlen
Arranged by Jay Althouse

Merrily We Sing Noel
(Celebrate a Happy Hanukkah)

SAB Voices and Piano with Opti...

Sight-Singing
Sight-sing this exercise on solfège and hand signs or numbers, then on *doom.* Use your usual lighter tone, then sing with a heavier tone. Do a step-touch motion, alternating first to the right, then to the left, as you sing.

Singing: "Have Your Lamps Gone Out?"
Many spirituals and African-American folk songs originated during the slavery period. The slaves used code words in songs to represent freedom and the land of freedom.

Tell what you know about how slaves escaped on the Underground Railroad. Then read the text of "Have Your Lamps Gone Out?" to discover the meaning of the song.

Now turn to the music for "Have Your Lamps Gone Out?" on page 22.

HOW DID YOU DO?
Reading music on your own gives you the freedom to share music with others whenever you want. Think about your preparation and performance of "Have Your Lamps Gone Out?"
1. Was your part mostly melody, mostly accompaniment, or a combination of the two. Are both important? Tell why you gave the answer you did.
2. Describe heavier and lighter tone. Can you sing equally well both ways? Sing a phrase from this lesson both with lighter and heavier tone.
3. There are solos and group parts in this piece. Which do you prefer to sing? Tell how it feels to sing solo or as part of a group.
4. How well do you think your ensemble performed this piece? What was good? What could be better? What should you work on next?

Des? 21

LESSON 3
Have Your Lamps Gone Out?
Based on a traditional African-American folk song
ARRANGER: Malcolm Dalglish

CHORAL MUSIC TERMS
accompaniment
melody
tone
solo/group

VOICING
SAB

PERFORMANCE STYLE
Swaying naturally
Accompanied by dulcimer or piano

FOCUS
- Read and sing melody and accompaniment parts.
- Sing with heavier tone.
- Sing solo and group parts.

Warming Up
Rhythm Drill
Read and clap the rhythm, then say it on *doom.* Notice the grace notes.
Try this:
- Sing the rhythm on D, or *do.*
- Sing it again on A, or *la.*
- Sing it using D and A, switching as you wish.
- Sing the rhythm on B, or *la.*
- Sing it using D, A and B, or *do, so,* and *la,* improvising a melody using just these pitches.

Vocal Warm-Up
Sing these pitches using solfège and hand signs or numbers, tuning the chords carefully. Now sing the exercise on *ee.*

Have Your Lamps Gone Out?
Based on a traditional African-American folk song
Voices and Hammer Dulcimer
Malcolm Dalglish

Baroque Period

1600–1750

COMPOSERS
Claudio Monteverdi (1567–1643)
Arcangelo Corelli (1643–1713)
Henry Purcell (1659–1695)
Antonio Vivaldi (1678–1741)
Georg Philipp Telemann (1681–1750)
Johann Sebastian Bach (1685–1750)
George Frideric Handel (1685–1759)

ARTISTS
El Greco (1541–1614)
Michelangelo da Caravaggio (c. 1565–1609)
Peter Paul Rubens (1577–1640)
Frans Hals (1580–1666)
Antonio Gherardi (c. 1597– c. 16...)
Guanbattista Guarini (1...)

After completing this lesson, you should be able to:
- Describe the general characteristics of Baroque visual arts.
- Discuss the most important differences between Renaissance music and Baroque music.
- Identify at least five new musical forms of the Baroque period.
- Identify at least four major composers of the Baroque period.

The artworks of the Renaissance reflect the ideas and ideals of the period. They are balanced and restrained, they communicate a sense of calm. The next period of European history—the Baroque period, which lasted from about 1600 until around 1750—was an age of reaction against the restraint and balance of the Renaissance. Baroque artists expressed the ideals of their own time by adding emotion, decoration, and opulence to their works.

A Time of Continued Development
The explorations and developments
into the Baroque period...
and Europe...

timeline: Galileo 1564–1642 | Henry Hudson explores the Hudson River 1609 | Pilgrims land in America 1620 | Isaac Newton 1643–1727 | Quakers arrive in Massachusetts 1656

1607 Jamestown, Virginia, established settlement | 1618–1648 Thirty Years' War | 1636 Harvard College founded | 1643–1715 Reign of Louis XIV as King of France

1608 Telescope invented in Holland

During this period, instrumental music gained in importance, both in the church and as music commissioned for the entertainment of the courts of Europe. Vocal music also underwent changes. Instrumental accompaniments were increasingly added to both sacred and secular vocal works, and several new musical forms developed.

Instrumental Forms
As instrumental music grew more important, the musical instruments themselves were refined and their uses changed. The violin, previously a solo instrument, was added to ensemble groups. The harpsichord and the organ became the most important keyboard instruments.

Longer instrumental works were composed during the Baroque period. Often, these compositions consisted of several *movements,* individual pieces that sound fairly complete within themselves but are part of a longer work.

One of the new instrumental forms of the Baroque period was the **concerto grosso.** This composition for a small chamber orchestra consists of several movements.

The ornate interior decor is reflected endlessly in the Hall of Mirrors, designed by François de Cuvilliés (1698–1768). Musical embellishment and ornamentation of the Baroque period provide similar stylistic elements in compositions by Johann Sebastian Bach and his contemporaries.

1734–39. François de Cuvilliés. Hall of Mirrors, Amalienburg, Munich, Germany.

and features a moving bass line and an elaborate melody. Most of the major Baroque composers wrote concerti grossi. Among the best known are the *Four Seasons* by Antonio Vivaldi and the set of six *Brandenburg Concertos* by Johann Sebastian Bach.

Another instrumental form that developed was the **suite,** a set of musical movements, usually inspired by dances, of contrasting tempos and styles. Suites and suite-related compositions were very popular during this time; the most famous suites were those composed by Bach.

Vocal and Mixed Forms
Vocal music became more varied and notably more dramatic during the Baroque period. Sacred music continued to be predominantly choral, but instrumental accompaniment added greater variety and strength to many compositions. One of the new forms of the Baroque period was the **chorale,** or *hymn tune.* Chorales were

140   Choral Connections   Level 3 Mixed Voices

Attention to detail, particularly in direct and reflected light in mirrors and doorways, characterizes this work of Diego Velázquez (1599–1660). The challenge to the viewer to find all the images in Los Meninas expands the challenge to comprehend the intricacies in a Bach fugue or concerto, representative musical works of the same period.

1649–51. Diego Velázquez. Las Meninas. 10 ft. 5 in. x 9 ft. ¾ in. (10'5" x 9'). Museo del Prado, Madrid, Spain.

Historical Connections Overhead from Resource Binder

Each text is divided into three sections:

1. *Teaching Lessons* systematically build skills and concepts

Each lesson includes:

- Focus
- Choral Music Terms
- Warm-Up Exercises
- Sight-Singing Exercises
- Assessment

Vocal Warm-Up 2
Sing this exercise using solfège or numbers. Repeat, using the last pitch (*re*) as *do*. After the first few, do this by ear. Hear the relationships so the new tonic chord is in tune.

Sight-Singing
Sight-sing this exercise using solfège. Notice that when more than one part is written on a staff, the direction of stems tells you which noteheads are your part.

LESSON 5
The Road Less Traveled

COMPOSER: Carl Strommen
TEXT: Carl Strommen

CHORAL MUSIC TERMS
key changes
phrase release
sixteenth notes

VOICING
SAB

PERFORMANCE STYLE
With feeling
Accompanied by piano

FOCUS
- Read and clap rhythms, including sixteenth notes
- Recognize and sing key changes accurately
- Perform correct phrase releases

Warming Up
Rhythm Drill
Practice reading and clapping these rhythms. Use Maelzel's metronome of ♩=76 as a tempo. Create longer phrases by clapping different combinations, one pattern after another.

Vocal Warm-Up 1
Sing this chordal warm-up on solfège and hand signs or numbers by half steps. Tune each chord quickly.

The Road Less Traveled
SAB Voices and Piano

Words and Music by
Carl Strommen

♪ BAROQUE CONNECTIONS
Listening to...
Baroque Music

CHORAL SELECTION

Handel — *Messiah,* "Hallelujah" Chorus
George Frideric Handel (c. 1685–1759) was a contemporary of Johann Sebastian Bach. Handel's compositions, great in number, were mostly English oratorios and Italian operas. Of all of his works, *Messiah* is the most well known. It is also exceptional in that it has no plot and is based on Old and New Testament passages of the Bible. *Messiah* was written in less than a month and was first performed in Ireland in 1741. It did not gain favor in England until a decade after its first performance in 1742. However, since that time it has grown to have tremendous popularity, being one of the favorite musical works of the Christmas and Easter holiday seasons.

INSTRUMENTAL SELECTION

Bach — Organ Fugue in G Minor (Little Fugue)
Johann Sebastian Bach (c. 1685–1750) was born into a family of musicians. Through his lifetime, he held many positions as organist and church musician. The longest standing being at Weimar, Cothen, and Leipzig. During his employment at Cothen, Bach composed mostly secular works (at the request of the prince, his benefactor). For nearly all of his career as a composer he wrote music for the organ. His organ music has a characteristic use of the obbligato pedals, contributing yet again to the elaborate style that we associate with music from the Baroque period.

♪ BAROQUE CONNECTIONS
Introducing...
"Werfet Panier Auf Im Lande"

Georg Philipp Telemann

Setting the Stage
"Werfet Panier Auf Im Lande," attributed to Georg Philipp Telemann, is based on Jeremiah's prophecy in the Bible predicting the destruction of Babylon because of its sinful ways. Keep this theme in mind so that you don't become carried away with the danceable quality of the music. If Telemann meant for there to be any joy in the music, it is in troops marching to war accompanied by the stirring music of a military band with its trumpet calls.

Meeting the Composer
Georg Philipp Telemann
In his own time, Georg Philipp Telemann (c. 1681–1767) was one of the most highly esteemed of all German musicians. Although he was one of the most prolific composers of all time, he composed in the shadows of Bach and Handel. Perhaps for this reason, this great Baroque composer is hardly more than a name in the twentieth century. Telemann's output of music includes some 40 operas, 700 church cantatas, 44 Passions, 600 French overtures, and innumerable other orchestral, chamber, and harpsichord compositions.

♪ Singing: "Werfet Panier Auf Im Lande"
Music is often played when people gather for special events. Describe the music you would expect to hear at a football game. What kind of music would you expect to hear at a wedding? Describe the music you would expect to hear at a funeral. If selected appropriately, music can enhance the mood of any occasion.

Now turn to the music for "Werfet Panier Auf Im Lande" on page 146.

HOW DID YOU DO? Think about your preparation and performance of "Werfet Panier Auf Im Lande."
1. Describe how you perform 6/8 meter. Choose a phrase to sing to demonstrate your ability to perform in 6/8 meter.
2. Describe the mood of "Werfet Panier Auf Im Lande," and tell how you performed the music to enhance the mood.
3. Where might you suggest that this piece be performed?
4. Tell why you think this piece is considered an exemplary model of Baroque vocal music. Give specific musical characteristics.

---

2. *Making Historical Connections*

- Historical narrative
- Listening selections accompanied by listening maps
- Historical literature

BAROQUE LESSON
Werfet Panier Auf Im Lande

COMPOSER: Georg Philipp Telemann (1681–1767)
TEXT: Jeremiah 51:27–29

CHORAL MUSIC TERMS
articulation
Baroque
interpretation
mode
motet
6/8 meter

VOICING
SATB

PERFORMANCE STYLE
Rhythmically, like a march
A cappella

FOCUS
- Read and sing in 6/8 meter.
- Interpret a piece to convey a specific mood.

Warming Up
Vocal Warm-Up
Before you begin singing, concentrate on relaxing the jaw and muscles that surround the jaw area, including your neck muscles. Roll your shoulders forward and backward, shake out your arms, move your head/neck area forward, back, and from side to side.
Now, sing this exercise on *mah* or *näh* to develop a resonant tone. Separate the repeated tones for clarity. Move up or down by half steps on each repeat.

Sight-Singing
Before singing this exercise out loud, sing it in your mind. Look at the key signature, meter signature, rhythms, and melodic leaps. Where will you need to really work for accuracy? Now sight-sing this exercise using solfège and hand signs or numbers. What mood does it convey? What can you do to help your singing enhance this mood?

---

3. *Additional Performance Selections*

- Patriotic
- Holiday
- Multicultural
- Proven Audience Pleasers

TEACHER WRAPAROUND EDITIONS

SAVE TIME, BUILD SKILLS, DELIVER EXCELLENT PERFORMANCE

1. Flexible Lesson Design

Clear, logical, yet flexible directions.

Each lesson, linked to one musical selection, includes:

- **Focus**
- **Objectives—clear and measurable**
- **Choral Music Terms**
- **Warm-Ups develop rhythm, vocal, and sight-singing skills**
- **Suggested Teaching Sequence builds skills and concepts**
- **Assessments match objectives**

2. Three Assessment Options

- **Allow informal checkpoints and formal assessments**
- **Can be compiled to create a portfolio showing growth**
- **May be done by teacher, student, peers, or a combination**

The Extension section of each lesson offers:

- Teaching strategies
- Background information
- Vocal development strategies
- Music literacy activities
- Enrichment Extensions
- Curriculum Connections

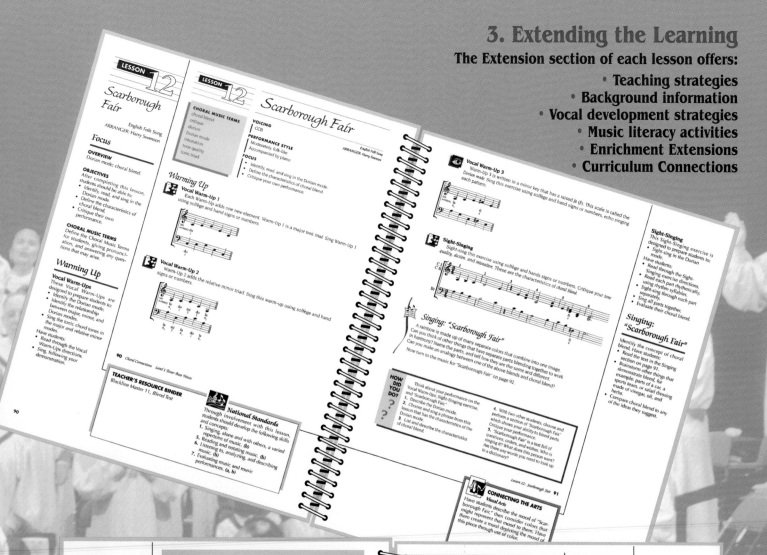

ADDITIONAL RESOURCES
- ADD DEPTH, ALTERNATIVES AND OPTIONS
- INVOLVE STUDENTS IN THEIR OWN LEARNING
- DEVELOP LISTENING, NOTATION, AND CRITICAL THINKING SKILLS

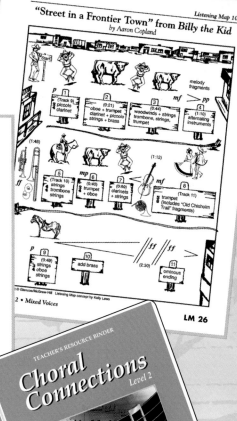

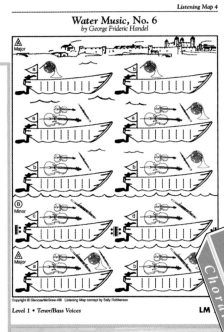

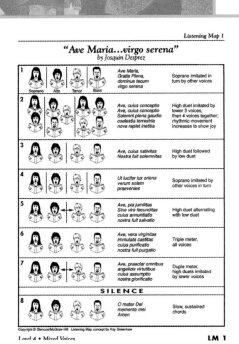

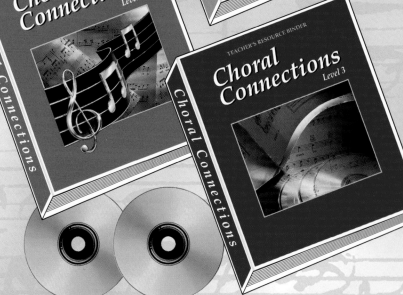

The Listening Program

Available as an optional CD program, the listening selections include:
- **Two selections from each historical period, accompanied by listening maps**
- **A correlation chart to the lessons**

The Teachers Resource Binder

A separate set of teaching tools involve students in their own learning. The binder, which accompanies each level, includes:

- Full-color fine art transparencies to enhance the historical narratives.
- Reproducible blackline masters providing:
  - basic resource information
  - music theory worksheets
  - pronunciation guides
  - listening maps
  - assessment masters

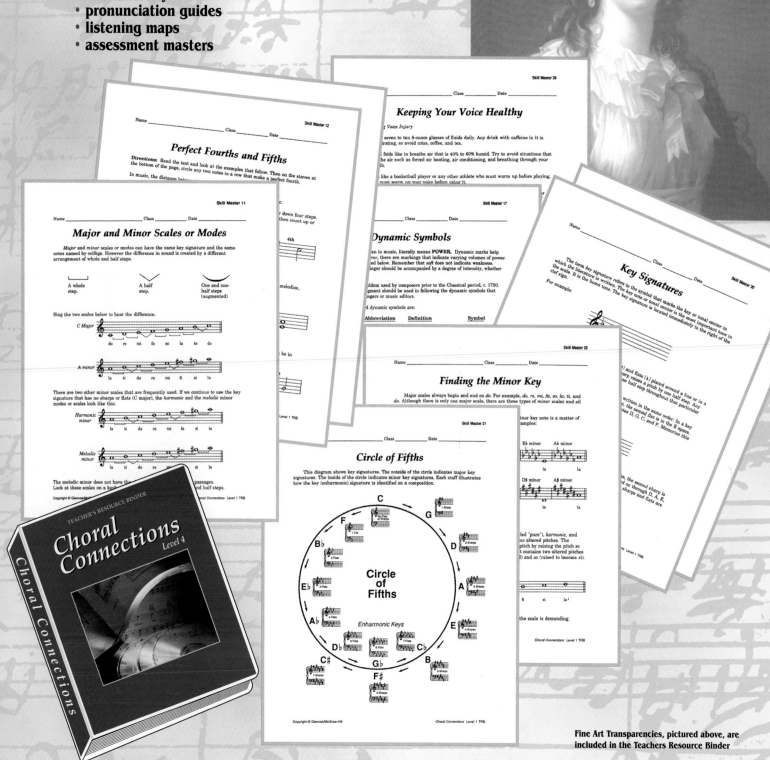

Fine Art Transparencies, pictured above, are included in the Teachers Resource Binder

PERFORMANCE LITERATURE AND TEACHING LESSONS

BEGINNING LEVEL 1 MIXED VOICES

24 selections

LESSONS

1. Bound for Jubilee-*Joyce Elaine Eilers*
2. A Red, Red Rose-*Daniel Burton*
3. Over There-*Jerry Ray*
4. Dare to Dream!-*Niel Lorenz and Mary Lynn Lightfoot*
5. The Tiger-*Sherri Porterfield*
6. Shalom, My Friends-*Douglas E. Wagner*
7. Whisper! Whisper!-*Jay Althouse*
8. Mansions in the Sky-*Carl Strommen*
9. Down by the Riverside-*Brad Printz*
10. Something Told the Wild Geese-*Sherri Porterfield*
11. Praise Ye the Lord, All Nations-*Johann S. Bach*
12. Wiegenlied-*Johannes Brahms and Sherri Porterfield*
13. Nightfall-*Lou Williams-Wimberly*
14. Riu, Riu, Chiu-*Linda Steen Spevacek*

MAKING HISTORICAL CONNECTIONS

Renaissance Period
Kyrie Eleison-*Antonio Lotti*

Baroque Period
Alleluia from *For Us a Child Is Born*-*Johann S. Bach*

Classical Period
Dies Irae from *Requiem*-*Wolfgang A. Mozart*

Romantic Period
In Stiller Nacht-*Johannes Brahms*

Contemporary Period
River, Sing Your Song-*Eugene Butler*

ADDITIONAL PERFORMANCE SELECTIONS
I Hear Liberty Singing-*Greg Gilpin*
It's Time to Fly Away-*Joyce Elaine Eilers*
Shenandoah-*Arranger Brad Printz*
Three Yoruba Native Songs of Nigeria-
Arrangers Henry Leck and Prince Adeniyi
The Tree of Peace-*Arranger Fred Bock*

FEATURED LISTENING SELECTIONS
Cantate Ninfe-*Luca Marenzio*
Saltarello-*Anonymous*
Cantata No. 80, A Mighty Fortress is Our God, No. 8
Brandenburg Concerto No. 2, First Movement-
Johann S. Bach
Non So Pui from *The Marriage of Figaro*, Act 1,
Scenes 6 and 7-*Wolfgang A. Mozart*
Eine kleine Nachtmusik, First Movement-
Wolfgang A. Mozart
Habanera from *Carmen*, Act 1-*Georges Bizet*
The Great Gate of Kiev and The Hut on Fowl's Legs
from *Pictures at an Exhibition*-
Modest Mussorgsky
Mister Tambourine Man-*Bob Dylan*
The Young Person's Guide to the Orchestra-
Benjamin Britten

BEGINNING LEVEL 1 TENOR-BASS VOICES

26 selections

LESSONS

1. The Colorado Trail-*Arranger Jennifer B. Scoggin*
2. Lord, In the Morning-*R. Paul Drummond*
3. Me Gustan Todas-*Arranger Donald W. Crouch*
4. Drink to Me Only with Thine Eyes-
Arranger Robert Lawrence
5. I'm Bound Away-*Donald Moore*
6. Viva Tutti-*Ralph Hunter*
7. My Love Is Like a Rose-*Eugene Butler*
8. Emmanuel's Birth-*Arranger Bobby L. Siltman*
9. My Highland Lassie, O!-*Tullye B. Norton*
10. Bound for Jubilee-*Joyce Elaine Eilers*
11. Masters In This Hall-*Chartres/Arranger David Burger*
12. Scarborough Fair-*Arranger Harry Swenson*
13. Something Told the Wild Geese-*Sherri Porterfield*
14. Sing Me a Song of a Lad That Is Gone-
Sherri Porterfield
15. Steal Away-*Arranger Bobby L. Siltman*

MAKING HISTORICAL CONNECTIONS

Renaissance Period
Ah, Robin, Gentle Robin-*William Cornysh*

Baroque Period
Praise the King-*George Frideric Handel*

Classical Period
Praise We Sing to Thee-*Franz Joseph Haydn*

Romantic Period
Abendlied-*Felix Mendelssohn*

Contemporary Period
Jubilate Deo-*Linda Steen Spevacek*

ADDITIONAL PERFORMANCE SELECTIONS
Old Dan Tucker-*Arranger Pat Willet*
Medley for Christmas-*Arranger Bobby L. Siltman*
Vive l'Amour-*Arranger Bobby L. Siltman*
Now Is the Month of Maying-*Thomas Morley*
My Lord, What a Morning-*Arranger Lois B. Land*
I Want to Be a Sailor-*Joseph M. Martin*

FEATURED LISTENING SELECTIONS
Kyrie from *L'homme armé* Mass-*Guillaume Dufay*
Saltarello-*Anonymous*
Cantata No. 80, A Mighty Fortress is Our God,
No. 5-*Johann S. Bach*
Water Music, No. 6-*George Frideric Handel*
Trio from *The Marriage of Figaro*, Act 1, Scenes
6 and 7-*Wolfgang A. Mozart*
Piano Concerto in G Major, First Movement-
Wolfgang A. Mozart
Children's Chorus from *Carmen*, Act I-
Georges Bizet
Symphonie fantastique, Fifth Movement-
Hector Berlioz
Mister Tambourine Man-*Bob Dylan*
Symphonic Dances from *West Side Story*-
Leonard Bernstein

BEGINNING LEVEL 1 TREBLE VOICES

27 selections

LESSONS

1. This Train Goes Marching In-*Arranger Sandy Feldstein*
2. Lift Up Your Voice, Alleluia-*Sally K. Albrecht*
3. No Well, No Well!-*Steve Kupferschmid*
4. Peace in Twelve Languages-*Thomas Knight*
5. Sing a Joyful Song-*Sally K. Albrecht*
6. Kwanzaa-*Teresa Jennings*
7. We Sing Feliz Navidad-*Carl Strommen*
8. In the Meadow-*Arranger Beatrice P. Krone*
9. Dear Nightingale, Awake-*Arranger Gerhard Track*
10. The First Noel/Pachelbel's Canon-*Johann Pachelbel*
11. Annabel Lee-*Edna Lewis and John Mitri Habash*
12. A la Nanita Nana-*Arranger David Eddleman*
13. For the Beauty of the Earth-*John Rutter*
14. Joshua Fit the Battle of Jericho-
Arranger Warren Williamson
15. The Ash Grove-*Arranger Thurlow T. Steffy*

MAKING HISTORICAL CONNECTIONS

Renaissance Period
Non Nobis, Domine-*William Byrd*

Baroque Period
Sound the Trumpet-*Henry Purcell*

Classical Period
Ave Verum Corpus-*Wolfgang A. Mozart*

Romantic Period
Evening Song (Abendlied)-*Felix Mendelssohn-
Bartholdy*

Contemporary Period
Linden Lea-*Ralph Vaughan Williams*

ADDITIONAL PERFORMANCE SELECTIONS
Alexander's Ragtime Band-*Irving Berlin*
America, of Thee I Sing!-*Mary Donnelly and
George L. O. Strid*
Let Freedom Sing!-*Mary Lynn Lightfoot*
'Round the Riverside-*Arranger Saundra Berry Musser*
Chumbara-*Arranger Aden G. Lewis*
The Kalanta of the New Year-*Malcolm Dalglish*
Three Sephardic Folk Songs
  I. Irme Quiero-*Arranger The Western Wind*
  II. Rahelica Baila-*Arranger Lawrence Bennett*
  III. Xinanáy-*Elliot Z. Levine*

FEATURED LISTENING SELECTIONS
Fair Phyllis-*John Farmer*
Saltarello-*Anonymous*
There Were Shepherds from *Messiah*-
George Frideric Handel
Prelude and Fugue in C Minor, from *The Well-
Tempered Clavier*, Book 1-*Johann S. Bach*
Non So Pui from *The Marriage of Figaro*, Act 1,
Scenes 6 and 7-*Wolfgang A. Mozart*
Piano Sonata in C Minor (*Pathétique*), First
Movement-*Ludwig van Beethoven*
Dans l'Air from *Carmen*, Act I-*Georges Bizet*
A Midsummer Night's Dream, Overture-
Felix Mendelssohn
My Funny Valentine-*Richard Rodgers*
Music for Strings, Percussion and Celesta, Fourth
Movement-*Béla Bartók*

BEGINNING LEVEL 2 MIXED VOICES

27 selections

LESSONS

1 The Lord of All Creation-*Johann Michael Haydn*
2 In These Delightful Pleasant Groves-*Henry Purcell*
3 Have Your Lamps Gone Out?-*Arranger Malcolm Dalglish*
4 O Won't You Sit Down-*Arranger Arthur Hardwicke*
5 The Road Less Traveled-*Carl Strommen*
6 Carol of the Bells-*Mikola D. Leontovich*
7 Cantate Domino-*John Carter*
8 Agnus Dei-*Wolfgang A. Mozart*
9 Early One Morning-*Arranger Noble Cain*
10 Domine Deus-*Jacob Regnart*
11 Sanctus-*Franz Joseph Haydn*
12 Scarborough Fair-*Arranger Willard A. Palmer*
13 Agnus Dei-*Audrey Snyder*
14 Zamba for You-*Ariel Ramirez*

MAKING HISTORICAL CONNECTIONS

Renaissance Period
My Heart Is Offered Still to You-*Orlande de Lassus*

Baroque Period
Gloria in Excelsis-*Antonio Vivaldi*

Classical Period
Gloria from *Heiligmesse*-*Franz Joseph Haydn*

Romantic Period
Song of the Lark-*Felix Mendelssohn*

Contemporary Period
The Snow-White Messenger-*Arranger Lloyd Pfautsch*

ADDITIONAL PERFORMANCE SELECTIONS
Ezekiel's Wheel-*Philip Kern*
Like an Eagle-*Carl Strommen*
Merrily We Sing Noel-*B. Dardess*
Stormy Weather-*Harold Arlen*
South African Suite-*Henry Leck*
  I. Tshotsholoza
  II. Siyahamba
  III. Gabi Gabi
Dindirin, Dindirindaña-*Anonymous*
Freedom Is Coming-*Henry H. Leck*
Hymn of Promise-*Natalie Sleeth*

FEATURED LISTENING SELECTIONS
Gloria from *Pope Marcellus* Mass-*Giovanni Pierluigi da Palestrina*
Two Dances-*Tylman Susato*
Hallelujah! from *Messiah*-*George Frideric Handel*
Spring, from *The Four Seasons*, Third Movement-*Antonio Vivaldi*
Credo from *Lord Nelson Mass*-*Franz Joseph Haydn*
Symphony No. 100 in G Major (*Military*), Second Movement-*Franz Joseph Haydn*
The Song of the Earth, Third Movement-*Gustav Mahler*
Symphony No. 5 in C Minor, First Movement-*Ludwig van Beethoven*
Alexander Nevsky, Seventh Movement-*Sergei Prokofiev*
Street in a Frontier Town from *Billy the Kid*, Scene 1-*Aaron Copland*

INTERMEDIATE LEVEL 3 MIXED VOICES

25 selections

LESSONS

1 Dream a Dream-*Ed Robertson*
2 The Road Less Traveled-*Carl Strommen*
3 Nginani Na-*Arranger Caroline Lyon*
4 Music, When Soft Voices Die-*Philip Young*
5 Cantaremos-*Ramón Noble*
6 Laudate Nomen Domini-*Christopher Tye*
7 Pål På Haugen-*Arranger Bradley Ellingboe*
8 It Was a Lover and His Lass-*Michael Larkin*
9 I Hear a Sky-Born Music-*Lois Land*
10 Four Spanish Christmas Carols-*Arranger Noe Sanchez*
11 Alleluia-*Will James*
12 Flow Gently, Sweet Afton-*Arranger John Leavitt*
13 Jesu Dulcis Memoria-*Tomás Luis de Victoria*
14 May the Road Rise to Meet You-*David Hamilton*
15 In Memoria Aeterna-*Antonio Vivaldi*

MAKING HISTORICAL CONNECTIONS

Renaissance Period
O Domine Jesu Christe-*Giovanni Pierluigi da Palestrina*

Baroque Period
Werfet Panier Auf Im Lande-*Georg Philipp Telemann*

Classical Period
Sanctus-*Luigi Cherubini*

Romantic Period
If I Should See You All Alone-*Felix Mendelssohn*

Contemporary Period
Still, Still, Still-*Arranger John Rutter*

ADDITIONAL PERFORMANCE SELECTIONS
Shut De Do-*Randy Stonehill*
The River-*Garth Brooks and Victoria Shaw*
Look-A That Star-*Jay Althouse*
A Holiday Wish-*Jay Althouse*
El Progreso Honduras-*Elliot Z. Levine*

FEATURED LISTENING SELECTIONS
As Vesta Was Descending-*Thomas Weelkes*
Ricercar in the Twelfth Mode-*Andrea Gabrieli*
Hallelujah Chorus from *Messiah*-*George Frideric Handel*
Organ Fugue in G Minor (*Little Fugue*)-*Johann S. Bach*
Là Ci Darem la Mano from *Don Giovanni*, Act I-*Wolfgang A. Mozart*
Symphony No. 40 in G Minor, First Movement-*Wolfgang A. Mozart*
La Donna è Mobile from *Rigoletto*, Act III-*Guiseppe Verdi*
Symphonie fantastique, Fourth Movement (March to the Scaffold)-*Hector Berlioz*
Tonight from *West Side Story*-*Leonard Bernstein*
Theme and Variations on "Simple Gifts" from *Appalachian Spring*, Section 7-*Aaron Copland*

INTERMEDIATE LEVEL 3 TENOR-BASS VOICES

26 selections

LESSONS

1 An Irish Blessing-*Donald Moore*
2 Ah, Robin, Gentle Robin-*William Cornysh*
3 Blow, Blow, Thou Winter Wind-*Sherri Porterfield*
4 Who Are the Brave-*Joseph M. Martin*
5 Streets of Laredo-*Arranger Merrilee Webb*
6 Two Folk Songs for Male Voices-*Arranger John Rutter*
7 Down in the Valley-*Arranger George Mead*
8 Sanctus-*Franz Schubert*
9 Ya Viene la Vieja-*Arranger Jim Leininger*
10 There Comes a Ship Full-Laden-*Heinrich Schütz*
11 Workin' on the Railroad!-*Arranger Donald Moore*
12 My Love for You-*Ludwig van Beethoven*
13 Two Humorous Songs-*Joseph Haydn/Christian Felix Weisse*
14 Come, Praise the Lord-*William Crotch*
15 Gloria-*Franz Schubert*

MAKING HISTORICAL CONNECTIONS

Renaissance Period
Let Thy Merciful Ears, O Lord-*Thomas Weelkes*

Baroque Period
Exsultate Justi-*Lodovico Viadana*

Classical Period
Come, O Jesus, Come to Me-*Maria Luigi Cherubini*

Romantic Period
Schön Blümelein-*Robert Schumann*

Contemporary Period
Do You Fear the Wind?-*Leland B. Sateren*

ADDITIONAL PERFORMANCE SELECTIONS
Hail to Our Audience!-*Ralph Wilkinson*
Dance of the One-Legged Sailor-*Brent Pierce*
Deshi-*Brent Pierce*
The Crawdad Song-*Arranger Aden Lewis*
O Mary, Don't You Weep-*Arranger Raymond Rhea*
Echo Carol-*Arranger Paul Royer*

FEATURED LISTENING SELECTIONS
As Vesta Was Descending-*Thomas Weelkes*
Ricercar in the Twelfth Mode-*Andrea Gabrieli*
For unto Us a Child Is Born from *Messiah*-*George Frideric Handel*
Brandenburg Concerto No. 5 in D Major, Third Movement-*Johann S. Bach*
Catalog Aria from *Don Giovanni*, Act I-*Wolfgang A. Mozart*
Trumpet Concerto in E Flat Major, Third Movement-*Franz Joseph Haydn*
Erlkönig (Erlking)-*Franz Schubert*
Transcendental Étude No. 10 in F Minor-*Franz Liszt*
Tonight from *West Side Story*-*Leonard Bernstein*
Concerto Grosso 1985, First Movement-*Ellen Taaffe Zwilich*

PERFORMANCE LITERATURE AND TEACHING LESSONS
(continued)

INTERMEDIATE LEVEL 3 TREBLE VOICES

25 selections

LESSONS
1 The Rainbow Comes and Goes-*Lois Land*
2 Behold, a Tiny Baby-*Arranger Mary Lynn Lightfoot*
3 Whispering Pine-*Eugene Butler*
4 Joseph's Lullaby-*Russell Schulz-Widmar*
5 Welcome Now in Peace-*Arranger Judith Herrington*
6 Silent the Forests-*Eugene Butler*
7 My Beloved-*Johannes Brahms*
8 Fresh Is the Maytime-*Johann Hermann Schein*
9 Who Has Seen the Wind?-*Robert E. Kreutz*
10 I Never Saw a Moor-*Michael Larkin*
11 Arruru-*Ruth Dwyer/Thomas Gerber*
12 Peace Today Descends from Heaven-
   Alessandro Grandi
13 Os Justi-*Eleanor Daley*
14 Dance On My Heart-*Allen Koepke*

MAKING HISTORICAL CONNECTIONS
Renaissance Period
   I Go Before, My Charmer-*Thomas Morley*

Baroque Period
   O Death, None Could Conquer Thee-
   Johann Sebastian Bach

Classical Period
   Holy, Holy, Holy-*Wolfgang A. Mozart*

Romantic Period
   Grüss-*Felix Mendelssohn*

Contemporary Period
   Nigra Sum-*Pablo Casals*

ADDITIONAL PERFORMANCE SELECTIONS
   Gloria-*Joseph Haydn*
   I Wonder as I Wander-*Richard Osborne*
   Native American Spring Songs-*Nancy Grundahl*
   Festival Alleluia-*Allen Pote*
   Wisdom and Understanding-*Kent A. Newbury*
   Beautiful Yet Truthful-*Lloyd Pfautsch*

FEATURED LISTENING SELECTIONS
   As Vesta Was Descending-*Thomas Weelkes*
   Ricercar in the Twelfth Mode-*Andrea Gabrieli*
   Chorale from Cantate No. 140 (*Wachet auf, ruft uns
   die Stimme*), Seventh Movement-*Johann S. Bach*
   Suite No. 3 in D Major, Air-*Johann S. Bach*
   Lá Ci Darem la Mano from *Don Giovanni*, Act I-
   Wolfgang A. Mozart
   Symphony No. 94 in G Major (*Surprise*),
   Second Movement-*Franz Joseph Haydn*
   Quartet from *Rigoletto*, Act III-*Giuseppe Verdi*
   Romance in G Minor for Violin and Piano No. 2-
   Clara Schumann
   Lost Your Head Blues-*Bessie Smith*
   The Firebird, Scene 2-*Igor Stravinsky*

ADVANCED LEVEL 4 MIXED VOICES

29 selections

LESSONS
1 The One Who Stands Alone-*Joseph Martin*
2 Siyahamba-*Donald Moore*
3 The Prayer of Saint Francis-*René Clausen*
4 Starlight Lullaby-*Philip Lane*
5 God Rest You Merry, Gentlemen-
   James Neal Koudelka
6 Papillon, Tu Es Volage-*Jonathan Thompson*
7 I Saw Three Ships-*Edwin Fissinger*
8 African Noel-*André J. Thomas*
9 The Lord Is My Shepherd-*Allen Pote*
10 Forest Cool, Thou Forest Quiet-*Johannes Brahms*
11 Keep Your Lamps!-*André J. Thomas*
12 Blessed Are the Pure of Heart-*Woldemar Voullaire*
13 V'amo di Core-*Wolfgang A. Mozart*
14 I Will Lay Me Down in Peace-*Healey Willan*
15 The Cloths of Heaven-*Adolphus Hailstork*
16 Ave Maria-*Franz Biebl*

MAKING HISTORICAL CONNECTIONS
Renaissance Period
   Ave Regina Coelorum-*Orlande de Lassus*

Baroque Period
   Alleluia-*Giovanni Battista Pergolesi*

Classical Period
   Come, Lovely Spring-*Franz Joseph Haydn*

Romantic Period
   So Wahr die Sonne Scheinet-*Robert Schumann*

Contemporary Period
   I Hear America Singing-*André J. Thomas*

ADDITIONAL PERFORMANCE SELECTIONS
   Over the Rainbow-*Harold Arlen*
   Three Canticles for Treble Voices-*Paul Liljestrand*
   Who Is He in Yonder Stall?-*Robert H. Young*
   42nd Street-*Harry Warren*
   Blue Moon-*Richard Rodgers*
   Desde el Fondo de Mi Alma-*Domingo Santa Cruz*
   Georgia on My Mind-*Hoagy Carmichael*
   Love Never Ends-*Elizabeth Volk*

FEATURED LISTENING SELECTIONS
   Ave Maria-*Josquin Desprez*
   The Most Sacred Queene Elizabeth, Her Galliard-
   John Dowland
   Zion Hört die Wächter Singen from Cantate
   No. 140 (*Wachet auf, ruft uns die Stimme*),
   Fourth Movement-*Johann S. Bach*
   La Primavera from *The Four Seasons*, First
   Movement-*Antonio Vivaldi*
   Dies Irae from *Requiem-Wolfgang A. Mozart*
   Piano Concerto No. 23 in A Major: First Movement-
   Wolfgang A. Mozart
   A German Requiem, Fourth Movement-
   Johannes Brahms
   The Moldau-*Bedřich Smetana*
   Symphony of Psalms, First Movement-
   Igor Stravinsky
   Sacrificial Dance from *Le Sacre du printemps*-
   Igor Stravinsky

Glencoe/McGraw-Hill
A Division of The McGraw-Hill Companies

**For more information contact
your nearest regional office or
call 1-800-334-7344.**

Northeast Region
Glencoe/McGraw-Hill
15 Trafalgar Square #201 • Nashua, NH 03063-1968
603-880-4701 • 800-424-3451 • Fax: 603-595-0204
(CT, MA, ME, NH, NY, RI, VT)

Mid-Atlantic Region
Glencoe/McGraw-Hill
P.O. Box 458 • Hightstown, NJ 08520-0458
609-426-5560 • 800-553-7515 • Fax: 609-426-7063
(DC, DE, MD, NJ, PA)

Atlantic-Southeast Region
Glencoe/McGraw-Hill
Brookside Park • One Harbison Way, Suite 101
Columbia, SC 29212
803-732-2365 • 800-731-2365 • Fax: 803-732-4582
(KY, NC, SC, VA, WV)

Southeast Region
Glencoe/McGraw-Hill
6510 Jimmy Carter Blvd. • Norcross, GA 30071-1705
770-446-7431 • 800-982-3992 • Fax: 770-446-2356
(AL, FL, GA, TN)

Mid-America Region
Glencoe/McGraw-Hill
936 Eastwind Drive • Westerville, OH 43081-3374
614-890-1111 • 800-848-1567 • Fax: 614-899-4905
(IN, MI, OH)

Great Lakes Region
Glencoe/McGraw-Hill
2122 York Road, Suite 130 • Oak Brook, IL 60521
630-954-5917 • 800-762-4876 • Fax: 630-954-6616
(IL, MN, WI)

Mid-Continent Region
Glencoe/McGraw-Hill
1066 Executive Parkway, Suite 106 • St Louis, MO 63141
314-514-0015 • 800-541-0491 • Fax: 314-514-0524
(IA, KS, MO, ND, NE, SD)

Southwest Region
Glencoe/McGraw-Hill
4360 Beltway Place, Suite 230 • Arlington, TX 76018
817-784-2113 • 800-828-5096 • Fax: 817-784-2116
(AR, AZ, LA, MS, NM, OK)

Texas Region
Glencoe/McGraw-Hill
4360 Beltway Place, Suite 230 • Arlington, TX 76018
817-784-2100 • 800-828-5096 • Fax: 817-784-2116
(TX)

Western Region
Glencoe/McGraw-Hill
709 E. Riverpark Lane, Suite 150 • Boise, ID 83706
208-368-0300 • 800-452-6126 • Fax: 208-368-0303
(AK, CO, ID, MT, NV, OR, UT, WA, WY)

California Region
Glencoe/McGraw-Hill
21600 Oxnard Street, Suite 500
Woodland Hills, CA 91367
818-615-2600 • 800-423-9534 • Fax: 818-615-2697
(CA, HI)

Glencoe Catholic School Region
Glencoe/McGraw-Hill
25 Crescent St., 1st Floor • Stamford, CT 06906
203-964-9109 • 800-551-8766 • Fax: 203-967-3108

Canada
McGraw-Hill Ryerson Ltd.
300 Water Street • Whitby, Ontario
L1N 9B6, Canada
905-430-5000 • Fax: 905-430-5194

International
The McGraw-Hill Companies
Educational & Professional Publishing
International Marketing • 28th Floor
1221 Avenue of the Americas • New York, NY 10020-1095
212-512-3641 • Fax: 212-512-2186

DoDDS and Pacific Territories
McGraw-Hill School Publishing • Margaruite Smith
600 Delran Parkway, Suite 640 • Delran, NJ 08075
609-764-4586 • Fax: 609-764-4587

INTERMEDIATE
LEVEL 3

Choral Connections

Mixed Voices

Teacher's Wraparound Edition

Teacher's Manual

Glencoe
McGraw-Hill

New York, New York   Columbus, Ohio   Woodland Hills, California   Peoria, Illinois

Meet the Authors

SENIOR AUTHOR

Mollie G. Tower - As Coordinator of Choral and General Music of the Austin Independent School District for 21 years, Mollie Tower was recently nominated "Administrator of the Year." She is very active in international, national, regional, and state music educators' organizations. Ms. Tower was contributing author, consultant, and reviewer for the elementary textbook programs *Share the Music*, and *Music and You*. Senior author of *Música para todos*, *Primary and Intermediate Dual Language Handbooks for Music Teachers*, she has also written and consulted for many other publications. A longtime advocate for music education, Mollie is a popular clinician who conducts workshops across the country.

Milton Pullen
Professor of Music and Director of Choirs

After attending Texas A & I University where he acquired a Bachelor of Music Education in voice, Milton Pullen attended the University of Houston, where in 1976 he received a Master of Music in conducting. He has taught at the middle and high school level for 24 years and for the last nine years has taught at the university level. He is now Professor of Music and Director of Choirs at Pepperdine University in Malibu, California.

Ken Steele
Director of Choral Activities

Ken Steele has taught secondary choral music for 23 years, having directed choirs at the middle school and high school levels. He received the Bachelor of Music degree from Stetson University in DeLand, Florida, and went on to the University of Texas in Austin to earn the Master of Music in Choral Literature and Conducting in 1971, studying with Dr. Morris J. Beachy. A member of Texas Music Educators Association, Texas Choral Directors Association, Texas Music Adjudicators Association, and a lifetime member of the American Choral Directors Association, he is currently the director of choral activities at L. C. Anderson High School, in Austin, Texas.

Gloria J. Stephens
Director of Choral Activities

With 25 years of teaching experience, Gloria Stephens is presently the Director of Choral Activities at Ryan High School in Denton, Texas. Mrs. Stephens earned her Bachelor of Music Education and Master of Music Education degrees from the University of North Texas in Denton. She has also done post-graduate work at Texas Woman's University in Denton, the University of Texas at Arlington, and Westminster Choir College in Princeton, New Jersey.

Contributing Writers

Dr. Susan Snyder has taught all levels of vocal music over the last 25 years. She holds a B.S. in music education from the University of Connecticut and an M.A. from Montclair State College. She holds a Ph.D. in curriculum and instruction from the University of Connecticut and advanced professional certificates from Memphis State University and the University of Minnesota. Teaching at Hunter College and City University of New York, Dr. Snyder was coordinating author of the elementary music program, *Share the Music*, and a consultant on *Music and You*. She has published many articles on music education and integrated curriculum and is an active clinician, master teacher, and guest conductor.

Vocal Development, Music Literacy
Katherine Saltzer Hickey, D.M.A.
University of California at Los Angeles
Los Angeles, California
Choir Director
Pacific Chorale Children's Choruses
Irvine, California

The National Standards for Music Education are reprinted from *National Standards for Arts Education* with permission from Music Educators National Conference (MENC). Copyright ©1994 by MENC. The complete National Standards and additional materials relating to the Standards are available from Music Educators National Conference, 1806 Robert Fulton Drive, Reston, Virginia 22091. (Telephone 800-336-3768.) A portion of the sales of this material goes to support music education programs through programs of the Music Educators National Conference.

Glencoe/McGraw-Hill
A Division of The McGraw-Hill Companies

Send all inquiries to:
Glencoe/McGraw-Hill
21600 Oxnard Street, Suite 500
Woodland Hills, California 91367

ISBN 0-02-655613-8 (Student's Edition)
ISBN 0-02-655614-6 (Teacher's Wraparound Edition)

Printed in the United States of America.

1 2 3 4 5 6 7 8   045   04 03 02 01 00 99 98

Table of Contents

Selection	Concepts and Skills	1	2	3	4	5	6	7	8	9	Teacher's Resources
TEACHING LESSONS											
Dream a Dream	Posture and breathing; scale tones and altered tones; syncopated rhythm.	a, b, c				a, b		a	b	c	📁
The Road Less Traveled	Posture; intervals.	a				a, b	a				📁
Nginani Na	12/8 meter; call-and-response form; block chord harmony; South African vocal tone color.	a, c		b, c		a, b	a, e	a	c	a, d	📁
Music, When Soft Voices Die	Phrasing; legato; dynamics; unison; harmony.	b				a	a	a	c	c	
Cantaremos	Form; rhythms in 2/4 meter; stepwise and skipwise melodic movement.	a, b, c				b	a	a	c	d	📁
Laudate Nomen Domini	Texture; sight-singing.	a, b, c				b	a, c		a, c		📁
Pål På Haugen	Tonic chord tones; sequence; repetition; Norwegian pronunciation.	a, b, c				b	a	a	c	d	📁
It Was a Lover and His Lass	Sixteenth notes; scalewise passages; madrigal style.	a, b, c				b	f	a	c	d	📁
I Hear a Sky-Born Music	Vocal tone color; tone painting.	a, b, c			a	e	c	a, b, c	a		
Four Spanish Christmas Carols	Characteristic style of Spanish music; Spanish pronunciation.	a, b, c				b	a		c	a, d	📁
Alleluia	Rhythmic motif; phrase; performance evaluation.	a, b, c				b	a, c, f	a	c		
Flow Gently, Sweet Afton	3/4 meter; legato style.	a, b, c				a	b	a		a, c, d	
Jesu Dulcis Memoria	Text; tonality; tone color; and mood.	a, b, c		b		a, b	f	a, b	c		📁
May the Road Rise to Meet You	Ascending melodic skips; legato style.	a, b, c				b		a	c		
In Memoria Aeterna	Round and fugal forms.	a, b, c				e	a, b	a	c		📁

T4

SECTION		National Standards									Teacher's Resources	
Selection	Concepts and Skills	1	2	3	4	5	6	7	8	9		
HISTORICAL LESSONS												
Renaissance Period	Understanding the development of choral music during the Renaissance period.						c		a, b, c, d, e	a, c, d		
O Domine Jesu Christe	Homophonic texture.	a, b, c				b	a		a, c			
Baroque Period	Understanding the development of choral music during the Baroque period.			b			c		a, b	a, b, c		
Werfet Panier Auf Im Lande	6/8 meter; mood.	a, b, c				b	a		a, c			
Classical Period	Understanding the development of choral music during the Classical period.						a, b, c	a	a, b, c, d, e	a, c, d, e		
Sanctus	Melodic steps and leaps; bright tone quality.	a, b, c				b	e		a, c	d		
Romantic Period	Understanding the development of choral music during the Romantic period.						a, b, c	a	a, b, c, d, e	a, c, d, e		
If I Should See You All Alone	3/4 meter; dotted rhythms; major keys; key signature.	a, b, c				a, b	e		a, c	a		
Contemporary Period	Understanding the development of choral music during the Contemporary period.		c		b, c		a, c		a, b			
Still, Still, Still	Humming with energy; dynamic contrast.	a, b, c				a, b	e					

ADDITIONAL PERFORMANCE SELECTIONS

Shut De Dō

The River

Look-A That Star

A Holiday Wish

 The folder icon indicates that Teacher Resources (such as listening maps, blackline masters, etc.) are available to support the learning process.

 The transparency projector icon indicates that there are overhead transparencies available to enhance learning.

 The headset icon indicates that there are listening selections specifically chosen to aurally illustrate the music of the period.

National Standards High School Grades 9-12

The National Standards for Music Education were developed by the Music Educators National Conference. Reprinted by permission.

MUSIC

The study of music contributes in important ways to the quality of every student's life. Every musical work is a product of its time and place, although some works transcend their original settings and continue to appeal to humans through their timeless and universal attraction. Through singing, playing instruments, and composing, students can express themselves creatively, while a knowledge of notation and performance traditions enables them to learn new music independently throughout their lives. Skills in analysis, evaluation, and synthesis are important because they enable students to recognize and pursue excellence in their musical experiences and to understand and enrich their environment. Because music is an integral part of human history, the ability to listen with understanding is essential if students are to gain a broad cultural and historical perspective. The adult life of every student is enriched by the skills, knowledge, and habits acquired in the study of music.

Every course in music, including performance courses, should provide instruction in creating, performing, listening to, and analyzing music, in addition to focusing on its specific subject matter.

1. **Content Standard:** Singing, alone and with others, a varied repertoire of music

   Achievement Standard, Proficient:
   Students
   a. sing with *expression and *technical accuracy a large and varied repertoire of vocal literature with a *level of difficulty of 4, on a scale of 1 to 6, including some songs performed from memory
   b. sing music written in four parts, with and without accompaniment
   c. demonstrate well-developed ensemble skills

   Achievement Standard, Advanced:
   Students
   d. sing with expression and technical accuracy a large and varied repertoire of vocal literature with a level of difficulty of 5, on a scale of 1 to 6
   e. sing music written in more than four parts
   f. sing in small ensembles with one student on a part

2. **Content Standard:** Performing on instruments, alone and with others, a varied repertoire of music

   Achievement Standard, Proficient:
   Students
   a. perform with expression and technical accuracy a large and varied repertoire of instrumental literature with a level of difficulty of 4, on a scale of 1 to 6
   b. perform an appropriate part in an ensemble, demonstrating well-developed ensemble skills
   c. perform in small ensembles with one student on a part

   Achievement Standard, Advanced:
   Students
   d. perform with expression and technical accuracy a large and varied repertoire of instrumental literature with a level of difficulty of 5, on a scale of 1 to 6

3. **Content Standard:** Improvising melodies, variations, and accompaniments

   Achievement Standard, Proficient:
   Students
   a. improvise stylistically appropriate harmonizing parts
   b. improvise rhythmic and melodic variations on given pentatonic melodies and melodies in major and minor keys
   c. improvise original melodies over given chord progressions, each in a consistent *style, *meter, and *tonality

   Achievement Standard, Advanced:
   Students
   d. improvise stylistically appropriate harmonizing parts in a variety of styles
   e. improvise original melodies in a variety of styles, over given chord progressions, each in a consistent style, meter, and tonality

4. **Content Standard:** Composing and arranging music within specified guidelines

   Achievement Standard, Proficient:
   Students
   a. compose music in several distinct styles, demonstrating creativity in using the *elements of music for expressive effect
   b. arrange pieces for voices or instruments other than those for which the pieces were written in ways that preserve or enhance the expressive effect of the music
   c. compose and arrange music for voices and various acoustic and electronic instruments, demonstrating knowledge of the ranges and traditional usages of the sound sources

   Achievement Standard, Advanced:
   Students
   d. compose music, demonstrating imagination and technical skill in applying the principles of composition

5. **Content Standard:** Reading and notating music

   Achievement Standard, Proficient:
   Students
   a. demonstrate the ability to read an instrumental or vocal score of up to four *staves by describing how the elements of music are used

Students who participate in a choral or instrumental
ensemble or class

    b. sightread, accurately and expressively, music with a
level of difficulty of 3, on a scale of 1 to 6

Achievement Standard, Advanced:

Students

    c. demonstrate the ability to read a full instrumental or
vocal score by describing how the elements of music
are used and explaining all transpositions and clefs

    d. interpret nonstandard notation symbols used by some
20th-century [sic] composers

Students who participate in a choral or instrumental
ensemble or class

    e. sightread, accurately and expressively, music with a
level of difficulty of 4, on a scale of 1 to 6

6. Content Standard: Listening to, analyzing, and
describing music

Achievement Standard, Proficient:

Students

    a. analyze aural examples of a varied repertoire of music,
representing diverse *genres and cultures, by describing the uses of elements of music and expressive devices

    b. demonstrate extensive knowledge of the technical
vocabulary of music

    c. identify and explain compositional devices and tech-
niques used to provide unity and variety and tension
and release in a musical work and give examples of
other works that make similar uses of these devices
and techniques

Achievement Standard, Advanced:

Students

    d. demonstrate the ability to perceive and remember
music events by describing in detail significant events[3]
occurring in a given aural example

    e. compare ways in which musical materials are used in a
given example relative to ways in which they are used
in other works of the same genre or style

    f. analyze and describe uses of the elements of music in a
given work that make it unique, interesting, and expressive

7. Content Standard: Evaluating music and music performances

Achievement Standard, Proficient:

Students

    a. evolve specific criteria for making informed, critical
evaluations of the quality and effectiveness of performances, compositions, arrangements, and improvisations and apply the criteria in their personal
participation in music

    b. evaluate a performance, composition, arrangement, or im-
provisation by comparing it to similar or exemplary models

Achievement Standard, Advanced:

Students

    c. evaluate a given musical work in terms of its aesthetic
qualities and explaining the musical means it uses to
evoke feelings and emotions

8. Content Standard: Understanding relationships between
music, the other arts, and disciplines outside the arts

Achievement Standard, Proficient:

Students

    a. explain how elements, artistic processes (such as
imagination or craftsmanship), and organizational
principles (such as unity and variety or repetition
and contrast) are used in similar and distinctive
ways in the various arts and cite examples

    b. compare characteristics of two or more arts within
a particular historical period or style and cite examples from various cultures

    c. explain ways in which the principles and subject
matter of various disciplines outside the arts are
interrelated with those of music[4]

Achievement Standard, Advanced:

Students

    d. compare the uses of characteristic elements,
artistic processes, and organizational principles
among the arts in different historical periods
and different cultures

    e. explain how the roles of creators, performers,
and others involved in the production and presentation of the arts are similar to and different
from one another in the various arts[5]

9. Content Standard: Understanding music in relation to
history and culture

Achievement Standard, Proficient:

Students

    a. classify by genre or style and by historical period
or culture unfamiliar but representative aural
examples of music and explain the reasoning
behind their classifications

    b. identify sources of American music genres,[6]
trace the evolution of those genres, and cite
well-known musicians associated with them

    c. identify various roles[7] that musicians perform,
cite representative individuals who have func-
tioned in each role, and describe their activities
and achievements

Achievement Standard, Advanced:

Students

    d. identify and explain the stylistic features of a given
musical work that serve to define its aesthetic
tradition and its historical or cultural context

    e. identify and describe music genres or styles that
show the influence of two or more cultural traditions, identify the cultural source of each influence, and trace the historical conditions that
produced the synthesis of influences

Terms identified by an asterisk (*) are explained further in the glossary of
National Standards for Arts Education, published by Music Educators
National Conference, © 1994.

3. E.g., fugal entrances, chromatic modulations, developmental devices
4. E.g., language arts: compare the ability of music and literature to convey images, feelings, and meanings; physics: describe the physical basis of tone
production in string, wind, percussion, and electronic instruments and the
human voice and of the transmission and perception of sound
5. E.g., creators: painters, composers, choreographers, playwrights; performers: instrumentalists, singers, dancers, actors; others: conductors, costumers,
directors, lighting designers
6. E.g., swing, Broadway musical, blues
7. E.g., entertainer, teacher, transmitter of cultural tradition

INTRODUCTION

Choral Connections is a four-level series designed to build music literacy and promote vocal development for all students and voice categories in grades 6–12. The series is a multi-textbook program supported with print materials and audio listening components. This enables students to develop music skills and conceptual understanding, and provides teachers with a flexible, integrated program.

Choral Connections presents beginning, intermediate, and advanced-level literature for various voice groupings: mixed, treble, and tenor-bass. This comprehensive choral music program includes student texts, teacher's wraparound editions, teacher's resource binders, and optional audio recordings designed to enhance student learning while reducing teacher preparation time.

Choral Connections is a curriculum that provides your students with a meaningful, motivating choral music experience, and will help you and your students make many connections. This choral music program …

Connects to . . . the National Standards

The National Standards are correlated to each lesson for quick-and-easy identification and reference. The performance standards related to singing and reading notations are explicit in each lesson, and by using the extension activities, teachers can connect the musical elements through improvisation and composition. Analysis and evaluation are an active and consistent component of lessons throughout the series. Additional student activities connect the lessons to the other arts, as well as provide a consistent historical and cultural context.

Connects to . . . Skill Development

Through vocal warm-ups and sight-singing exercises, students build vocal skills and master the vocal and sight-reading skills necessary to perform each piece. Rhythmic melodic and articulation skills are developed as needed for expressive interpretation. Students are encouraged to develop listening skills and use their perceptions to improve individual and group performance.

Connects to . . . Performance

Fundamental to a quality choral music program is the student performance of the literature. Student performance provides opportunities for young musicians to demonstrate musical growth, to gain personal satisfaction from achievement, and to experience the joy of music making. To help develop skills, *Choral Connections* provides exercises in warming-up and sight-singing which help prepare students to successfully sing each piece.

Conceptual understanding is built throughout the teaching/learning sequence, as the performance is prepared.

Connects to . . . the Arts and Other Curriculum Areas

Choral music provides a rich opportunity to connect the musical experience to other art disciplines (dance, visual arts, theatre), and to enhance the learning in other subject areas. It also provides a vehicle to help students gain knowledge and understanding of historical and cultural contexts across the curriculum.

PROGRAM PHILOSOPHY

Responding to Trends in Choral Music Education

Choral Connections is consistent with current educational philosophy that suggests:

- Performance is a product which should be the end result of a sound educational process, building conceptual understanding and skills as the performance is prepared.

- Students are motivated through materials and concepts that are connected to their own lives and interests, and they should be exposed to high-quality, challenging musical literature.

- Students learn best when they are active participants in their learning, and when they clearly understand and help set the goals of the learning process.

- Students understand concepts better when they have background information and skills which allow them to place their learning into a larger context.

- Students need to actively manipulate musical concepts and skills through improvisation and/or composition in order to fully assimilate and understand them.

- Students improve when they receive fair, honest, and meaningful feedback on their successes and failures.

- Students should be encouraged to assess themselves individually and as a group, learning to receive and process constructive criticism, which leads to independent self-correction and decision making.

Scope and Depth of Music Literature

Most students are capable of performing more difficult material than they can sight-sing. Therefore, the literature in *Choral Connections* is drawn from many periods and styles of music. The wide range of composers and publishers ensures variety, and allows for various skills and concepts to be developed as each new piece is encountered. The high standards set in *Choral Connections* provides selections that are inherently powerful and exciting for students. Rather than working with contrived songs to teach skills or concepts, students learn through discovery and interaction with quality literature.

Addressing the National Standards

The National Standards for Arts Education, published in 1994 and reprinted with permission on pages T6–T7, launched a national effort to bring a new vision to arts education for all students. The National Standards provides a framework for achievement in music, with outcomes suggested for grades 4, 8, and 12. *Choral Connections* addresses the National Standards in several ways.

The most obvious and predominant National Standards addressed in choral ensemble are: (1) singing and (5) reading notation. However, good performance requires musical understanding which only occurs when all aspects of musical experience are incorporated. The preparation of vocal performance is enriched and deepened by involvement in all nine of the National Standards.

As you teach with *Choral Connections*, there will be frequent opportunities to deepen or extend student learning through: (2) playing through and creating accompaniments, (3) improvisation, (4) composition and arranging, (6) analyzing, (7) assessing, (8) linking with other arts and other academic disciplines, and (9) understanding historical and cultural contexts. The National Standards identified for each lesson and the Teacher's Wraparound extension activities help you become aware of the National Standards, and the depth of learning that will occur as you implement this choral music program.

Promoting Music Literacy

Choral Connections promotes music literacy. Literacy includes oral and aural aspects of music communication—reading, writing, singing, and listening. Each lesson begins with a *vocal warm-up* during which the student builds vocal skills through singing and listening. The lesson then proceeds to *sight-singing exercise(s)*, emphasizing reading development. These exercises may be rhythmic, melodic, harmonic, or a combination thereof; and emphasize the musical elements which are the objectives of the lesson. The sight-singing exercises lead directly into the *musical selection*. Students are encouraged to sight-sing in every lesson, and are assessed in an increasingly rigorous way as the text progresses from lesson to lesson. Sight-singing is approached as a challenge, and a means to the student's musical independence.

Literacy goes beyond reading pitch and rhythm and extends to the expressive elements of music and appropriate interpretation. Students are frequently asked to explore interpretive aspects of music making, and encouraged to suggest their own ideas for phrasing, dynamics, and so on. Through careful listening and constructive critique of their own work, they will gradually become more discriminating about the quality of performance, and the impact of that performance on the audience.

Including Authentic Student Assessment

The assessment in *Choral Connections* is systematic, objective, and authentic. There is ongoing *informal assessment* by teacher observation throughout the lessons. The text is written as a series of action steps for the student, so there are many opportunities for the director to hear and see the level of accomplishment.

Students will find objectives at the beginning of each lesson, and two types of assessment questions at the end. First, factual questions that check for understanding of concepts and skills are presented. Next, there are questions which require higher-level thinking through analysis, synthesis, and/or evaluation. The questions are always related directly to the lesson objectives, and allow students to demonstrate their understanding. By answering the questions, and demonstrating as suggested, students are involved in *self-assessment*. Many times students are involved in their own assessment, constructing rubrics or critiquing their performance, and identifying their next challenge.

The Teacher's Wraparound Edition includes lesson objectives and each lesson is taught so the concepts and skills are experienced, labeled, practiced, and reinforced, then measured through *formal assessment*. These assessment tasks match the lesson objectives, allowing students to demonstrate understanding of concepts and skills through performance, composition, or writing. Students are frequently required to produce audio or video tapes. This authentic assessment technique keeps testing of rote learning to a minimum, and allows measurement of higher-level application of knowledge and skills. A portfolio can be constructed for individual students, groups, or the whole ensemble; demonstrating growth over time.

Connecting the Arts and Other Curriculum Areas

Lessons in *Choral Connections* integrate many appropriate aspects of musical endeavor into the preparation of a piece. Students compose, improvise, conduct, read, write, sing, play, listen/analyze, and assess on an ongoing basis that builds understanding, as well as high standards. In this way, the many aspects of music are integrated for deeper learning.

As one of the arts, music can be linked to other arts through similarities and differences. Throughout the text, and particularly in the historical section, music is compared and contrasted with other arts to determine aspects of confluence, and the unique features of each art.

As one way of knowing about the world, music can be compared with concepts and skills from other disciplines as seemingly different as science or mathematics. The integrations between music and other disciplines are kept at the conceptual level, to maintain the integrity of both music and the other subjects. For example, mathematical sets of 2, 3, 4, 5, and 6 might be explored as a link to pieces with changing meter; or the text of a piece might become a starting point for exploration of tone painting. In Making Historical Connections, a time line connects music to social studies, and a list of authors for each period provides a link to language and literature.

Providing a Variety of Student Activities

Choral Connections begins with the choral experience, and builds understanding through active participation in a range of activities including singing, playing, improvising, composing, arranging, moving, writing, listening, analyzing, assessing, and connecting to cultures, periods, or disciplines. Lessons are written with the heading "Have students … ," so there is always an emphasis on learning by doing.

Fitting Your Classroom Needs

Effective classrooms are characterized by many features, including student participation, a positive environment, clear sense of purpose, challenging content, high motivation, and a sense of sharing between teacher and student. These probably describe your choral ensemble classroom, and Choral Connections will allow you to make the most of these characteristics.

With Choral Connections, your students will be clear about purpose and direction, have multiple routes to success, and be involved in their own learning. The lessons will guide you and your students to share in the excitement of music making, and help you to grow together. The lessons are written the way you teach, and allow you to maintain and strengthen your routines, while adding flexibility, variety, and depth.

ORGANIZATION AND FLEXIBILITY

Each Choral Connections text is divided into the following sections:
• Preparatory Materials

• Lessons
• Making Historical Connections
• Additional Performance Selections

Preparatory Materials

Preparatory Materials introduce such basic concepts as notes and their values, rests and their values, rhythm patterns, breathing mechanics, solfège and hand signs, frequently found intervals, and pitch. Activities provided in the Teacher's Wraparound Edition suggest ways to use these materials as beginning exercises if your students have little or no music background. If your students are familiar with choral music, these Preparatory Materials can be both a quick review and a convenient reference.

Lessons

The Lessons are designed to be taught over a period of time. Each lesson is developed around a piece of quality authentic music literature. The lesson includes warm-ups, sight-singing, and rhythmic or melodic drills, all of which are directly related to preparation of the piece. Objectives are clearly stated, and a motivational opening activity or discussion is provided. The Teacher's Wraparound Edition outlines a carefully sequenced approach to the piece, with multiple entry points, and clear assessment opportunities to document achievement and growth.

Making Historical Connections

Making Historical Connections provides narrative, listening, and choral experiences for each of the five main historical periods. A narrative lesson provides a brief and interesting exposition of the main characteristics of the period, leading from the previous period, and outlining the achievements and new styles that emerged. A time line guides the student to place the musical characteristics into a larger historical and cultural context. The listening lesson includes both vocal and instrumental listening selections from the period, with listening maps and teacher wraparound lessons to guide student listening. The third component, a literature lesson, rounds out the student experience through a preparation of a piece to be sung from the period.

Additional Performance Selections

Additional Performance Selections provide a range of additional literature featuring popular pieces and multicultural selections that can be used to enhance the repertoire of your choral music performance. Warm-up exercises and suggestions to help you guide your students through the score are given, as well as program tips.

Lesson Objectives

Each lesson has objectives that emphasize and build conceptual understanding and skills across the lessons. The objectives in this book are:

LESSON OBJECTIVES	
LESSON 1 Dream a Dream	• Read and sing in four parts using proper posture and breathing. • Recognize and read scale tones and altered pitches. • Describe and read syncopated rhythms.
LESSON 2 The Road Less Traveled	• Identify and use correct singing posture. • Visually and aurally identify intervals. • Read, write, and sing intervals of M2, M3, P4, P5, M6 and octave.
LESSON 3 Nginani Na	• Read and sing in 12/8 meter. • Identify and sing in call-and-response form. • Sing block chord harmonies. • Describe and sing using South African vocal tone color.
LESSON 4 Music, When Soft Voices Die	• Sing legato phrasing. • Identify and perform dynamics using control. • Sing in unison and harmony.
LESSON 5 Cantaremos	• Identify ABA form. • Read and clap simple rhythms in 2/4 meter. • Identify, read, and sing stepwise and skipwise melodic movement.
LESSON 6 Laudate Nomen Domini	• Identify and compare homophonic and polyphonic texture. • Sing homophonic and polyphonic texture. • Sight-sing pitches in G major.
LESSON 7 Pål På Haugen	• Recognize, read, and sing the pitches of the tonic chord. • Identify sequence and repetition within a melodic line. • Sing, using correct Norwegian pronunciation.
LESSON 8 It Was a Lover and His Lass	• Read and sing rhythms with sixteenth notes. • Read and sing scalewise patterns with flexibility. • Identify and perform in a madrigal style.
LESSON 9 I Hear a Sky-Born Music	• Identify and select correct vocal tone colors for different songs. • Demonstrate various combinations of articulation, dynamics, and volume as choices in vocal tone color. • Describe an analogy between painting a picture and composing, arranging, or performing a piece of music.
LESSON 10 Four Spanish Christmas Carols	• Sing, using correct Spanish pronunciation. • Identify and perform characteristic styles of Spanish songs.
LESSON 11 Alleluia	• Identify rhythmic motifs. • Identify and sing musical phrases, using dynamic shading. • Listen to and evaluate group performance.
LESSON 12 Flow Gently, Sweet Afton	• Read and sing in 3/4 meter. • Conduct in 3/4 meter. • Sing, using a legato style.

LESSON OBJECTIVES (continued)

LESSON 13 Jesu Dulcis Memoria	• Read and sing in C major and C minor. • Explore the relationship between text, tonality, and tone color to create mood.
LESSON 14 May the Road Rise to Meet You	• Read and sing ascending melodic skips. • Sing in legato style.
Lesson 15 In Memoria Aeterna	• Identify round and fugal form. • Distinguish between round and fugal form. • Sing in fugal form.
RENAISSANCE PERIOD	• Describe some characteristics of Renaissance architecture, fine art, and music. • Explain the difference between sacred music and secular music. • Discuss the major musical forms of the Renaissance period. • Identify some of the key composers of the Renaissance period.
O Domine Jesu Christe	• Visually and aurally identify homophonic texture. • Sing homophonic texture. • Sing a Renaissance piece a cappella.
BAROQUE PERIOD	• Describe the characteristics of Baroque architecture, fine art, and music. • Discuss the most important differences between Renaissance music and Baroque music. • Identify at least five new musical forms of the Baroque period. • Identify at least four major composers of the Baroque period.
Werfet Panier Auf Im Lande	• Read and sing in 6/8 meter. • Interpret a piece to convey a specific mood.
CLASSICAL PERIOD	• Describe characteristics of architecture, fine art, and music of the Classical period. • Discuss the most important musical forms of the Classical period. • Identify the key Classical composers.
Sanctus	• Read and sing melodic leaps with supported tone. • Sing with bright vocal tone quality.
ROMANTIC PERIOD	• Describe the characteristics of architecture, fine art, and music of the Romantic period. • Identify the major musical forms of the Romantic period. • Explain the importance of nationalism in Romantic music. • Identify at least three major Romantic composers.
If I Should See You All Alone	• Read and clap rhythms in 3/4 meter including dotted rhythms. • Sight-sing in a major key. • Identify key signatures for major keys.
CONTEMPORARY PERIOD	• Describe characteristics of architecture, fine art, and music of the Contemporary period. • Discuss at least five musical forms of the Contemporary period. • Identify at least four Contemporary composers. • Explain the importance of fusion in Contemporary music.
Still, Still, Still	• Hum with energy and accurate intonation. • Sing with dynamic contrast.

Student Text

Lessons

The lessons, through which students systematically build musical skills and conceptual understanding, comprise the majority of the text. These lessons are structured as follows:

- **FOCUS** . . . tells the student the main concepts and skills addressed in the lesson. By having only a few main goals, students and teacher will keep focused on these objectives as work progresses.

- **SIGHT-SINGING EXERCISES** . . . build rhythmic, melodic, and expressive sight-singing skills through exercises that are directly related to some aspect of the upcoming musical selection. Through sight-singing practice every day, students gain confidence and skills to become independent readers.

- **CHORAL MUSIC TERMS** . . . give the students an opportunity to build a musical vocabulary essential for clarity of thought in communicating about music to others.

- **WARM-UP EXERCISES** . . . allow the students to warm-up their bodies, voices, and minds at the beginning of every class, while immediately exploring the main rhythmic, melodic, and skill issues that will arise in preparing the piece. These exercises are designed to sequentially build skills.

- **SINGING** . . . provides a motivating introduction to the piece of music, related to the student's perspective, which begins with a familiar idea and asks the student to think about or explore some concept or skill. Through interest and active participation, the student is then led logically into the piece.

- **STUDENT SELF-ASSESSMENT—HOW DID YOU DO?** . . . gives the student ways to assess accomplishment, growth, and needs, for both self and group. Beginning with recall, comprehension and application questions, the final questions ask for analysis, synthesis, and evaluation, guiding the student to higher-level thinking and the ability to self-assess.

Making Historical Connections

The Historical section of the text provides a survey of Western music history through exploration of the culture and music of the five overarching periods: Renaissance, Baroque, Classical, Romantic, and Contemporary. Each period is addressed in the following ways:

- **Historical Narrative Lesson** . . . provides a brief, student-oriented historical context of the period through visual art, architecture, historical events, musical developments, artistic characteristics, musical personalities, and listening selections. Students are encouraged to imagine this time period as if they were living in it, and experience the music from the perspective of the period.

- **Historical Listening Lesson** . . . provides one choral and one instrumental listening selection, to give students an aural experience with the styles, sounds and forms of the period. Listening maps are provided in the Teacher's Resource Binder so the student can follow along as a visual guide to listening.

- **Historical Literature Lesson** . . . is paired with the narrative lesson for each period, and provides the opportunity to perform a piece with appropriate characteristics and performance style. The selected materials reflect the period, and provide a concrete example of those characteristics introduced in the previous narrative.

Additional Performance Selections

Each book provides additional performance selections which meet the various needs of the ensemble and director. Each selection is accompanied by a specifically designed warm-up to build appropriate vocal skills.

- **Patriotic Selections** . . . provide excellent openers and closers for concerts, and are particularly useful when performing at patriotic celebrations.

- **Holiday Selections** . . . acknowledge the need for performance literature appropriate for winter holidays and during the spring season.

- **Multicultural selections** . . . provide an opportunity for performance of music that has different criteria than Western art music, allowing exploration of different languages, vocal tone color, styles, movement, and cultural characteristics.

- **Proven Audience-Pleaser Selections** . . . allow you to round out your programs with appropriate rousing or sentimental pieces that provide a change of pace or variety.

Glossary

The glossary provides brief, accurate definitions of musical terms used in the text.

TEACHER'S WRAPAROUND EDITION

National Standards Connections

Choral Connections affords multiple opportunities to address the National Standards. Correlations between lesson content, extension activities, and bottom-page activities are listed to show the relationship between lesson activities and the standards.

Teaching Sequence

Each lesson is organized to follow a logical progression from warm-ups through assessment, while providing maximum flexibility of use for your individual situation. Each lesson is linked to one musical selection, and provides learning opportunities based on the inherent concepts and skills required to understand and perform the piece. The lessons of the Teacher Wraparound Edition are structured as follows:

- **Focus** . . . gives the teacher a brief overview of concepts and skills which form the content of the objectives and assessments in the lesson.

- **Objectives** . . . provides concrete, measurable objectives allowing an interconnected approach to lesson segments. Each objective will be assessed in three ways during the lesson.

- **Choral Music Terms** . . . identifies the terms used during the lesson to build understanding and skills.

- **Warming Up** . . . includes rhythm and vocal warm-up exercises, as well as sight-singing exercises. The vocal warm-ups are designed to sequentially develop vocal skills, and start each class immediately with singing. The sight-singing exercises are designed to systematically build sight-singing skills, and lead directly into the upcoming piece. The purpose of each exercise is stated clearly for the teacher and student at the beginning of the lesson. These exercises may all be done before the piece is introduced, or they may be presented cumulatively, one each day, and concurrent with developing understanding of the piece.

- **Singing** . . . provides motivation and an entree to the piece of literature. Many different approaches are utilized, but they all draw the student into the piece through active learning and thinking.

- **Suggested Teaching Sequence** . . . returns to each warm-up activity and reviews, then guides you directly from the warm-up into the piece of literature. In this way, you have multiple entry points, so your approach is new and different each day the ensemble works on the piece. Specific rehearsal techniques, based on sight-singing, sectional work, and analysis of difficulties build skills and conceptual understanding as the performance is refined day after day. Each lesson includes recommended steps for organizing students into small groups by voice part to sight-sing the song separately before coming together in full ensemble to perform the selection.
- **Assessment** . . . provides Informal Assessment, Student Self-Assessment, and Individual Performance Assessment. There is appropriate assessment for each lesson objective.

Assessment

Informal Assessment is accomplished through teacher observation during the lesson. Each objective is observable, and the text indicates the checkpoint for teacher assessment.

Student Self-Assessment is accomplished through oral or written response to questions in the Student Text.

Individual Performance Assessment requires the student to demonstrate a skill or understanding through individual assessment. This is frequently done through audio or video taping, creation of rubrics to assess the quality of the performance, or a written exercise to demonstrate understanding. Individual Performance Assessment can be done by the teacher, student, peers, or a combination thereof. The tapes may be compiled into a portfolio which shows growth and development of understanding.

Extensions and Bottom-Page Activities

Extensions and bottom-page activities in each lesson afford a plethora of background information, teaching strategies, and enrichment opportunities.
- **Enrichment activities** in the side columns provide opportunities for movement, improvisation, composition, and analysis based on lesson and selection content.
- **Vocal development strategies** give detailed information about specific techniques that facilitate vocal production, style, and negotiation of difficult passages within the piece.
- **Music literacy strategies** help students expand their ability to read and analyze music.
- **Teaching strategies** are available to reinforce concepts or skills that may be difficult for students,

or elaborate on classroom management techniques suggested within the lesson.
- **More about** boxes provide background historical, cultural, and/or biographical information to give deeper understanding of the piece.
- **Curriculum connections** provide strategies to help students build bridges between music and other disciplines.

Performance Tips

In the Additional Performance Selection section, you are provided with performance suggestions that identify specific strategies that have worked successfully for choral music teachers, and potential "hot spots" you may need to address. Each selection is accompanied by a suggested program, including selections from the book. These recommendations should be extremely helpful for the beginning choral director, and provide many interesting alternatives for the experienced conductor.

TEACHER'S RESOURCE BINDER

The Teacher's Resource Binder contains teaching materials designed to reduce teacher preparation time and maximize students' learning. The following categories are provided to assist with meeting the individual needs and interests of your students.

Skill Masters. The *Skill Masters* provide sequential musical concepts that can be used to review and reinforce musical concepts in the areas of rhythm and pitch, music literacy, vocal development, and pronunciation guides.

Blackline Masters. The *Blackline Masters* are designed to enhance the concepts presented in the student text lessons.

Assessment. Assessment activities provide performance assessment criteria, rubrics, and other activity pages to help teachers with individual and group assessment.

Fine Art Transparencies. Full color overhead transparencies of the visual art pieces that introduce each of the historical sections are provided.

Listening Maps. Blackline masters of listening maps are provided and feature choral and instrumental selections. These help reinforce learning about the five major historical periods. Teachers may wish to make a transparency of the blackline master and have students follow along as the teacher points to the overhead transparency.

OPTIONAL CD LISTENING PROGRAM

Music: An Appreciation, 6th edition, by Roger Kamien, is correlated to this text to provide students with an exemplary listening experience. Two selections, one choral and one instrumental, are featured with each of the five historical periods in the Making Historical Connections section of this book (pages 124 to 192). The Teacher's Wraparound Edition provides the CD number and track at point of use for each selection. Additionally, the following correlation shows you how to use the Kamien series to supplement and reinforce related concepts in the Lessons.

LESSON TITLE	RELATED CONCEPTS	CD TRACK AND TITLE
LESSON 1 Dream a Dream	• syncopated rhythms	CD 1, Track 45 "I Got Rhythm" by George Gershwin
LESSON 2 The Road Less Traveled	• aural identification of intervals	CD 8, Track 43 "Tonight" from West Side Story by Leonard Bernstein
LESSON 3 Nginani Na	• sung block chord	CD 2, Track 34 Cantata No. 140, Seventh Movement, by J. S. Bach
LESSON 4 Music, When Soft Voices Die	• legato singing • good phrasing • dynamics	CD 6, Track 19 A German Requiem, Fourth Movement, by Johannes Brahms
LESSON 5 Cantaremos	• identifying ABA form	CD 3, Tracks 5–13 Symphony No. 40 by Mozart
LESSON 6 Laudate Nomen Domini	• homophonic and polyphonic textures	CD 2, Tracks 28–30, 34 Cantata No. 140 by J. S. Bach
LESSON 7 Pål På Haugen	• pitches of the tonic chord	CD 2, Tracks 31–33 Cantata No. 140, Fourth Movement, by J. S. Bach
LESSON 8 It Was a Lover and His Lass	• sixteenth notes in a madrigal style	CD 1, Track 78 "Now Is the Month of Maying" by Thomas Morley
LESSON 9 I Hear a Sky-Born Music	• how musical elements affect a vocal piece	CD 4, Tracks 48–53 "Erlkönig" by Franz Schubert
LESSON 10 Four Spanish Christmas Carols	• characteristic styles of Spanish dance music	CD 7, Tracks 8–11 "Bolero" by Maurice Ravel
LESSON 11 Alleluia	• rhythmic motifs • dynamic shading	CD 5, Tracks 1–2 "Chiarina" from Carnaval by Robert Schumann
LESSON 12 Flow Gently, Sweet Afton	• 3/4 meter • legato singing	CD 6, Track 19 A German Requiem, Fourth Movement, by Johannes Brahms
LESSON 13 Jesu Dulcis Memoria	• setting mood with tempo, rhythm, tone color, dynamics, and tonality	CD 7, Tracks 28–32 Wozzeck, Act III, by Alban Berg
LESSON 14 May the Road Rise to Meet You	• ascending melodic skips • legato style	CD 2, Tracks 31–33 Cantata No. 140, Fourth Movement, by Bach
LESSON 15 In Memoria Aeterna	• identifying fugal form	CD 2, Tracks 11–13 Organ Fugue by J. S. Bach

INTERMEDIATE
LEVEL 3

Choral Connections

Mixed Voices

Teacher's Wraparound Edition

Glencoe
McGraw-Hill

New York, New York   Columbus, Ohio   Woodland Hills, California   Peoria, Illinois

Cover Photos: Peter Samels Photography

Glencoe/McGraw-Hill

*A Division of The **McGraw·Hill** Companies*

Send all inquiries to
Glencoe/McGraw-Hill
21600 Oxnard Street, Suite 500
Woodland Hills, CA 91367

ISBN 0-02-655613-8 (Student's Edition)
ISBN 0-02-655614-6 (Teacher's Wraparound Edition)

Printed in the United States of America.

1 2 3 4 5 6 7 8 9   045   04 03 02 01 00 99 98

Meet the Authors

Mollie G. Tower, Senior Author
As Coordinator of Choral and General Music of the Austin Independent School District for 21 years, Mollie Tower was recently nominated as "Administrator of the Year." She is very active in international, national, regional, and state music educators' organizations. Ms. Tower was contributing author, consultant, and reviewer for the elementary textbook programs, *Share the Music* and *Music and You*. Senior author of *Música para todos, Primary and Intermediate Dual Language Handbooks for Music Teachers*, she has also written and consulted for many other publications. A longtime advocate for music education, Mollie is a popular clinician who conducts workshops across the country.

Milton Pullen
Professor of Music and Director of Choirs
After attending Texas A & I University where he acquired a Bachelor of Music Education in voice, Milton Pullen attended the University of Houston, where in 1976 he received a Master of Music in conducting. He has taught at the middle and high school levels for 24 years and for the last nine years has taught at the university level. He is now Professor of Music and Director of Choirs at Pepperdine University in Malibu, California.

Ken Steele
Director of Choral Activities
Ken Steele has taught secondary choral music for 23 years, having directed choirs at the middle school and high school levels. He received the Bachelor of Music degree from Stetson University in DeLand, Florida, and went on to the University of Texas in Austin to earn the Master of Music in Choral Literature and Conducting in 1971, studying with Dr. Morris J. Beachy. A member of Texas Music Educators Association, Texas Choral Directors Association, Texas Music Adjudicators Association, and a lifetime member of the American Choral Directors Association, he is currently the director of choral activities at L. C. Anderson High School, in Austin, Texas.

Gloria J. Stephens
Director of Choral Activities
With 25 years of teaching experience, Gloria Stephens is presently the Director of Choral Activities at Ryan High School in Denton, Texas. Mrs. Stephens earned her Bachelor of Music Education and Master of Music Education degrees from the University of North Texas in Denton. She has also done postgraduate work at Texas Woman's University in Denton, the University of Texas at Arlington, and Westminster Choir college in Princeton, New Jersey.

Consulting Author

Dr. Susan Snyder has taught all levels of vocal music over the last 25 years. She holds a B.S. in music education from the University of Connecticut and an M.A. from Montclair State College. She holds a Ph.D. in curriculum and instruction from the University of Connecticut and advanced professional certificates from Memphis State University and the University of Minnesota. Teaching at Hunter College and City University of New York, Dr. Snyder was coordinating author of the elementary music program, *Share the Music*, and a consultant on *Music and You*. She has published many articles on music education and integrated curriculum and is an active clinician, master teacher, and guest conductor.

Consultants

Choral Music
Stephan P. Barnicle
Choir Director
Simsbury High School
Simsbury, Connecticut

Vocal Development, Music Literacy
Katherine Saltzer Hickey, D.M.A.
University of California at Los Angeles
Los Angeles, California
Choir Director
Pacific Chorale Children's Choruses
Irvine, California

Music History
Dr. Kermit Peters
University of Nebraska at Omaha
College of Fine Arts
Department of Music
Omaha, Nebraska

Contributors/Teacher Reviewers

Dr. Anton Armstrong
Music Director and Conductor, St. Olaf Choir
St. Olaf College
Northfield, Minnesota

Jeanne Julseth-Heinrich
Choir Director
James Madison Middle School
Appleton, Wisconsin

Caroline Lyon
Ethnomusicologist
University of Texas at Austin
Austin, Texas

Caroline Minear
Supervisor
Orange County School District
Orlando, Florida

Judy Roberts
Choir Director
Central Junior High School
Moore, Oklahoma

Dr. A. Byron Smith
Choir Director
Lincoln High School
Tallahassee, Florida

Table of Contents

Preparatory Material

Using the Preparatory Material

The preparatory material found on these pages is designed to build a basic rhythmic, melodic, and sight-singing vocabulary. By working through the challenges, students will build the skills required for successful work in the upcoming lessons.

- If your students have little or no music background, take a day or two to introduce this musical vocabulary. Have them sing a few rounds to get them familiar with basic conducting, breathing, and working together.
- If your students have a rich music background, and have participated in a solid elementary and/or middle-school music program, review these challenges quickly, stopping to answer questions and clarify any misunderstandings. Then proceed to Lesson 1. Refer back to these pages during lessons when necessary.

Notes and Rests

The alignment of notes and rests on this page show the relationship between notes or rests of different value. Encourage students to learn these concepts early.

Notes and Note Values

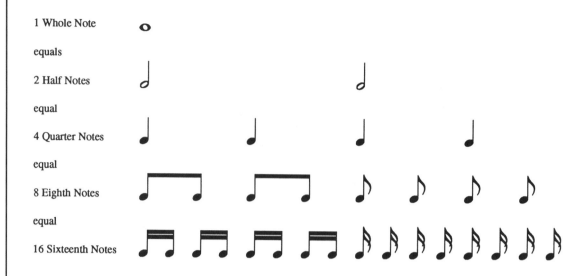

1 Whole Note	o
equals	
2 Half Notes	
equal	
4 Quarter Notes	
equal	
8 Eighth Notes	
equal	
16 Sixteenth Notes	

Rests and Rest Values

1 Whole Rest	
equals	
2 Half Rests	
equal	
4 Quarter Rests	
equal	
8 Eighth Rests	
equal	
16 Sixteenth Rests	

Rhythm Challenge in 4/4 Meter

Directions: Accurately count and/or perform the following rhythms without stopping!

Asymmetric Meter

Rhythm Challenges

When presenting a rhythm challenge, allow students the chance to read through the whole challenge first, answering any questions, and helping them resolve any concerns. Then offer students the opportunity to perform the challenge without pressure.

At the beginning of the year, too much pressure for those with little or no previous experience might discourage them for the rest of their lives! Some techniques to consider are:

- Have students design a chart in the form of a graph with approximately 15 columns that represent the same number of trials. One or more trials can be attempted at the beginning of each class. After each trial, each student should record the number of the measure where the first mistake was made. After fifteen trials, most students should show, by a line graph, considerable improvement.
- Encourage students to design their own method of tracking their improvement.

Asymmetric Meters

Asymmetric meters are those with odd numbered beats in patterns of unequal groupings of notes within a measure. Some examples of asymmetric meters are 5/4, 7/4, 5/8, 7/8, and 9/8. Accents, beams, ties, and other articulations define the groupings of the notes.

Read asymmetric meters by identifying what note equals one beat. Speak or phonate the rhythm while keeping the beat by tapping or conducting. Clap or use an instrument to express the rhythm while counting the beats. Note any accents or articulations to define the groupings of the notes.

Have students write an example of asymmetric rhythm by choosing a meter and writing rhythms to equal the beat and subdivisions of the beat. Include accents and other articulations to show how they want their notes to be grouped. Students might perform their asymmetric meter with a variety of instruments or timbres.

More Rhythm Challenges

To increase students' skill at reading rhythms, have them:

- Speak or clap each rhythm challenge as a group or in small ensembles, isolating and practicing measures and phrases that pose difficulty.
- Practice in small groups for a predetermined amount of time, such as 5 minutes. At the end of that time, assess rhythmic reading in one of the following ways: each student speaks and claps the pattern; each group speaks and claps the pattern; the whole class speaks and claps the pattern.
- Students should keep a record of their progress by recording the first measure where an error is made on each successive attempt.

Rhythm Challenge in 6/8 Meter

Directions: Accurately count and/or perform the following rhythms without stopping!

x

Breathing Mechanics

Singing well requires good breath control. Support for singing comes from correct use of the breathing mechanism. Deep, controlled breathing is needed to sustain long phrases in one breath. Also, correct breathing will support higher, more difficult passages.

Posture
Posture is very important in breath support.
- Keep your body relaxed, but your backbone straight.
- To stretch your back: Bend over and slowly roll your back upward until you are standing straight again. Do this several times.
- Hold your rib cage high, but keep your shoulders low and relaxed.
- Facing front, keep your head level. Imagine you are suspended by a string attached to the very top of your head.
- When you stand, keep your knees relaxed, but do not "lock" them by pushing them all the way back. Keep your feet slightly apart.
- When you sit, keep both feet flat on the floor and sit forward on the edge of your chair.

Inhaling
- Expand the lungs out and down, pushing the diaphragm muscle down.
- Inhale silently without gasping or making any other noise.
- Keep the throat and neck muscles relaxed to maintain a feeling of space in the back of the mouth (picture a reverse megaphone).
- Imagine taking a cool sip of air through a straw, lifting the soft palate.
- Expand your entire waistline, keeping the chest high, and the shoulders relaxed, feeling the breath low in the body.

Breath Control
To help you develop breath control do the following:
- Hold one finger about six inches from your mouth imagining that your finger is a birthday candle. Now blow out a steady stream of air to blow out the flame of the candle.

Summary

STANDING
Feet slightly apart, one
slightly forward
Knees relaxed
Backbone straight
Rib cage high
Shoulders low
Head level

SITTING
Feet on the floor
Sit on edge of chair
Backbone straight
Rib cage high
Shoulders low
Head level

xi

Breathing Mechanics
Remind students that vocal tone, resonance, and intonation are affected by posture and breathing. Basic singing posture is a relaxed, but firm, body stance. Have students read through the text on this page and practice correct posture and breathing.

Diaphragmatic Breathing
Have students:
- Feel the sensation of muscle expansion by placing thumbs above the small of the back with fingers pressing the top of the hips. Sip a long, deep breath and feel the action of the muscles.
- Feel the action of the diaphragm muscle by pressing the fingertips of both hands into the midsection of the torso just below the rib cage. Take a startled, quick surprise breath and feel the action of the muscle. Ask: How did the diaphragm react?
- Feel the diaphragm muscle expand outward as they sip a long, cool breath.
- Pant like a dog or bark like a dog (use *arf* and *woof*). Feel the action of the diaphragm.
- Use unvoiced consonants, such as *sh, f, p, t,* and *k* in different rhythms and tempos to create the diaphragmatic action.

xi

What is Signing?

Signing in music describes the use of hand signals to represent relative sounds of pitches. The signs were used by Reverend John Curwen from a method developed by Sarah Glover of Norwich in the nineteenth century. The *do* is movable and was intended to teach beginners to sing accurate pitches. The system has been adopted by the Kodaly approach and Tonika-Do system in Germany.

Intervals

Help students remember intervals by relating them to the first two pitches of the following familiar songs:

Major 2nd —"Frère Jacques"
Major 3rd—"Taps"
Perfect 4th—"Here Comes the Bride"
Perfect 5th—"Twinkle, Twinkle Little Star"
Major 6th—"My Bonny Lies Over the Ocean"
Octave—"Somewhere, Over the Rainbow"

Have students:

- Challenge one another in pairs, one singing an interval, the other telling what interval was heard.
- Check any disagreements with another pair.
- Take turns singing intervals.

Composing with Frequently Found Intervals

Have students:

- Compose an exercise of eight measures, using at least three different intervals shown on this page.
- Notate their melodies.
- Describe their piece and perform it to a classmate.

Solfège and Hand Signs

Solfège is a system designed to match notes on the staff with specific interval relationships. Hand signs provide additional reinforcement of the pitch relationships.

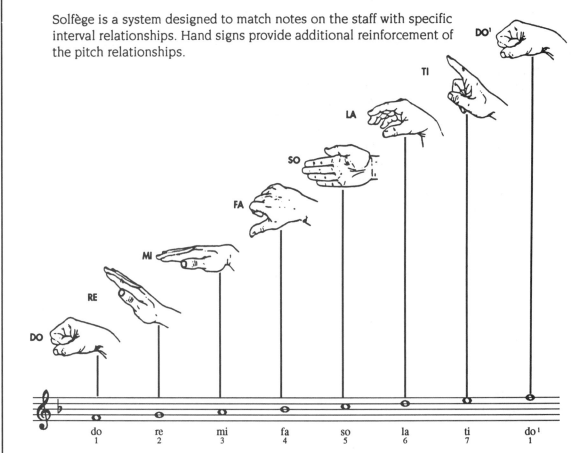

Frequently Found Intervals

An interval is the distance between two notes.

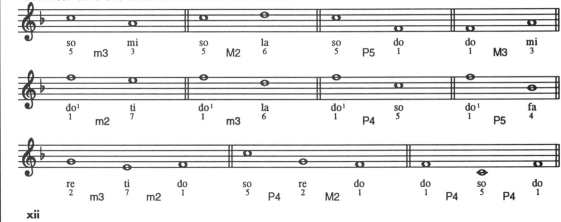

Pitch Challenge

Directions: Accurately sing each measure on solfège using hand signs and without stopping! During the measure of rest, look ahead to the next challenge.

Testing Pitch Accuracy

The best way to get better at pitch accuracy is to get feedback about which pitches are sung flat or sharp. The following activity is excellent for both the singer and listener. However, use confident volunteers only, as students will be critiqued openly in front of peers.

Have students:

- Listen to volunteers who are willing to have their pitch accuracy assessed as they perform the Pitch Challenge on this page with a partner.
- If the pitch is accurate, listeners should point thumbs to the side; if sharp, point thumbs up; and if flat, point thumbs down.
- Repeat this activity with as many volunteers as time permits.

Lessons

Dream a Dream

TEXT: Ed Robertson
COMPOSER: Ed Robertson

Focus

OVERVIEW
Posture and breathing; scale tones and altered tones; syncopated rhythm.

OBJECTIVES
After completing this lesson, students will be able to:
- Read and sing in four parts using proper posture and breathing.
- Recognize and read scale tones and altered pitches.
- Describe and read syncopated rhythms.

CHORAL MUSIC TERMS
Define the Choral Music Terms for students, giving pronunciation, and answering any questions that may arise.

Warming Up

Rhythm Drill
This Rhythm Drill is designed to prepare students to:
- Read and clap rhythms in 4/4 meter, including syncopation.
- Improvise with scat syllables to loosen up and feel phrases.
- Sing scale tones in rhythm in the Vocal Warm-up.

Have students:
- Read through the Rhythm Drill directions.
- Perform the drill.

Dream a Dream

COMPOSER: *Ed Robertson*
TEXT: *Ed Robertson*

CHORAL MUSIC TERMS
altered pitches
breath support
posture
scale tones
syncopation

VOICING
SATB

PERFORMANCE STYLE
Gently
Accompanied by piano

FOCUS
- Read and sing in four parts using proper posture and breathing.
- Recognize and read scale tones and altered pitches.
- Describe and read syncopated rhythms.

Warming Up

Rhythm Drill
Echo these patterns, then clap the whole line with repeats. Take a good breath, and "scat" the rhythm using *doom*, *daka*, and *dah*. You choose when to say which scat syllables—just let it happen naturally. Use one breath for the whole pattern—with repeats!

Vocal Warm-Up 1
Sing the scale below using solfège and hand signs or numbers. Now sing one scale tone for each measure of the Rhythm Drill.

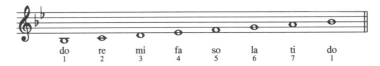

| do | re | mi | fa | so | la | ti | do |
| 1 | 2 | 3 | 4 | 5 | 6 | 7 | 1 |

Vocal Warm-Up 2
Sing the exercise below on *doo*, *mah*, or other scat syllables. Snap on the offbeats as you repeat the exercise up or down a half step. Notice the altered pitch, and the syncopated rhythm in the last measure of each line. Make it swing gently.

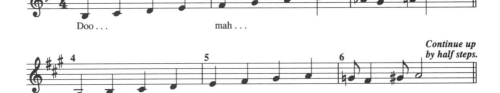

Doo . . .   mah . . .

Continue up by half steps.

TEACHER'S RESOURCE BINDER
Skill Master 8, *Scales and the Solfège System*, page 30
Blackline Master 1, *Simple to Complex Rhythms*, page 77

National Standards
In this lesson, students should develop the following skills and concepts:

1. Singing a varied repertoire of music. (**a, b, c**)
5. Reading and notating music. (**a, b**)
7. Evaluating music. (**a**)
8. Understanding relationships between music, the other arts, and disciplines outside the arts. (**b**)
9. Understanding music in relation to history and culture. (**c**)

Sight-Singing

First clap the rhythm, then sight-sing this exercise using solfège and hand signs or numbers. Sing each line with one breath. Follow the *da capo al fine*, and *fine* markings.

Singing: "Dream a Dream"

People all over the world dream of ways to make things better. Everyone has a choice to work for his or her dreams, and hope that these dreams will come true.

What might you dream for that would make the world a better place? What does Ed Robertson, the composer and lyricist of "Dream a Dream," wish for? Read the text and find out.

Now turn to the music for "Dream a Dream" on page 4.

HOW DID YOU DO?
? ? ?

Dreams take hard work, commitment, and dedication to come true, and so does good singing.

Think about your preparation and performance of "Dream a Dream."
1. What did you learn about posture and breathing in this lesson? Demonstrate good posture and breathing as you sing Warm-Up 1.
2. Sing the B♭ scale again, then tell about the altered tones in "Dream a Dream." What

pitches were altered? Choose a part of "Dream a Dream" to sing that will demonstrate that you can sing the altered tones in tune.
3. Describe syncopated rhythm, then clap a few measures to show how it sounds.
4. Is your ensemble able to sing in four parts? How do you sound? How do you know? What is the next step to a better performance?

Vocal Warm-Ups

These Vocal Warm-Ups are designed to prepare students to:
• Recognize and sing scale tones and altered tones.
• Sing using syncopated rhythm.
• Pulse the offbeat.
Have students:
• Read through the set of Vocal Warm-Up directions.
• Sing, following your demonstration.

Sight-Singing

This Sight-Singing exercise is designed to prepare students to:
• Sight-sing using solfège and hand signs or numbers.
• Read scale tones and altered tones.
• Follow *da capo al fine* and *fine* markings.
Have students:
• Read through the Sight-Singing exercise directions.
• Read each voice part rhythmically, clapping the rhythms.
• Sight-sing through each part separately using solfège and hand signs or numbers.
• Sing all parts together using solfége and hand signs or numbers.
• Sing each line with one breath, and follow the markings.

Singing: "Dream a Dream"

Interpret the text of "Dream a Dream."
Have students:
• Read the text on page 3.
• Discuss what dreams they have that would make the world a better place.
• Read the text of "Dream a Dream," and then identify the dreams of the composer, comparing them to the ones they named.

Suggested Teaching Sequence

1. Review Rhythm Drill.

Have students:

- Review the Rhythm Drill on page 2, first echoing, and then clapping the whole pattern.
- Scat the patterns with *doom, daka,* and *dah,* building a feeling for the rhythms.
- Identify ways to assure good breath support, including correct posture and breathing techniques for singing. (See page 9 in your Teacher's Wraparound Edition.)
- Repeat the scat rhythms using good breath support.

2. Review Vocal Warm-Ups 1 and 2.

Have students:

- Review Vocal Warm-Up 1 on page 2, using solfège and hand signs or numbers.
- Sing each pitch of the scale for one measure of the Rhythm Drill.
- Review correct singing posture and breathing techniques, and then apply them to the drill.
- Listen as you play the B♭ scale in whole notes, with A♭ in place of A.
- Describe the altered pitch, write the scale on the board, and identify the syllable *te* instead of *ti.*

Have students:

- Review Vocal Warm-Up 2 on page 2, using solfège and hand signs or numbers.
- Identify the altered tone, and remember it is called *te.*
- Review the solfège system using Skill Master 8, *Scales and the Solfège System,* in the TRB.
- Sing Vocal Warm-Up 2 again, using correct posture and breathing, and singing pitches in tune.

Dream a Dream

Words and Music by
Ed Robertson

V 7701

4 *Choral Connections   Level 3 Mixed Voices*

new   to - mor - row   when the   peo - ple   learn   to   love   their   fel - low
world   u - nit - ted   when the   na - tions choose to   lay   their   wea - pons

new   to - mor - row   when the   peo - ple   learn   to   love   their   fel - low
world   u - nit - ted   when the   na - tions choose to   lay   their   wea - pons

B

man. _____   Dare   to   hope   for   a
down. _____   Dare   to   hope   for   a

man. _____   Dare   to   hope   for   a
down. _____   Dare   to   hope   for   a

Dare   to   hope   for   a
Dare   to   hope   for   a

Dare   to   hope   for   a
Dare   to   hope   for   a

B

Dream a Dream **5**

3. Review Sight-Singing.
Read scale and altered tones using solfège and hand signs or numbers. Review breathing and phrases.
Have students:
- Review the Sight-Singing exercise on page 3, first clapping the rhythm, then singing using solfège and hand signs or numbers.
- Identify the altered tones and be certain to sing them in tune.
- Sing each line with a good breath and support.

4. Sight-sing "Dream a Dream" using solfège and hand signs or numbers.
Have students:
- Divide into voice sections (SATB) and read each part rhythmically, using rhythm syllables.
- Still in sections, sing with solfège and hand signs or numbers, identifying and working on problem areas.
- Sing the piece through, using solfège and hand signs or numbers, with full ensemble.
- Divide into sections and recite the text rhythmically for each voice part.
- Sing the piece through with text as a full ensemble.

Assessment

Informal Assessment

During this lesson, students showed the ability to:

• Read rhythms with syncopation in the Rhythm Drill.

• Demonstrate correct posture and breathing in Vocal Warm-Up 1.

• Identify, read, and sing altered pitches in Vocal Warm-Up 2.

• Sing altered pitches and use correct posture and breathing for singing in the Sight-Singing exercise.

• Sing "Dream a Dream" with syncopated rhythms and altered pitches, using correct posture and breathing.

Student Self-Assessment

Have students:

• Evaluate their performance with the How Did You Do? section on page 3.

• Answer the questions individually. Discuss them in pairs or small groups and/or write their responses on a sheet of paper.

Individual Performance Assessment

To further demonstrate accomplishment, have each student:

• Read simple to complex syncopated rhythms in pairs, assessing one another's accuracy, using Blackline Master 1, *Simple to Complex Rhythms.*

• Identify altered pitches using Skill Master 8, *Scales and the Solfège System,* in the TRB.

Student Evaluation Process

You will find three different evaluation procedures in each lesson. The first is informal, and done by teacher observation at specific checkpoints during the lesson. The second, student self-evaluation, helps students reflect upon what learning has taken place, and self-assess where more work is necessary. Finally, the formal assessment requires each student to make a response or perform in a way that is individually measurable. By mixing techniques, you should be able to construct an objective grading system for students that has many components. Share your assessment plans with students, so they will know the benchmarks of success.

VOCAL DEVELOPMENT

To encourage vocal development, have students:

- Energize sustained tones by increasing the breath support and dynamic level on words such as *dream, hope, true,* and *soon.*
- Listen for tall vowels and alter the vowel sounds when necessary, such as *man, love,* and *come.*
- Demonstrate the correct singing of the *r* consonant after a vowel; it should be almost silent, as in *world, dare, morning, together,* and *work.*
- Listen for diphthongs (two vowel sounds when one vowel is written) in words such as *day* and *way.* Sing or sustain the first vowel sound and barely sing the second vowel sound with the next syllable.
- Create a ringing resonance on the words with the *oo* vowel sound, as in *true, soon,* and *new.*
- Balance the chords between the parts by listening to them. Have students try adding more weight to one part to determine the effect on the chord.
- Articulate the different rhythmic patterns at section D by speaking the text clearly and emphasizing the rhythm strongly.

CURRICULUM CONNECTIONS
Photography

From the beginning of the school year, have students photograph important successes, both individual and schoolwide. Plan "Dream a Dream" as an end-of-the-year program piece, and create a slide presentation to go with it, highlighting the year's events and successes.

Extension

Composing Using Altered Tones

Have students:

- Compose short pieces, up to 32 measures, that have scale tones and altered tones. They may use the B♭ scale and A♭ altered tone as in "Dream a Dream," or choose another scale and altered tone with which to experiment.
- Share the piece with a classmate, and get feedback.
- Revise the piece accordingly, and then share with others.
- Continue the revision and consultation process until they are satisfied with the piece.
- Practice and perform the melody for the ensemble or another audience.

Substituting Syncopated Rhythms

Have students:

- Clap the rhythm of the Sight-Singing exercise.
- In groups, choose a measure and substitute a syncopated rhythm for any two successive beats. Adjust the pitches to fit, adding a repeated pitch or two if necessary.
- Next, add syncopated rhythm to two measures of any line.
- Then add syncopated rhythm to the first three measures of any line.

8 *Choral Connections Level 3 Mixed Voices*

National Standards

The following National Standards are addressed through the Extension and bottom-page activities:

3. Improvising melodies, variations, and accompaniments. **(b)**

4. Composing and arranging music within specified guidelines. **(a)**

5. Reading and notating music. **(a)**

7. Evaluating music and music performances. **(a)**

8. Understanding relationships between music, the other arts, and disciplines outside the arts. **(a, b)**

9. Understanding music in relation to history and culture. **(b)**

may-be we _____ can make it hap- pen

free and dreams come true. _____ Dream a

some - time dreams come true. _____ Dream a

some - time dreams come true. _____ Dream a

E

soon. may-be

dream of a new to-mor-row may-be

dream of a new to-mor-row may-be

dream of a new to-mor-row may-be

E

TEACHING STRATEGY
Guiding Composition

Guiding student composition is a delicate balance. The writing process used in language instruction offers a series of steps which can become a process for composition. The first step is planning, then creating a first draft. Next is a peer consultation and revision of step one. This process continues until the student feels that he or she is close to the final product. At this point, a conference is scheduled with you. There is more revision resulting in a final product, which is then published. In the case of music, *published* means both written and performed. By establishing this process, the student begins to understand that a first draft is not a final product.

TEACHING STRATEGY
Posture and Breathing

Posture and breathing are the foundation of good tone in singing. Establish good habits and insist on them whenever students are singing.

To establish good posture, have students:

- Stand with feet apart, one foot slightly ahead of the other, weight evenly distributed, knees unlocked, as if getting ready to ski downhill.
- Tuck in abdomen; body should be held firmly.
- Roll the shoulders forward and backward while counting aloud. Let shoulders drop easily and naturally.
- Turn head side to side gently without moving any other part of the body. Tip head forward to chest and backward in the same manner. Head should rest comfortably on shoulders with chin level.

To promote proper breath support, have students:

- Begin with good body alignment.
- Sip in a long (deep) breath of air, as if sipping through a straw. Hold it with a good facial look, release with an energetic long hiss.
- Sip in a long breath, hold, and release with short hisses.

To practice breath control in many different ways, have students:

- Sip in a long breath, releasing the air as if blowing on a candle, without blowing it out.
- Sip in a long breath; sing "America" on one breath.
- Sip in a long breath; count as high as possible while exhaling slowly.
- Energize sound with hisses followed by vocalizations on *hoo, whoo, whoa,* and *wow* sounds.
- Vocalize sounds from the head register downward.

9

some - day we can see our dreams come true.

some - day we can see our dreams come true.

some - day we can see our dreams come true.

some - day we can see our dreams come true.

slight rit.

The Road Less Traveled

COMPOSER: *Carl Strommen*
TEXT: *Carl Strommen*

CHORAL MUSIC TERMS
intervals
Major 2nd
Major 3rd
Perfect 4th
Perfect 5th
Major 6th
octave
posture

VOICING
SAB

PERFORMANCE STYLE
With feeling
Accompanied by piano

FOCUS
- Identify and use correct singing posture.
- Visually and aurally identify intervals.
- Read, write, and sing intervals of M2, M3, P4, P5, M6, and octave.

Warming Up

Movement Warm-Up
Use your imagination to do this warm-up. *Stand, pretending a birthday cake is balanced on each shoulder. Be sure the cakes don't fall to the ground as you walk carefully around the room, making pathways through shared space.* By doing this, you are demonstrating the correct posture for singing.

 Vocal Warm-Up
Sing this exercise using solfège and hand signs or numbers. Then sing it on *loo*, in a legato style. Repeat, moving up by half steps.

do mi so mi re so do
1 3 5 3 2 5 1

 Sight-Singing
Have fun sight-singing this exercise, using solfège and hand signs or numbers. Sing each line by itself. Can you find the stepwise intervals? Thirds? Where is the Perfect 5th?

Ⓐ
do mi so mi fa so la so fa mi do re do
1 3 5 3 4 5 6   5 4 3 1 2 1

Ⓑ
do re mi fa so mi re mi fa so do
1 2 3 4 5   3 2 3 4 5 1

Ⓒ
do mi fa so mi re do mi re do
1 3 4 5   3 2 1 3 2 1

Lesson 2: The Road Less Traveled **11**

TEACHER'S RESOURCE BINDER
Blackline Master 2, *Primary Intervals*, page 78

 National Standards
Through involvement with this lesson, students will develop the following skills and concepts:
1. Singing, alone and with others, a varied repertoire of music. **(a)**
5. Reading and notating music. **(a, b)**
6. Listening to, analyzing, and describing music. **(a)**

LESSON 2

The Road Less Traveled

COMPOSER: Carl Strommen
TEXT: Carl Strommen

Focus

OVERVIEW
Posture; intervals.

OBJECTIVES
After completing this lesson, students will be able to:
- Identify and use correct singing posture.
- Visually and aurally identify intervals.
- Read, write, and sing intervals of M2, P3, P4, P5, M6, and octave.

CHORAL MUSIC TERMS
Define the Choral Music Terms for students, giving pronunciation, and answering any questions that may arise.

Warming Up

Movement Warm-Up
This Movement Warm-Up is designed to prepare students to:
- Use correct singing posture.
Have students:
- Read through the Movement Warm-Up directions.
- Perform the exercise.

Vocal Warm-Up
This Vocal Warm-Up is designed to prepare students to:
- Read and sing steps and skips.
- Sing in legato style.
Have students:
- Read through the Vocal Warm-Up directions.
- Sing, following your directions.

Sight-Singing

The Sight-Singing exercise on page 11 is designed to prepare students to:
- Sight-sing in both clefs using solfège and hand signs or numbers.
- Sing and identify melodic intervals of a second, third, and fifth.

Have students:
- Read through the Sight-Singing exercise directions.
- Read each line rhythmically, using rhythm syllables.
- Sight-sing through each line separately, using solfège and hand signs or numbers.
- Sing all parts together using solfége and hand signs or numbers.
- Identify the Major 3rds and Perfect 5th.

Singing: "The Road Less Traveled"

Identify the interval as a measure of distance between pitches. Have students:
- Read the text on page 12.
- Give examples of common measurements used to measure distance. (inches, meters, fathoms, light-years, and so on)
- Watch as you show examples of intervals on the board, labeling Major 2nd, Major 3rd, Perfect 4th, Perfect 5th, Major 6th, and octave.
- Use Blackline Master 2, *Primary Intervals*, to read, hear, write, and identify these intervals.

Singing: "The Road Less Traveled"

Whether the road is more or less traveled, people usually keep track of how far they have gone. How do they measure distance? What measurement terms do they use?

In music, the term *interval* is used to measure the distance from one pitch to another. You can hear intervals when they are played or sung, and you can see intervals in notation.

Turn to the music for "The Road Less Traveled" on page 13 and find the intervals in measures 2–9.

HOW DID YOU DO?

Think about your preparation and performance of "The Road Less Traveled."
1. Describe how you learned to establish correct posture. Does correct posture help your singing? How?
2. Tell what an interval is, then write the intervals of a Major 2nd, Major 3rd, Perfect 4th, Perfect 5th, Major 6th, and octave, using E♭ as the tonic pitch.
3. Sing the intervals you have written for a partner, and assess each other's accuracy.
4. Describe the intervals in measures 2–9 of "The Road Less Traveled."
5. Is knowing about intervals important for singing well? Defend your answer with a logical point of view.

Composer Carl Strommen

A background in music and education led Carl Strommen to become a teacher, then a high school choir director. His love of teaching and choral music originated in the 1970s when he began arranging music for a high school choir. Since then, he has had a prolific career writing and arranging music for school choirs and bands. Currently the band director at a New York high school, Strommen is highly respected by his students, peers, and audiences for his articulate words, beautiful melodies, and effective choral arrangements.

The Road Less Traveled

Words and Music by
Carl Strommen

SAB Voices and Piano

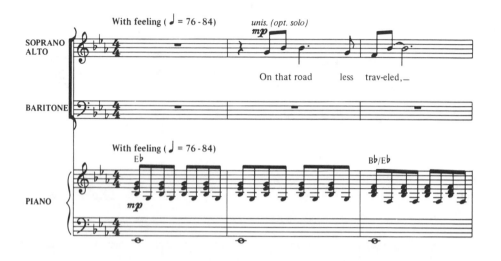

Also available for S.A.T.B., Level Four (11344), and 2-part/S.S.A., Level Two (11346).
SoundTrax Cassette available (11855).

The Road Less Traveled **13**

Suggested Teaching Sequence

1. Review Movement Warm-Up.
Identify and practice correct posture.
Have students:
- Review the Movement Warm-Up on page 11.
- Move through shared space using correct posture.

2. Review Vocal Warm-Up.
Have students:
- Review the Vocal Warm-Up on page 11, using solfège and hand signs or numbers.
- Identify legato style as smoothly connecting note to note.
- Sing on *loo*, in legato style.

3. Review Sight-Singing.
Read melodic steps and skips. Identify seconds, thirds, and fifth. Read in treble and bass clefs.
Have students:
- Review the Sight-Singing exercise on page 11 using solfège and hand signs or numbers.
- Identify the intervals in each part. (Use Blackline Master 2, *Primary Intervals*, to help students identify and read intervals.)
- Sing each line with good posture and in-tune intervals.

TEACHING STRATEGY
Moving Through Shared Space
If students are not used to moving in class, they might feel awkward or conspicuous in this situation. Give them guidelines to provide structure to the experience. Begin with one person moving through space without bumping into anyone or anything. Then add one person, then two more, and so on, until everyone is up and moving. This type of movement will become a real challenge when they are singing in four parts independently, moving through space, and hearing other parts around them. So, this is indeed a preparation not only for posture, but for future challenges.

4. Sight-sing "The Road Less Traveled" using solfège and hand signs or numbers.

Have students:

- Divide into voice sections (SAB) and read each part rhythmically, using rhythm syllables.
- Still in sections, sing with solfège and hand signs or numbers, identifying and working on problem areas.
- Sing the piece through, using solfège and hand signs or numbers, with full ensemble.
- Divide into sections and recite the text rhythmically for each voice part.
- Sing the piece through with text as a full ensemble.

 CURRICULUM CONNECTIONS

Poetry

"The Road Less Traveled" might open the door to Robert Frost's famous poem, "The Road Not Taken."

Have students:

- Read the text of the song, and the text of the poem.
- Discuss the meaning of each text separately.
- Compare and contrast the messages of the two texts.
- Discuss how a composer might set Frost's poem, and if the same type of setting would work as "The Road Less Traveled." Why or why not?

Assessment

Informal Assessment

During this lesson, students showed the ability to:

- Move, demonstrating correct posture in Movement Warm-Up.
- Sing in legato style in the Vocal Warm-Up.
- Aurally and visually identify and read intervals in the Sight-Singing exercise and on Blackline Master 2, *Primary Intervals*.
- Demonstrate correct posture and singing of in-tune intervals in "The Road Less Traveled."

Student Self-Assessment

Have students:

- Evaluate their performance with the How Did You Do? section on page 12.
- Answer the questions individually. Discuss them in pairs or small groups and/or write their responses on a sheet of paper.

Individual Performance Assessment

To further demonstrate accomplishment, have each student:

- Aurally or visually identify specific intervals by circling them on Blackline Master 2, *Primary Intervals*.
- In a small group or individually, sing intervals as directed by you.

TEACHING STRATEGY

Intervals

Help students remember intervals by relating them to the first two pitches of familiar songs. Major 2nd —"Frère Jacques"; Major 3rd—"Taps"; Perfect 4th—"Here Comes the Bride"; Perfect 5th—"Twinkle, Twinkle, Little Star"; Major 6th—"My Bonny Lies Over the Ocean"; Octave—"Somewhere, Over the Rainbow."

Have students:

- Challenge one another in pairs, one singing an interval, the other telling what interval was heard.
- Check any disagreements with another pair.
- Take turns singing intervals.

VOCAL DEVELOPMENT

To encourage vocal development, have students:

- Energize sustained tones by increasing the breath support and dynamic level on words such as *traveled, wide, flight, own, go, star, far,* and so on. Releases should occur on the first beat rest of the ensuing measure.

- Demonstrate the correct singing of the *r* consonant after a vowel; it should be almost silent, as in *far, star, here, never,* and *dark.*

- Listen for diphthongs (two vowel sounds when one vowel is written) in words such as *wide, flight, own, miles,* and *fly.* Always sing or sustain the first vowel sound and barely sing the second vowel sound with the next syllable.

- Create a ringing resonance on the words with the *oh* or *oo* vowel sound, as in *rainbow, go, road, know,* and *to.*

- Balance the unison sections and the chordal sections by listening to them. Encourage students to experiment by adding more weight to one part to determine the effect on the music.

- Articulate the rhythm patterns precisely with clear enunciation of the text.

- Sustain the phrases with long, supported breath, carrying the phrases to the rests.

16 *Choral Connections   Level 3 Mixed Voices*

MUSIC LITERACY

To help students expand their music literacy, have them:

- Clap and speak the rhythms of "The Road Less Traveled" precisely.
- Conduct and speak the text precisely in rhythm.
- Identify the unison and part sections. Listen carefully to balance the dynamics when singing from parts to unison passages.
- Analyze the form by comparing the phrases and sections. Ask: Which sections repeat?

been,   to that se - cret place you know,   where your dreams be -

gin.   Fare-thee-well   and God-speed   'till we meet a-

gain.   On that dark   and wind - ing road

Composing Using Primary Intervals

Have students:

- Compose an exercise of eight measures, using at least three different intervals learned in this lesson.
- Notate their melodies.
- Describe their piece and perform it to a classmate.

The Road Less Traveled **17**

National Standards

The following National Standards are addressed through the Extension and bottom-page activities:

4. Composing and arranging music within specified guidelines. **(a)**

6. Listening to, analyzing, and describing music. **(a)**

8. Understanding relationships between music, the other arts, and disciplines outside the arts. **(a)**

there are miles to go.   Wrap your dreams___   in a

rain-bow.___   Hang your hopes___   on a star.___

On the wings___   of song I___ fly   to that place so

far. Wrap your dreams_ in a rain-bow._

Hang your hopes_ on a star._____ On the wings_ of

song I__ fly to that place so far.

Nginani Na

Traditional South African Song
ARRANGED BY: *Caroline Lyon*

CHORAL MUSIC TERMS
block chords
call-and-response form
improvisation
12/8 meter
vocal tone color

VOICING
SATB and soloist

PERFORMANCE STYLE
Swaying
Clapping shaker and drum accompaniment

FOCUS
• Read and sing in 12/8 meter.
• Identify and sing in call-and-response form.
• Sing block chord harmonies.
• Describe and sing using South African vocal tone color.

Warming Up

 Rhythm Drill
Perform each line from the bottom up, using body percussion. Feel the sway of 12/8 meter, swaying as you step the bottom line. Divide into four groups and put the four parts together. How does 12/8 meter work?

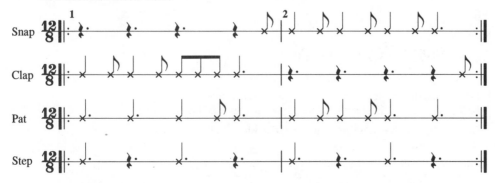

Now echo clap rhythms in 12/8 meter, using the bottom line of this Rhythm Drill as an accompaniment.

 Vocal Warm-Up
Sing each "call" using solfège and hand signs or numbers. Then have one person sing each call, with the whole ensemble singing the echo. Sing first on *loo*, then on *nyah*. How is your sound different using these two syllables?

Lesson 3: Nginani Na **21**

TEACHER'S RESOURCE BINDER
Blackline Master 3, *Translation and Pronunciation Guide for "Nginani Na,"* page 79

 National Standards
In this lesson, students should develop the following skills and concepts:
1. Singing, alone and with others, a varied repertoire of music. **(a, c)**
3. Improvising melodies, variations, and accompaniments. **(b, c)**
5. Reading and notating music. **(a, b)**
6. Listening to, analyzing, and describing music. **(a, e)**
7. Evaluating music and music performances. **(a)**
8. Understanding relationships between music and other disciplines. **(c)**
9. Understanding music in relation to history and culture. **(a, d)**

LESSON 3

Nginani Na

Traditional South African Song
ARRANGED BY: Caroline Lyon

Focus

OVERVIEW
12/8 meter; call-and-response form; block chord harmony; South African vocal tone color.

OBJECTIVES
After completing this lesson, students will be able to:
• Read and sing in 12/8 meter.
• Identify and sing in call-and-response form.
• Sing block chord harmonies.
• Describe and sing using South African vocal tone color.

CHORAL MUSIC TERMS
Define the Choral Music Terms for students, giving pronunciation, and answering any questions that may arise.

Warming Up

Rhythm Drill
This Rhythm Drill is designed to prepare students to:
• Identify and perform 12/8 meter patterns.
• Feel the sway of 12/8 meter.
• Experience taking turns between parts, preparing call-and-response form.
• Lead echo patterns in 12/8 meter.
Have students:
• Read through the Rhythm Drill directions.
• Perform the drill.

Vocal Warm-Up

The Vocal Warm-Up on page 21 is designed to prepare students to:
- Sing using solfège and hand signs or numbers.
- Sing solo and in ensemble.
- Echo and improvise answers in response to a "call."
- Sing and identify vocal tone colors created by the syllables *loo* and *nyah*.

Have students:
- Read through the Vocal Warm-Up directions.
- Sing, following your demonstration.

Sight-Singing

This Sight-Singing exercise is designed to prepare students to:
- Sight-sing in both clefs using solfège and hand signs or numbers.
- Read in 12/8 meter.
- Sing block chords in rhythm.
- Feel the sway of 12/8 meter.

Have students:
- Read through the Sight-Singing exercise directions.
- Read each voice part rhythmically, using rhythm syllables.
- Sight-sing through each part separately using solfège and hand signs or numbers.
- Sing all parts together.

Singing: "Nginani Na"

Identify and compare the vocal tone color characteristics of South African and Western choral music.

Have students:
- Read the text on student page 22.
- In groups, predict and chart how they think the sound will be the same and how it will be different.
- Listen to a recording of "Nginani Na."
- Describe what they heard using specific musical terms, and compare their findings to their predictions.
- Discuss how accurate their predictions were.

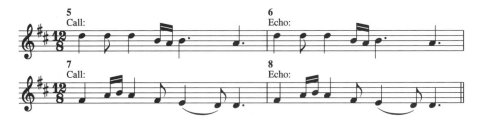

In call-and-response form, the ensemble part is not an echo, but an answer. Sing your own answer to each call on *nyah*, using combinations of these pitches: *do, re, mi, so, la,* and *do'*.

Sight-Singing

Sight-sing each voice part using solfège and hand signs. Then sing the block chords together slowly. Repeat the exercise, increasing in speed a little each time, until you are swaying slowly as you sing.

Singing: "Nginani Na"

You are going to perform music from South Africa.

Predict what this music might sound like. Make a chart that shows how you think it might be the same as, and different than, pieces you have sung in this ensemble.

Listen to "Nginani Na." After you listen, describe what you heard, and compare it with your predictions.

Now turn to the music for "Nginani Na" on page 23.

HOW DID YOU DO? ? ?

Each experience with a new culture helps you understand the similarities and differences that enrich the world.

Think about your preparation and performance of "Nginani Na."

1. Describe 12/8 meter, and clap the Rhythm Drill with three classmates to show your ability to perform in this meter.

2. How is call-and-response form used in "Nginani Na"?

3. What are block chords and where are they found in "Nginani Na"?

4. Describe the characteristics of "Nginani Na," and the characteristics of your performance style that are typical of South African music.

5. If you went to South Africa, do you think all music would sound like "Nginani Na"? What other music might you hear? How could you find out more?

MORE ABOUT...

Caroline Lyon

Caroline Lyon is a performer and teacher of choral and vocal music of several different styles. Her studies of South African choral music, West African drum and dance, and Latin American and Caribbean musical genres have permeated her jazz and salsa bands, small vocal ensembles, community choirs, and integrated performances. These studies have also inspired scholarly inquiry: she holds a Bachelors degree from Dart- mouth College, and a Master of Music degree from the University of Texas at Austin where she studied Ethnomusicology. She directed the Afro-Caribbean ensemble at the University of Texas in Austin; the choir at the Naropa Institute in Boulder, Colorado; and founded a community choir in Austin. She has taught numerous choral workshops for all education levels in Colorado, California, and Texas.

Nginani Na

What do I have? Why am I sick?

Traditional South African
Arranged by Caroline Lyon

SATB and Soloist

Meaning/context:
To be cured in the Sangoma tradition of South Africa, the sick person is being treated by a sangoma (healer). The worried patient thinks, "What do I have?"

Pronunciation:
Solo part: Wuh-meh-meh soon-goh-mah {"z" is allided with the next word}
(d)neen-deh-chloh-koh (d)neen-deh-chlah-bah

[Where "(d)" is almost hummed with the lips and teeth parted and the tongue against the hard palate, and where "ch" is like the German sound, passing between the tongue and hard palate with much force and air]

Chorus: (n)dee-yah-goo-lah (n)jee-nah-nee-nah
{the n is silent, but you should still make the shape}

© 1995 Cultural Bridge Choral Innovations

Nginani Na **23**

TEACHING STRATEGY
Improvising in the Pentatonic Scale

The Vocal Warm-Up in this lesson requires students to improvise using tones of the pentatonic scale. At first, it would seem that this would produce a dissonant mess, but the tones of the pentatonic scale, sounding together, avoid the clashes produced by the half steps of *fa* and *ti*, and actually sound quite nice together. The more students improvise this way, the more they will realize the safety of exploring in a cacophony of sound. Mistakes are not heard, and good combinations can be remembered for a later time.

Suggested Teaching Sequence

1. Review Rhythm Drill.
Have students:
- Review the Rhythm Drill on page 21, performing all lines with body percussion.
- Discuss 12/8 meter, identifying the technical definition of 12 eighth notes in each measure, and the feeling of four main pulses, each with three subdivisions, producing a swaying feeling.
- With a small group performing the bottom two lines, each student leading several patterns of 12/8 rhythm with the ensemble echoing. (See the Teaching Strategy on page 24 for help.)

2. Review Vocal Warm-Up.
Have students:
- Review the Vocal Warm-Up on page 21, reading each pattern, and then echoing it.
- Compare the *loo* and *nyah* sounds to identify the frontal, nasal, tone color of *nyah* that is typical of the South African vocal tradition.
- Sing a scale pattern from *so* to *do* on *nyah*.
- Improvise answers to the "calls" in this exercise, using the pitches of the pentatonic scale (*do, re, mi, so, la,* and *do'*), which will sound fine in combination with one another. (See the Teaching Strategy at the bottom of this page.)

3. Review Sight-Singing.
Have students:
- Review the Sight-Singing exercise on page 22 using solfège and hand signs or numbers, one line at a time, and then all together.
- Increase the tempo until they are swaying on the first and third beats of the measure. (This may turn into a step-touch pattern, which is fine.)

4. Sight-sing "Nginani Na" using solfège and hand signs or numbers.

Have students:

- Scan the piece, identifying the rhythm, call-and-response form, block chords, and overall form. (Performance instructions are to sing A twice, B four times, and then repeat the entire song at least once more.)
- Divide into voice sections (SATB) and read each part rhythmically, using rhythm syllables.
- Still in sections, sing with solfège and hand signs or numbers, identifying and working on problem areas.
- Learn the text with Blackline Master 3, *Translation and Pronunciation Guide for "Nginani Na,"* practicing with frontal nasal production, and echoing back passages until they are secure.
- Rehearse the text and music at a slow tempo, working for precise pronunciation and rhythm.
- Sing the piece through with full ensemble using text.

VOCAL DEVELOPMENT

To encourage vocal development, have students:

- Energize sustained tones by increasing the breath support and dynamic level.
- Speak and sing the text with open vowel sounds of the African text.
- Feel the 12/8 rhythm. Conduct and speak the text. Sway in tempo and sing the music.
- Balance the parts of the chordal sections by listening to them. Encourage students to try adding more weight to one part to determine the effect on the music.
- Articulate the rhythm patterns precisely with clear enunciation of the text.

Performance notes:
The soloist may take liberties with her part. The drums should be played with sticks.
Suggested form: A(2x); B (4x); repeat entire song at least one more time.

24 *Choral Connections Level 3 Mixed Voices*

 TEACHING STRATEGY

Improvisation

If students are unfamiliar or uncomfortable improvising, have them:

- Echo in the rhythm or tone set they will be using.
- Lead patterns, beginning with just the basic pulse, ♩., or tonal center, *do*.
- Continue leading patterns, adding only one rhythmic or melodic element at a time. Rhythmically, use only ♩. and ♩♪, and then add one more element at a time. Melodically, move from just the tonic to the tonic triad, *do-mi-so*. Gradually add *la, do'*, and *re*. Each new element is a choice, not a requirement.
- Lead patterns first in pairs, then small groups, and finally the whole ensemble.

Wo-i-shi-

Ndi - nen - hlo- ko Ndi-ne - hla - ba

ya - gu la Ngi-na - ni Na

Ndi- ya - gu- la Ngi-na - ni Na

second low drum

Simile

Simile

Mid drum

Low drum

© 1995 Cultural Bridge Choral Innovations

"Nginani Na"

"Nginani Na" is a type of music that comes from an oral tradition. Therefore, the printed music is to be used only as a guide to a stylistically correct performance. Singers should not be afraid to experiment with different tone qualities when singing songs from unfamiliar cultures. The soloist may take liberties with the part, as heard in the recorded performance. There is an optional harmony part in measure 8 which is not included in the performed version. When the piece is memorized, put the score away, clap, and dance!

Assessment

Informal Assessment
During this lesson, students showed the ability to:
• Identify characteristics of South African vocal style.
• Describe and perform rhythms in 12/8 meter.
• Sing in call-and-response form in the Vocal Warm-Up.
• Sing block chords in the Sight-Singing exercise.
• Demonstrate 12/8 meter, call-and-response form, block chord harmony, and South African vocal tone color in "Nginani Na."

Student Self-Assessment
Have students:
• Evaluate their performance with the How Did You Do? section on page 22.
• Answer the questions individually. Discuss them in pairs or small groups and/or write their responses on a sheet of paper.

Individual Performance Assessment
Have each student:
• Demonstrate the ability to perform 12/8 meter, call-and-response form, block chord harmonies, and South African vocal tone color by performing "Nginani Na" in small ensembles, with no more than two to a part and a soloist.
• Signal by showing the index finger at the chest when hearing the correct style for this piece when sung by you.

Extension

Arranging for Unpitched Percussion Instruments

Have students:

- In groups, arrange the Rhythm Drill for four unpitched percussion instruments.
- Discuss possible combinations of instruments and what qualities would work best with different lines; for example: a ringing instrument might be appropriate for a part with lots of space, and a crisp wood sound might be good for parts with lots of quicker sounds. Lower sounds might be better for the bottom parts, and higher sounds for the upper two parts.
- Try out different combinations until a satisfactory arrangement is found.
- Perform for the class, and then discuss which combinations were effective.

Composing a Call-and-Response Exercise

Have students:

- Compose an exercise modeled after "Nginani Na," in the South African style, that employs call and response.
- Notate their exercises.
- Use these exercises with soloist and ensemble as warm-ups at the beginning of class or rehearsal.

Oral Tradition

Explain that at many times and in many cultures of the world, there was no means for notating or writing down music. Songs and games were passed down from generation to generation by oral transmission. That is, songs were sung and learned by rote. Naturally, alterations occurred in melody, rhythms, and/or the text as different people sang the songs in different ways. Musical notation or symbols of sound can take many shapes and forms. Challenge students to illustrate the sounds of a song using a new notation.

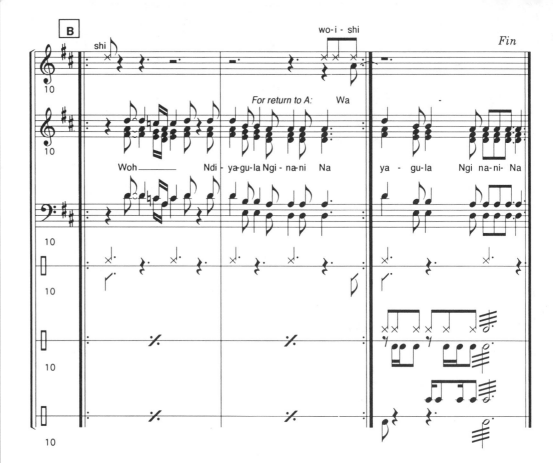

© 1995 Cultural Bridge Choral Innovations

National Standards

The following National Standards are addressed through the Extension and bottom-page activities:

2. Performing on instruments, alone and with others, a varied repertoire of music. **(b)**
3. Improvising melodies, variations, and accompaniments. **(b)**
4. Composing and arranging music within specified guidelines. **(b, c)**
8. Understanding relationships between music, the other arts, and disciplines outside the arts. **(c)**
9. Understanding music in relation to history and culture. **(c)**

Music, When Soft Voices Die

LESSON 4

Music, When Soft Voices Die

COMPOSER: *Philip M. Young*
TEXT: *Percy Bysshe Shelley (1792–1822)*

COMPOSER: Philip M. Young

TEXT: Percy Bysshe Shelley (1792–1822)

CHORAL MUSIC TERMS
dynamics
forte
legato
phrase
pianissimo

VOICING
SATB

PERFORMANCE STYLE
Expressively
Accompanied by piano

FOCUS
- Sing legato phrasing.
- Identify and perform dynamics using control.
- Sing in unison and harmony.

Focus

OVERVIEW
Phrasing; legato; dynamics.

OBJECTIVES
After completing this lesson, students will be able to:
- Sing legato phrasing.
- Identify and perform dynamics using control.

CHORAL MUSIC TERMS
Define the Choral Music Terms for students, giving pronunciation, and answering any questions that may arise.

Warming Up

 Vocal Warm-Up

Sing this exercise following the dynamic markings, creating a crescendo from *pianissimo* to *forte* and back again. Remember to use good posture and breath control.

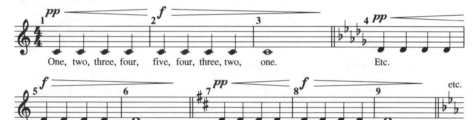

One, two, three, four, five, four, three, two, one. Etc.

Warming Up

Vocal Warm-Up
This Vocal Warm-Up is designed to prepare students to:
- Control the full dynamic range.
- Use pressure from the diaphragm to change dynamic level.
- Sing phrases.

Have students:
- Read through the Vocal Warm-Up directions.
- Sing, following your demonstration.

Lesson 4: Music, When Soft Voices Die **27**

TEACHER'S RESOURCE BINDER

National Standards
1. Singing a varied repertoire of music. **(b)**
5. Reading and notating music. **(a)**
6. Listening to, analyzing, and describing music. **(a)**
7. Evaluating music and music performances. **(a)**
8. Understanding relationships between music and other disciplines. **(c)**
9. Understanding music in relation to history and culture. **(c)**

Sight-Singing

This Sight-Singing exercise is designed to prepare students to:

- Identify and sing phrases.
- Interpret phrases using breath support and legato phrasing.
- Hear the difference between unison and harmony.

Have students:

- Read through the Sight-Singing exercise directions.
- Read each voice part rhythmically, using rhythm syllables.
- Sight-sing through each part separately using solfège and hand signs or numbers.
- Sing all parts together.

Singing: "Music, When Soft Voices Die"

Interpret poem text. Discuss composer options.

Have students:

- Read the text on student page 28.
- Write out the text of "Music, When Soft Voices Die," and then read it out loud several times.
- Interpret each phrase or stanza, and then construct one sentence that gives the overall message of the poem.
- Discuss possible musical treatments a composer might use.

Sight-Singing

Sight-sing this exercise using solfège and hand signs or numbers. Use good breath support, and shape the phrases with appropriate dynamics. Connect each pitch to the next smoothly, in legato style.

Singing: "Music, When Soft Voices Die"

Composers get inspiration from many sources. Sometimes a poem text creates an idea for just the right mood. Read the text of "Music, When Soft Voices Die" on page 29. Phrase by phrase, discuss what the words mean. Then try to communicate the meaning of the poem in one sentence. What musical treatment would you use to convey this meaning if you were the composer?

Now turn to the music for "Music, When Soft Voices Die" on page 29.

HOW DID YOU DO?

The composer, the performer, and the audience make a triangle of musical communication. Think about your preparation and performance of "Music, When Soft Voices Die."
1. As a performer, how did you know where the phrases were in this piece?
2. What did you learn about phrasing, legato singing, and dynamics that helped you interpret the piece?

3. Using the text and notation, describe what effect the use of unison and harmony had in this piece?
4. If you were going to grade the composer on interpretation of the poem, what grade would you assign? Give specific examples and reasons for your decision.

TEACHING STRATEGY

Dynamics

Have students:

- Identify the term *dynamics* as relating to the loudness or softness of a sound.
- List, or watch you list, the dynamic markings: *pp, p, mp, mf, f, ff.*
- Name and describe each marking:
  pp—pianissimo—very soft
  p—piano—soft
  mp—mezzo piano—medium soft

  mf—mezzo forte—medium loud
  f—forte—loud
  ff—fortissimo—very loud.

- Gradually going from soft to loud is called crescendo, and loud to soft is decrescendo. A phrase is shaped by making a crescendo to the peak, then decrescendo to the end of the phrase.

For the Choir of the First Baptist Church, Henderson, NC

Music, When Soft Voices Die

Music by Philip M. Young

Poem by Percy Bysshe Shelley

SATB with Piano Accompaniment

Music, When Soft Voices Die **29**

Suggested Teaching Sequence

1. Review Vocal Warm-Up.

Practice dynamics using good breath support.

Have students:

- Review the Vocal Warm-Up on page 27.
- Identify the dynamic markings. (See the Teaching Strategy on page 28.)
- Review good posture and how to breathe properly. (See the Teaching Strategy at the bottom of this page.)
- Sing the exercise again, demonstrating good posture, breath control, and dynamics.

2. Review Sight-Singing.

Read and sing in unison and harmony using solfège and hand signs or numbers. Sing in legato style.

Have students:

- Review the Sight-Singing exercise on page 28 using solfège and hand signs or numbers.
- Identify legato style and sing again, connecting pitches smoothly, and shaping the phrases using dynamics.
- Discuss the difference between the unison and harmonic versions in terms of emotional impact.
- Find these two phrases in "Music, When Soft Voices Die." Discuss possible reasons why the composer used one, then the other.

 TEACHING STRATEGY

Breath Support and Control

Have students:

- Feel the support of the breath by using a *burr* sound with vibration of the lips. It requires support in order to do it; coach students to feel the sensation of holding back the breath.

- Hiss on an *ss* or *f* sound in different rhythm patterns. Sing the rhythm of the song on the hissing sounds, then on an *oo* sound.

3. Sight-sing "Music, When Soft Voices Die" using solfège and hand signs or numbers.

Have students:

- Divide into voice sections (SATB) and read each part rhythmically, using rhythm syllables.
- Still in sections, sing with solfège and hand signs or numbers, identifying and working on problem areas.
- Sing the piece through, using solfège and hand signs or numbers, with full ensemble.
- Divide into sections and recite the text rhythmically for each voice part.
- Discuss legato singing and phrasing, and any places that present problems.
- Sing the piece through as a full ensemble, using correct legato phrasing and dynamics.

TEACHING STRATEGY

Interpreting the Poem

Have students read the poem out loud, paraphrase line by line, and then interpret the poem in one sentence.

Music, . . . memory. (The music of soft voices remains in the memory after the sound is gone.)

Odours, . . . quicken. (The impression of very sweet violet smells also remains in the memory.)

Rose leaves, . . . bed. (The dried rose is a Romantic symbol of love, and perhaps the memory of the rose smell permeates the feelings when imagining a bed prepared for the beloved.)

And so. . . slumber on. (The beloved's thoughts are like the rose leaves, and love remains like a dream—a memory of the beloved—when she is gone.)

Possible meaning: All dear and loved things remain in the memory when they are no longer present, including my beloved.

TEACHING STRATEGY

Irregular Phrases

Have students:

- Sing the piece, phrasing only where conducted to do so. (Break the phrases at any points other than normal.)
- Discuss this interpretation and decide whether they like it better this way, or the way they first performed it. Students should give concrete, factual reasons for their opinions. (Note: Be cautious not to express or impose your own opinion on this discussion. There are legitimate arguments for both points of view. You should monitor to see that legitimate facts are used to substantiate either point of view, and that *ideas* are argued, not personalities.)

CURRICULUM CONNECTIONS

Literature

Have students:

- Research and write a report on one of the English Romantic poets—Shelley, Keats, Byron, and the Brownings—and a composer who lived in the same country during the same period.
- Choose one poem of the poet, and one composition of the composer, comparing them for similarities and differences in musical or poetic elements, organization, or interpretation.
- Choose one poem of the poet and set it in the style of the composer.
- Choose one composition of the composer and analyze it for characteristics of the Romantic period.
- Summarize the reports for the class, using visuals and a performance.

VOCAL DEVELOPMENT

To encourage vocal development, have students:

- Energize sustained tones by increasing the breath support and intensity.
- Listen for tall vowels and alter the vowel sounds when necessary, such as *memory* (add *oo* to the *ee* sound), *beloved* (change *uh* to *awh*), and *love*.
- Demonstrate the correct singing of the *r* consonant after a vowel; it should be almost silent as in *odours*.
- An *r* consonant at the beginning of a word should be flipped once, especially in a British/English setting as in *rose*.
- Listen for word stresses at phrase endings such as *sicken*. Be sure to stress the first syllable only. Have students practice this feeling by using their arm to circle out away from their body while singing loud and then back in to their body while singing soft. This gesture and imagery will remind them of the concept of tapering off on an unstressed syllable at the end of a phrase.
- Listen for diphthongs (two vowel sounds when one sound is written) in words such as *voices* and *die*. Sustain the first vowel sound and barely sing the second vowel sound with the next syllable.
- Create a ringing resonance on the words with the *oo* vowel sound, as in *Music*.
- Balance the chords between the parts by listening to them.
- Contrast the contrapuntal entrances beginning at measure 26 with the chordal passages in the piece.

Assessment

Informal Assessment

During this lesson, students showed the ability to:

- Demonstrate good singing posture, breath control, and dynamics in the Vocal Warm-Up exercise.
- Identify and sing legato phrasing in the Sight-Singing exercise.
- Sing using correct legato phrasing and dynamics in "Music, When Soft Voices Die."

Student Self-Assessment

Have students:

- Evaluate their performance with the How Did You Do? section on page 28.
- Answer the questions individually. Discuss them in pairs or small groups and/or write their responses on a sheet of paper.

Individual Performance Assessment

To further demonstrate accomplishment, have each student:

- Signal the end of a correctly sung musical phrase as you sing examples that are both correct and incorrect.
- In a small ensemble, first describe, then demonstrate the following, using appropriate segments selected from the exercises and "Music, When Soft Voices Die": legato phrasing and controlled dynamics. Videotaping is optional.

CURRICULUM CONNECTIONS
Visual Arts

In setting the words to music, the composer uses organizational principles such as unison and harmony, consonance and dissonance, and repetition to further support the underlying message of the text.

Have students:

- Listen again to the poem, listing the major images, for example: music (voice), odours (violets), rose leaves (beloved's bed), slumbering love.
- Discuss how one might use these same organizational principles in a visual way to make a drawing, painting, or sculpture inspired by the poem.
- Use the poem as a source of inspiration, and draw, paint, or sculpt using at least one of these organizational principles.

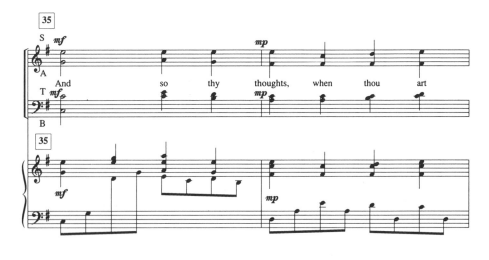

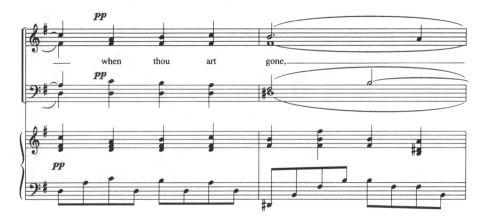

National Standards

The following National Standards are addressed through the Extension and bottom-page activities:

3. Improvising melodies, variations, and accompaniments. **(a)**
4. Composing and arranging music within specified guidelines. **(a)**
5. Reading and notating music. **(b)**
6. Listening to, analyzing, and describing music. **(a)**

7. Evaluating music and music performances. **(b)**
8. Understanding relationships between music, the other arts, and disciplines outside the arts. **(a, c, d, e)**
9. Understanding music in relation to history and culture. **(c, d)**

Extension

Identifying Dissonance as a Compositional Tool

Have students:

- Listen as you play dissonant intervals (2nds and 7ths) on an instrument.
- Sing some 2nds and 7ths in two parts.
- Listen to a tape of their performance of "Music, When Soft Voices Die," raising a hand when they hear dissonance between the parts.
- Discuss the effect of dissonance on the mood of the piece. (Dissonance creates tension, or a strangely melancholy irony, when it occurs in Romantic music. It is usually quickly resolved to a more consonant chord.)

Improvising Harmony for a Melody

Have students:

- Write a short, two-phrase melody in G major, beginning and ending on *do.*
- In pairs or small groups, construct a harmony line to go with the melody line, using experimentation and improvisation to find pitches that sound right together.
- Consider the use of dissonance at some points in the harmony, then choose whether or not to use it.
- Write the two parts, and perform it if they wish. (Note: These short compositions can be used in performance, before the piece, to alert the audience to the sound of unison and harmony, consonance and dissonance, phrasing and dynamics.)

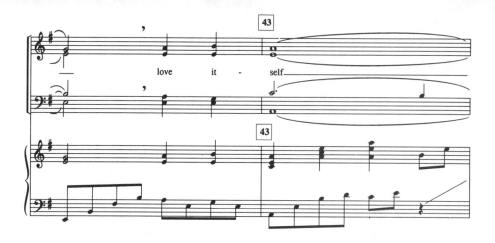

love it - self

Broader   *a tempo*

shall slum - ber on.

Broader

a tempo

p

Ped.

CURRICULUM CONNECTIONS
Dance

If there are students who are involved in modern dance or ballet, have them:

- Use their knowledge of choreography to construct a dance interpretation of the piece. (Help them avoid the literal translation of the text, and go for the more abstract ideas represented—memory and the lingering of sounds, smells, and love. Encourage use of levels, directionality, line, shape, and interaction.)
- Discuss how a dance interpretation mirrors musical phrasing and dynamics.

Cantaremos

Traditional Spanish Dance
ADAPTED BY: *Ramón Noble*
ARRANGER: *Ramón Noble*

CHORAL MUSIC TERMS
AB form
ABA form
a cappella
introduction
rhythm
rondo form
skipwise melodic movement
stepwise melodic movement

VOICING
SATB

PERFORMANCE STYLE
Very fast
A cappella

FOCUS
* Identify ABA form.
* Read and clap simple rhythms in 2/4 meter.
* Identify, read, and sing stepwise and skipwise melodic movement.

Warming Up

 Vocal Warm-Up 1
Sing the melody of "Happy Birthday," on the consonant *fff*. Hold one hand on your stomach, and feel your diaphragm controlling your breath.

 Vocal Warm-Up 2
Sing this exercise using solfège and hand signs or numbers, then sing again on *ta*. Repeat, moving up by half steps. The *t* sound should help "wake up your breathing." Repeat once more using *loo*, keeping the same feeling of breath support. Notice the syncopated rhythm.

Lesson 5: Cantaremos **35**

TEACHER'S RESOURCE BINDER
Blackline Master 4, *Translation and Pronunciation Guide for "Cantaremos,"* page 80
Blackline Master 5, *Understanding Form,* page 81

 National Standards
1. Singing a varied repertoire of music. **(a, b, c)**

5. Reading and notating music. **(b)**
6. Listening to, analyzing, and describing music. **(a)**
7. Evaluating music and performances. **(a)**
8. Understanding relationships between music, the other arts, and disciplines outside the arts. **(c)**
9. Understanding music in relation to history and culture. **(d)**

Cantaremos

Traditional Spanish Dance
ADAPTED BY: Ramón Noble
ARRANGER: Ramón Noble

Focus

OVERVIEW
Form; rhythms in 2/4 meter; stepwise and skipwise melodic movement.

OBJECTIVES
After completing this lesson, students will be able to:
* Identify ABA form.
* Read and clap simple rhythms in 2/4 meter.
* Identify, read, and sing stepwise and skipwise melodic movement.

CHORAL MUSIC TERMS
Define the Choral Music Terms for students, giving pronunciation, and answering any questions that may arise.

Warming Up

Vocal Warm-Ups
These Vocal Warm-Ups are designed to prepare students to:
* "Wake up" the diaphragm.
* Improve breathing and breath control.
* Read and sing in four parts using solfège and hand signs or numbers.
* Read syncopated rhythms.
Have students:
* Read through the set of Vocal Warm-Up directions.
* Sing, following your demonstration.

Sight-Singing

This Sight-Singing exercise is designed to prepare students to:
- Read simple rhythms in 2/4 meter.
- Read and sing stepwise and skipwise melodic movement, based mainly on the tonic chord tones.
- Identify and perform AB and ABA form.

Have students:
- Read through the Sight-Singing exercise directions.
- Read section A rhythmically, using rhythm syllables.
- Sight-sing through section A.
- Clap the B section.

Singing: "Cantaremos"

Identify and determine the form of a piece.

Have students:
- Read the text on page 36.
- Describe the form of an object and guess what form others are describing.
- Identify form as the sequential organization of sections in music.
- Clap the rhythm of the soprano/alto part in measures 10–17 of "Cantaremos," labeling this as A, and describing the style as lively and quick.
- Find a contrasting section (measures 19–26), and label this section as B, describing the style as legato or less active.
- Individually or in small groups, scan the entire piece and determine the form. (Introduction, ABA)

Sight-Singing

Sight-sing this exercise using solfège and hand signs or numbers. Notice the intervals that stay the same, move stepwise, and skip. Clap the B section rhythm. Combine these to create an ABA form.

Singing: "Cantaremos"

Think of the form of some object. Describe the form, without using the name. Can your classmates guess the object from your description?

Form is the organizing shape of something. In music, the form of a piece describes how many sections there are, in what order they are heard, and which are the same. Beginning with the letter A, each new idea is assigned the next letter of the alphabet. Some common forms are AB—binary form, ABA—ternary form, and ABACABA—rondo form.

Now turn to the music for "Cantaremos" on page 37. What is the form of "Cantaremos"?

HOW DID YOU DO?

Just as "Cantaremos" had a form which unfolded, so did your learning as you worked through this lesson.

Think about your preparation and performance of "Cantaremos."

1. As you read the piece, what rhythms and melodic patterns were easy for you? Which need more work?
2. Clap the rhythm of the B section in the Sight-Singing exercise, then make up your own eight-measure rhythm in 2/4 meter, showing your knowledge of rhythms, repetition, and contrast.

3. Describe melodic steps and skips, then sing a section of your choice from the Warm-Ups or "cantaremos" to show your ability to sing intervals in tune.
4. Describe how form occurs in music, and the form of "Cantaremos." Compare the sections, telling what was musically the same and different.
5. Listen to a taped performance of "Cantaremos" by your ensemble, and critique it. What was good? What needs work? What should you focus on to get better as an ensemble?

TEACHING STRATEGY
Diaphragmatic Breathing

- Feel the sensation of muscle expansion by placing thumbs above the small of the back with fingers pressing the top of the hips. Sip a long, deep breath and feel the action of the muscles.
- Feel the action of the diaphragm muscle by pressing the fingertips of both hands into the midsection of the torso just below the rib cage. Take a startled,

quick surprise breath and feel the action of the muscle. Which way did it react?
- Feel the diaphragm muscle expand outward as you sip a long, cool breath.
- Pant like a dog or bark like a dog (*arf* and *woof*). Feel the diaphragm action.
- Use unvoiced consonants such as *sh, f, p, t,* and *k* in various rhythms and tempos to create diaphragmatic action.

Cantaremos

Traditional Spanish Dance
Adapted and Arranged by Ramón Noble

SATB A cappella

Cantaremos **37**

Suggested Teaching Sequence

1. Review Vocal Warm-Ups.
Build correct breath support. Sing in four parts.
Have students:
- Review the Vocal Warm-Ups on page 35.
- Feel the diaphragm moving to force air from the lungs.
- Identify the syncopated rhythm, and practice clapping it for accuracy.
- Sing Vocal Warm-Up 2 again, using correct breath control and rhythmic accuracy.

2. Review Sight-Singing.
Read and sing simple rhythms and pitches using solfège and hand signs or numbers. Perform ABA form.
Have students:
- Review the Sight-Singing exercise on page 36 using solfège and hand signs or numbers.
- Find the intervals that stay the same, move by steps, and move by skips.
- Read and clap the rhythms accurately in the B section.
- Perform the exercise first in AB form, then ABA form.
- Discuss what would be needed to create a rondo (ABACABA) form. (a C section)

3. Sight-sing "Cantaremos" using solfège and hand signs or numbers.
Have students:
- Divide into voice sections (SATB) and read each part rhythmically, using rhythm syllables.
- Still in sections, sight-sing the pitches using solfège and hand signs or numbers, identifying and working on problem areas.
- Sing the piece through, using solfège and hand signs or numbers, with full ensemble.

TEACHING STRATEGY
Compare and Contrast Form
Have students:
- Find motifs in the room that are similar to AB, ABA, and rondo forms.
- Look back at "Dream a Dream" (page 4) and "Nginani Na" (page 23). Determine the form of each, and compare them to "Cantaremos." (Dream—ABA, Nginani—AB)

4. Learn the Spanish pronunciation and translation.

Have students:

- Read the translation on Blackline Master 4, *Translation and Pronunciation Guide for "Cantaremos,"* and decide if the text matches the spirit of the song.
- Use the pronunciation guide and echo the teacher or another Spanish speaker, saying each phrase slowly, then in rhythm.
- Speak the text of the song in rhythm, and in four parts.
- Sing "Cantaremos" with Spanish text, using correct pronunciation.

VOCAL DEVELOPMENT

To encourage vocal development, have students:

- Sing tall, open vowels for the phonetic Spanish diction.
- Clap and speak the rhythms, then speak the text in rhythm while conducting. The fast tempo demands clear, clean, quick words.
- Contrast the ostinato figures in the tenor and bass voices with the rhythmic intensity of the treble voices.
- Balance the chords between the parts by listening to them. Encourage students to try adding more weight to one part to determine the effect on the chord.

38 *Choral Connections Level 3 Mixed Voices*

CONNECTING THE ARTS
Dance

Have students:

- First alone, and then in pairs or small groups, improvise movement as they sing the piece.
- Divide into two groups and half watch as the other half improvises.
- Point out movements they found appropriate to the character of each section.

- Work together to choose two movements, one for each section, and develop a formation (concentric circles, lines, squares, scattered couples), adapting the movement until it becomes a dance.

Cantaremos **39**

Informal Assessment

During this lesson, students showed the ability to:

- Demonstrate good breath control and syncopated rhythm in the Vocal Warm-Ups.
- Identify stepwise and skip-wise melodic movement in the Sight-Singing exercise.
- Perform AB and ABA form in the Sight-Singing exercise.
- Sing using correct Spanish pronunciation in "Cantare-mos."

Student Self-Assessment

Have students:

- Evaluate their performances with the How Did You Do? section on page 36.
- Answer the questions individually. Discuss them in pairs or small groups and/or write their responses on a sheet of paper.

Individual Performance Assessment

To further demonstrate accomplishment, have each student:

- Use Blackline Master 5, *Understanding Form*, to demonstrate understanding of AB, ABA, and rondo forms.
- Point out places in his or her voice part of "Cantaremos" where it moves stepwise and skipwise, checked by a partner.
- Read or sing the text of either the A or B section of "Cantaremos" into a tape recorder, in an isolated area, to demonstrate correct Spanish pronunciation and breath control.

CURRICULUM CONNECTIONS
Multicultural Dances

Have students:

- Research other Hispanic dances, using folk dance books and recordings or resources in the community.
- Learn several of these dances, and compare the movements and musical characteristics to "Cantaremos."

- Learn the dances of several cultures, and then compare them to the melody of "Cantaremos," discovering similarities and differences between music and dance of two or more cultures.

Extension

Creating a Melody with Steps, Skips, and Repeats

Have students:

- Write a short song, no more than four phrases long, that uses skips, steps, and repeats.
- Describe their melody using musical terms related to meter, key, tempo, and character.
- Write a contrasting section of the same length, using opposite characteristics than those described.
- Determine a form for these two melodies. Share their pieces first with a classmate, then within a group, then with the teacher, revising after each consultation. Perform the final piece if they desire.

Arranging an Accompaniment for Unpitched Percussion in the Style of the Piece

Have students:

- Develop ostinato patterns taken from the song, and play them on claves, drums, maracas, or cowbell with the piece.
- Choose contrasting accompaniment ostinati and instruments for the B section.
- Practice and decide if the contrast works, or if it is too much.
- Refine the accompaniment until they are satisfied.

Arranging the Sight-Singing Exercise for Instruments

Have students:

- Determine which parts of the Sight-Singing exercise are pitched (A) and unpitched (B).
- Arrange both sections for instruments, with the only constraint being use of pitched instruments for A and unpitched for B. (Note: This is a good opportunity to use electronic keyboards with built-in percussion sounds.)

National Standards

The following National Standards are addressed through the Extension and bottom-page activities:

1. Singing, alone and with others, a varied repertoire of music. **(b)**
4. Composing and arranging music within specified guidelines. **(b, c)**
6. Listening to, analyzing, and describing music. **(c)**
8. Understanding relationships between music, the other arts, and disciplines outside the arts. **(a, d)**
9. Understanding music in relation to history and culture. **(a)**

Laudate Nomen Domini

Traditional Latin Text
COMPOSER: *Christopher Tye* (1553)

CHORAL MUSIC TERMS
homophonic
monophonic
polyphonic
texture

VOICING
SATB

PERFORMANCE STYLE
Moderately
Accompanied

FOCUS
* Identify and compare homophonic and polyphonic texture.
* Sing homophonic and polyphonic texture.
* Sight-sing pitches in G major.

Warming Up

 Vocal Warm-Up
Sing this exercise using solfège and hand signs or numbers, then sing again on *nah*. Repeat, moving up by half steps. Notice the tonic chord tones.

 Sight-Singing
Sight-sing this exercise using solfège and hand signs or numbers. Sing each line separately in unison; then combine, trying different voice parts on each line.

TEACHER'S RESOURCE BINDER
Blackline Master 6, *Polyphonic Texture,* page 82
Blackline Master 7, *Translation and Pronunciation Guide for "Laudate Nomen Domini,"* page 83

National Standards

In this lesson, students should develop the following skills and concepts:
1. Singing, alone and with others, a varied repertoire of music. **(a, b, c)**
5. Reading and notating music. **(b)**
6. Listening to, analyzing, and describing music. **(a, c)**
8. Understanding relationships between music, the other arts, and disciplines outside the arts. **(a, c)**

LESSON 6

Laudate Nomen Domini

Traditional Latin Text
COMPOSER: *Christopher Tye*
(1553)

Focus

OVERVIEW
Texture; sight-singing.

OBJECTIVES
After completing this lesson, students will be able to:
* Identify and compare homophonic and polyphonic texture.
* Sing homophonic and polyphonic texture.
* Sight-sing pitches in G major.

CHORAL MUSIC TERMS
Define the Choral Music Terms for students, giving pronunciation, and answering any questions that may arise.

Warming Up

Vocal Warm-Ups
These Vocal Warm-Ups are designed to prepare students to:
* Perform with good vocal resonance.
* Sing octave leaps in a melodic line.
* Sing pitches in the tonic chord.
Have students:
* Read through the set of Vocal Warm-Up directions.
* Sing, following your demonstration.

Sight-Singing

The Sight-Singing exercise on page 41 is designed to prepare students to:

- Practice reading and singing in the key of G major.
- Read in the treble and bass clefs.
- Sing three parts at the same time.

Have students:

- Read through the Sight-Singing exercise directions.
- Speak and clap each voice part rhythmically, using rhythm syllables.
- Sight-sing through each part separately using solfége and hand signs or numbers.
- Sing all parts together, trying different voice parts on each line.

Singing: "Laudate Nomen Domini"

Identify and determine texture. Have students:

- Read the text on page 42.
- Feel different fabrics, either from samples you have brought in, or sweaters and jackets that can be passed among the rows of singers.
- Describe the textures, and then read the definitions of texture in music.
- Listen to a recording of the first eight measures of Handel's "Hallelujah" Chorus, and identify the texture. (homophonic)
- Using Blackline Master 6, *Polyphonic Texture*, identify polyphony and motet; sing an example of polyphony.
- Look at the notation for the first page of "Laudate Nomen Domini," describing where they will be singing homophonically (measures 1–8) and where they will sing polyphonically (measure 8 on).

Singing: "Laudate Nomen Domini"

Think texture! Look at different fabrics, and compare their textures. Notice how one is rough, while another is smooth, depending upon the arrangement, size, and quality of the threads.

In music, texture is formed by the vertical and horizontal relationships of pitches.

- Monophony is a single line of melody.
- Homophony is created when there is more than one line and all the lines move at the same time.
- Polyphony is created when there is more than one line and each line has its own melody. The lines intertwine, moving at different times, creating harmony by the overlapping of pitches from each line.

Listen to some musical examples, and identify monophony, homophony, and polyphony.

Now turn to the music for "Laudate Nomen Domini" on page 43. What textures do you think you will find in "Laudate Nomen Domini"?

HOW DID YOU DO?

Think about your preparation and performance of "Laudate Nomen Domini."

1. How well could you sight-sing your part with your own group? Was it different with the whole ensemble? What is getting easy, and what is still difficult? What should you work on?

2. Describe the three musical textures you have learned. Plan a short lecture/demonstration with a small group, using musical examples from the lesson to illustrate each texture.

3. Choose either visual art or movement, and describe how monophony, homophony, and polyphony could be represented in this other art.

 Developing Vocal Resonance

Resonance is the unique sound of a voice which identifies it and gives it a rich beauty. To get resonance, there must be large spaces. Ask students to think about a time when they have been in a large marble or stone building like a cathedral or church. Sound has a huge place to resonate, or let the sound ring out. The sound is amplified without mechanical means when it can resonate in a large space with firm walls. The head is your resonating chamber for sound and needs large spaces with firm walls (your facial bone structure) to ring and sound

Laudate Nomen Domini

Music by
Christopher Tye, 1553
Traditional Latin text

Motet

Lau - da - te No - men Do - mi - ni, vos
O come, ye ser - vants of the Lord, And

ser - vi Do - mi - ni, ab
praise His ho - ly Name; From

ser - vi Do - mi - ni, ab or - tu
praise His ho - ly Name; From ear - ly

ser - vi - Do - mi - ni, ab or - tu so - lis us - que
praise His ho - ly Name; From ear - ly morn to set - ting

ser - vi Do - mi - ni, ab or - tu so - lis
praise His ho - ly Name; From ear - ly morn to

Laudate Nomen Domini **43**

Suggested Teaching Sequence

1. Review Vocal Warm-Ups.
Develop good resonance. Sing octave leaps.
Have students:
- Review the Vocal Warm-Ups on page 41.
- Discuss vocal resonance.
- Use vocal resonance especially when reaching over the top of the octave leap.

2. Review Sight-Singing.
Read and sing in G major using solfège and hand signs or numbers.
Have students:
- Review the Sight-Singing exercise on page 41 using solfège and hand signs or numbers.
- Sing any two parts at the same time. Then sing all three parts at the same time.
- Each begin on one line, and continue in a sequence from line 1, to 2, to 3, to 1 and so on.
- Describe the texture as homophony or polyphony, identifying the musical characteristics of each.

3. Sight-sing "Laudate Nomen Domini" using solfège and hand signs or numbers.
Have students:
- Divide into voice sections (SATB) and read each part rhythmically, using rhythm syllables.
- Still in sections, sing with solfège and hand signs or numbers, identifying and working on problem areas.
- Sing the piece through, using solfège and hand signs or numbers, with full ensemble.

---

out.
The resonance or tone placement of the voice is also called the mask. Have students:
- Focus the tone behind the nose, feeling a buzz or ring when singing an *ng*.
- Keep the buzzing feeling in the mask on every sound to keep a continuous focus.
- Use a hum, and vocalize with *m* and *ng* sounds to create resonance, then add different vowels.

4. Learn the Latin pronunciation.

Have students:

- Read the translation of "Laudate Nomen Domini."
- Use the pronunciation guide on Blackline Master 7, *Translation and Pronunciation Guide for "Laudate Nomen Domini"* and echo each phrase slowly, then in rhythm.
- Speak the text of the song in rhythm, in four parts.
- Sing "Laudate Nomen Domini" with Latin text, using correct pronunciation.

5. Use dynamics on polyphonic entrances.

Have students:

- Sing from measures 8–12.
- Discuss how dynamics can help the audience hear individual part entrances. Once a part has entered, it should decrescendo while the new entering voice part comes in, and continue until all parts have entered.
- Sing measures 8–12 again, practicing this technique.

Assessment

Informal Assessment

During this lesson, students showed the ability to:

- Distinguish between monophony, homophony, and polyphony using Blackline Master 6, *Polyphonic Texture.*
- Demonstrate good breath control and octave leaps in the Vocal Warm-Ups.
- Read and sing in G major, using solfège and hand signs or numbers, in the Sight-Singing exercise.
- Sight-sing in G major in four parts in "Laudate Nomen Domini."
- Sing with correct Latin pronunciation in "Laudate Nomen Domini."

Student Self-Assessment

Have students:

- Evaluate their performance with the How Did You Do? section on page 42.

44

 VOCAL DEVELOPMENT

To encourage vocal development, have students:

- Sing tall, open vowels for the Latin text.
- Energize and sustain the phrases with breath support and the feeling of moving forward. Sing forward to the climax of each phrase and carry to the end of the phrase. Feel the forward momentum.

- Use movement to illustrate the forward feeling of the music.
- Balance the chords by listening to each voice in the chords.
- Contrast the chordal (homophonic or homorhythmic because the parts move together) sections with the contrapuntal (polyphonic) sections. Feel the forward momentum in both types of writing.

Laudate Nomen Domini **45**

Individual Performance Assessment

Have each students

- Sing through the entire piece, raising the left hand when the texture is homophonic, and the right hand when it is polyphonic.
- In a small group, perform measures 8–12 and 26–38, demonstrating appropriate "entrance" dynamics for the different parts.
- In a quartet, read or sing the text of measures 1–18 into a tape recorder, in an isolated area, to demonstrate correct Latin pronunciation.

Extension

Texture in Today's Music

Have students:

- Find examples of musical textures on CDs, tapes, or records.
- Listen to environmental sounds for examples of texture.
- Make a large chart compiling their findings, labeled "Textured Sound All Around."

Creating a Homophonic Piece

Have students:

- Study a chord progression: for example, I-IV-V-I in G major.
- Assign each chord to one measure, choose a meter, and write a rhythm for each measure.
- In vocal part sections, choose one chord tone to sing for each measure, and sing those tones using the rhythms created above.
- In four groups, sing all four parts together to hear their homophonic piece.
- Identify the measures that work well, and where revision is needed to fill out the chords.
- Revise, practice, and perform again.

National Standards

The following National Standards are addressed through the Extension and bottom-page activities:

1. Singing, alone and with others, a varied repertoire of music. **(b)**
4. Composing and arranging music within specified guidelines. **(a)**

6. Listening to, analyzing, and describing music. **(a, c)**
9. Understanding music in relation to history and culture. **(a, c, d)**

LESSON 7

Pål På Haugen

Norwegian Folk Tune
ARRANGER: Bradley Ellingboe
TRANSLATED BY: Bradley Ellingboe

Focus

OVERVIEW
Tonic chord tones; sequence; repetition; Norwegian pronunciation.

OBJECTIVES
After completing this lesson, students will be able to:
- Recognize, read, and sing the pitches of the tonic chord.
- Identify sequence and repetition within a melodic line.
- Sing, using correct Norwegian pronunciation.

CHORAL MUSIC TERMS
Define the Choral Music Terms for students, giving pronunciation, and answering any questions that may arise.

Warming Up

Vocal Warm-Up
This Vocal Warm-Up is designed to prepare students to:
- Warm up the voice.
- Conduct in 4/4 meter.
- Sing with vocal resonance.
- Identify and sing repeated pitches.

Have students:
- Read through the Vocal Warm-Up directions.
- Sing, following your demonstration.

LESSON 7

Pål På Haugen

Norwegian Folk Tune
ARRANGER: Bradley Ellingboe
TRANSLATED BY: Bradley Ellingboe

CHORAL MUSIC TERMS
chord
repetition
scale
sequence
tonic
tonic chord

VOICING
SATB

PERFORMANCE STYLE
A cappella

FOCUS
- Recognize, read, and sing the pitches of the tonic chord.
- Identify sequence and repetition within a melodic line.
- Sing using correct Norwegian pronunciation.

Warming Up

 Vocal Warm-Up

Sing this exercise using solfège and hand signs or numbers, then on the *neh* syllables. Conduct in 4/4 meter as you sing. Move a half step up or down on each repeat. Notice the five repeated pitches at the beginning of each pattern.

 Sight-Singing

Sight-sing the two exercises below using solfège and hand signs or numbers. Sing each line separately in unison, then in these combinations: Soprano and alto sing part I with tenor and bass singing part II; tenor and soprano sing part I with bass and alto singing part II. Notice the tonic chord tones and melodic sequence in part I.

TEACHER'S RESOURCE BINDER
Skill Master 19, *Conducting Patterns*, page 42
Blackline Master 8, *Translation and IPA Pronunciation Guide for "Pål På Haugen,"* page 84

National Standards
1. Singing a varied repertoire of music. **(a, b, c)**
5. Reading and notating music. **(b)**
6. Listening to, analyzing, and describing music. **(a)**
7. Evaluating music and performances. **(a)**
8. Understanding relationships between music, the other arts, and disciplines outside the arts. **(c)**
9. Understanding music in relation to history and culture. **(d)**

Singing: "Pål På Haugen"

Listen to the three notes as given below. Can you name this tune in three notes?

These first three notes make up the tonic chord—*do, mi,* and *so.* Many melodies are centered around these three pitches, so if you recognize them, and hear their pitches in your head, they will be guideposts as you sight-sing music.

Now turn to the music for "Pål På Haugen" on page 48.

HOW DID YOU DO?

"Pål På Haugen" is a story of learning from your mistakes, and having courage to go on. When you are learning new things, this song has a good message to remember.

Think about your preparation and performance of "Pål På Haugen."

1. Describe the three syllables that make up the tonic chord. Can you hear these pitches in your head? Why is this important for sight-singing?

2. Tell what melodic sequence is, then sing something from the lesson to demonstrate sequence.

3. Find a place in the piece that has repeated pitches. Notice the text, and tell why it makes sense to have repeated tones at this point in the text.

4. How good is your Norwegian pronunciation? What could be better?

5. If you were to meet the arranger of this folk song, what advice would you give for his next arrangement, based on your feelings about this one? Give specific musical examples to support your ideas.

Sight-Singing

This Sight-Singing exercise is designed to prepare students to:
- Sight-sing using solfège and hand signs or numbers.
- Identify, hear, and sing tonic chord tones.
- Identify and sing melodic sequence.
- Sing in two parts, in different combinations.

Have students:
- Read through the Sight-Singing exercise directions.
- Read each voice part rhythmically, using rhythm syllables.
- Sight-sing through each part separately using solfége and hand signs or numbers.
- Sing all parts together.

Singing: "Pål På Haugen"

Identify the tonic chord tones. Have students:
- Read the text on page 47.
- Listen to the three pitches, and identify the tune. (One possibility is "Marine's Hymn.")
- Identify the first three pitches as the tonic chord tones *do, mi,* and *so.*

TEACHING STRATEGY
Conducting in 4/4 Meter

Have students:
- Take turns conducting the Vocal Warm-Up using the 4/4 conducting pattern. (See Skill Master 19 in the TRB.)
- Practice and then conduct "Pål På Haugen" after the ensemble is fairly secure. (Notice the meter changes and prepare carefully.)

Suggested Teaching Sequence

1. Review Vocal Warm-Up.
Conduct in 4/4 meter. Develop vocal resonance. Identify repeated tones.

Have students:
- Review the Vocal Warm-Up on page 46.
- Review vocal resonance.
- Identify the repeated tones and train themselves to recognize what the pitches sound like.
- Learn the conducting pattern for 4/4 meter, and conduct as they repeat the exercise. (See Skill Master 19, *Conducting Patterns,* in the TRB.)

2. Review Sight-Singing.
Sight-sing using solfège and hand signs or numbers. Identify tonic chord tones and melodic sequence.

Have students:
- Review the Sight-Singing exercise on page 46 using solfège and hand signs or numbers.
- Sing in the recommended two-part combinations.
- Identify the tonic chord tones in Part A, the first measure.
- Identify melodic sequence as the repetition of a pattern of pitches, beginning on a different pitch on each repetition.
- Visually and aurally identify the sequence in Part A. (the quarter note/two eighth note combination with the descending third, in measures 3 and 4)

For Anton Armstrong and the St. Olaf Choir

Pål På Haugen
Paul and His Chickens

Traditional Norwegian
Translated and Arranged by Bradley Ellingboe

SATB, A cappella

Used with Permission 1995/96.

"Pål På Haugen"

This piece, "Pål På Haugen," was written for the Saint Olaf choir and its director, Anton Armstrong. Armstrong and Bradley Ellingboe, the composer of the piece, know each other from their student days of singing together in that same choir.

hau - gen___ sprang; Pål kun - ne væl på___ hø - nom for - ne - me
noth - ing were wrong; Yet Paul could well on their fu - tures___ won - der,

hau - gen___ sprang; Pål for - ne - me
noth - ing were wrong; Yet Paul won - dered,

hau - gen___ sprang; Pål kun - ne væl på___ hø - nom for - ne - me
noth - ing were wrong; Yet Paul could well on their fu - tures___ won - der,

hau - gen___ sprang; Pål for - ne - me
noth - ing were wrong; Yet Paul won - dered,

re - ven var u - te med rum - pe så lang:
loose was the fox with his tail so___ long.

re - ven var u - te med rum - pe så lang:
loose was the fox with his tail so___ long.

re - ven var u - te med rum - pe så lang:
loose was the fox with his tail so___ long.

re - ven var u - te med rum - pe så lang:
loose was the fox with his tail so___ long.

3. Sight-sing "Pål På Haugen" using solfège and hand signs or numbers.

Have students:
- Listen to the soprano line in measures 1–8 of the piece played on the piano.
- Identify the tonic chord tones, repetition, and sequence.
- Repeat with other three part lines.
- Divide into voice sections (SATB) and read each part rhythmically, using rhythm syllables.
- Still in voice sections, sight-sing measures 1–8 using solfège and hand signs or numbers, identifying and working on problem areas.
- Then sing the measures as full ensemble.
- Continue this process with one section of the song at a time: measures 9–17; 18–26; 27–34; 34–46; 47–end.
- Sing the entire piece on solfège and hand signs or numbers as a full ensemble.

4. Learn the Norwegian pronunciation.

Have students:
- Study Blackline Master 8, *Translation and IPA Pronunciation Guide for "Pål På Haugen."*
- Pronounce the vowels as given in the examples.
- Pronounce the consonants as given in the examples.
- Apply the phonetic pronunciation to the text of "Pål På Haugen."
- Practice, then sing "Pål På Haugen" with correct Norwegian pronunciation.

 Arranger Bradley Ellingboe

Bradley Ellingboe is an Associate Professor of Music at the University of New Mexico, where he teaches voice and directs the university chorus. He is also the Music Director at Saint Paul Lutheran Church in Albuquerque, New Mexico.

Folk Songs and Stories of the Fox

Have students:

- Search for examples of songs and stories in literature of all cultures that have a story similar to "Pål På Haugen." (To get them started, suggest "The Fox Went Out One Chilly Night," "Rosie's Walk," and "Chicken Little.")
- Identify the common elements in the stories and songs collected.

- Speculate about why there are many songs and stories about this type of event.
- Construct a picture book, play, or pantomime for one of the songs or stories, then share it with a class of children at an elementary school.

13

Pål   han sprang   og vreng - de med au - gom:
Paul   jumped up   and fear   made him wide - eyed.

Pål   han sprang   og vreng - de med au - gom:
Paul   jumped up   and fear   made him wide - eyed.

Pål   han sprang   og vreng - de med au - gom:
Paul   jumped up   and fear   made him wide - eyed.

Pål   han sprang   og vreng - de med au - gom:
Paul   jumped up   and fear   made him wide - eyed.

13

"Nå tør eg in - kje kom - a heim   åt a mor!"
"Now   I don't dare   to go home   to my ma!"

"Nå tør   eg in - kje   kom heim åt   a mor!"
"Now I   don't dare to   go home to   my ma!"

"Nå tør   eg in - kje   kom heim åt   a mor!"
"Now I   don't dare to   go home to   my ma!"

"Nå tør   eg in - kje   kom heim åt   a mor!"
"Now I   don't dare to   go home to   my ma!"

Pål På Haugen **51**

Assessment

Informal Assessment
During this lesson, students showed the ability to:
- Identify repeated tones in the Vocal Warm-Up exercise.
- Visually and aurally identify tonic chord tones in the Sight-Singing exercise, Part I.
- Visually and aurally identify melodic sequence in the Sight-Singing exercise, Part I.
- Read and sing in four parts in "Pål På Haugen," using correct Norwegian pronunciation.

Student Self-Assessment
Have students:
- Evaluate their performance with the How Did You Do? section on page 47.
- Answer the questions individually. Discuss them in pairs or small groups and/or write their responses on a sheet of paper.

Individual Performance Assessment
To further demonstrate accomplishment, have each student:
- In a small group, identify all occurrences of tonic chord tones on an assigned page of "Pål På Haugen."
- In a small group, identify all occurrences of melodic repetition on an assigned page of "Pål På Haugen."
- In a small group, identify all occurrences of melodic sequence on one assigned page of "Pål På Haugen."

CURRICULUM CONNECTIONS
Social Studies

Because of Norway's geographical location and shape, most people live on or near the sea. Norway's seafaring history goes back a thousand years to the days of the Vikings. When the Vikings adopted Christianity, Norway was unified with the rest of the European world. These elements—the geography, the explorations of the Vikings, and early Christianity in Norway—are characteristics that are likely to be included in traditional Norwegian folk songs. Encourage students to discover more about Norwegian folk songs, especially the works of Norway's most famous composer, Edvard Grieg. Grieg based many of his orchestrations on traditional Norwegian folk songs.

Extension

The Conductor's Role

Have students:

- Identify the role of the conductor in keeping the group together and providing interpretation signals for such elements as phrasing, dynamics, and style.
- Watch concerts on television to learn about specific conductors, or invite a local conductor to come in and discuss the role of the conductor.
- Learn the conducting patterns for sets of two beats and three beats. (See Skill Master 19, *Conducting Patterns,* in the TRB.)
- Optional: Research conducting by watching and comparing several conductors, and reading conducting texts.

Exploring the Tonic Chord, Melodic Sequence, and Repeated Tones

Have students:

- Choose one or more of the elements—tonic chord, melodic sequence, and repeated tones; create a vocal warm-up exercise that demonstrates understanding of the concept.
- Describe the concept, and lead the warm-up at the beginning of a rehearsal.

National Standards

The following National Standards are addressed through the Extension and bottom-page activities:

3. Improvising melodies, variations, and accompaniments. **(b, c)**
4. Composing and arranging music within specified guidelines. **(a)**
7. Evaluating music and music performances. **(b)**
8. Understanding relationships between music, the other arts, and disciplines outside the arts. **(a, b, c)**
9. Understanding music in relation to history and culture. **(a, c)**

52

Improvising on the Tonic Chord Tones

One way to solidify the sound of the tonic chord tones, and an easy way to begin improvisation, is to limit the tone set to just the three tonic chord tones, over a strong tonic or open fifth accompaniment. Place the tonic chord tones in a comfortable key on the board.

Have students:

- Listen as you provide an ostinato accompaniment with a strong sense of beat, in any meter and style you choose, using either the tonic at an octave (tonic accompaniment), or the tonic and fifth (bordun).
- Vocally or at the keyboard, improvise rhythmically on just the tonic pitch, *do,* using the solfège name.
- Add *so,* then *mi,* allowing students to freely improvise on one pitch for a long time before moving to another, and gradually moving between the pitches more frequently and comfortably.
- Begin using passing tones only if they are ready.
- Share with a partner by taking turns and listening to one another if they wish.

It Was a Lover and His Lass

COMPOSER: Michael Larkin

TEXT: William Shakespeare (1564–1616)

Focus

OVERVIEW
Sixteenth notes; scalewise passages; madrigal style.

OBJECTIVES
After completing this lesson, students will be able to:
- Read and sing rhythms with sixteenth notes.
- Read and sing scalewise patterns with flexibility.
- Identify and perform in a madrigal style.

CHORAL MUSIC TERMS
Define the Choral Music Terms for students, giving pronunciation, and answering any questions that may arise.

Warming Up

Movement Warm-Up
This Movement Warm-Up is designed to:
- Prepare students for singing by stretching and relaxing the body.

Have students:
- Read through the Movement Warm-Up directions.
- Perform the exercise.

CHORAL MUSIC TERMS
dotted eighth-sixteenth rhythm
madrigal style
scalewise melodic patterns
sixteenth notes

It Was a Lover and His Lass

COMPOSER: *Michael Larkin*
TEXT: *William Shakespeare (1564–1616)*

VOICING
SATB

PERFORMANCE STYLE
Playfully
Accompanied by piano

FOCUS
- Read and sing rhythms with sixteenth notes.
- Read and sing scalewise patterns with flexibility.
- Identify and perform in a madrigal style.

Warming Up

Movement Warm-Up
You sing best when you are relaxed. Imitate your teacher or a classmate hanging up a load of laundry on a clothesline. Be sure to include bending to pick clothes out of the basket, stretching up to the clothesline, reaching to get the clothespins out of a bag, and pinning various widths of clothes to the line. Bending and stretching will relax your body.

 Vocal Warm-Up
Sing this exercise clearly on *da*. Repeat, moving up by half steps. Feel the sixteenth notes over a steady beat, and keep them even. Notice that the melody moves in scalewise patterns.

Continue up by half steps.

Da da . . .

 Sight-Singing
Remember to keep a good supply of air as you sing this little tune. Sight-sing first using solfège and hand signs or numbers, then try the words. Think about this text, and decide what style characteristics to use.

Come a - way my love and hear the birds sing, come a - way for now it is spring.

TEACHER'S RESOURCE BINDER
Blackline Master 9, *Mad About Madrigals*, page 86

National Standards
1. Singing a varied repertoire of music. **(a, b, c)**
5. Reading and notating music. **(b)**
6. Listening to and describing music. **(f)**
7. Evaluating music and performances. **(a)**
8. Understanding relationships between music and other disciplines. **(c)**
9. Understanding music in relation to history and culture. **(d)**

Singing: "It Was a Lover and His Lass"

You know what attire is correct for different occasions. Picture yourself at a concert, at a football game, and then at your grandparents' wedding anniversary party. Describe your attire at each of these events. Does the style of your clothes match the occasion?

In music, composers sometimes write in a style because it is popular at the time, or they might match the style to the text. During the Renaissance, many poems were written about love. Sometimes they were happy and sometimes sad.

Read the text of the Sight-Singing exercise. What is the mood? What musical style would match? Read the text of "It Was a Lover and His Lass." If it has the same mood as the exercise, use the same style of singing.

Now turn to the music for "It Was a Lover and His Lass" on page 62.

HOW DID YOU DO?
?
?

Think about your preparation and performance of "It Was a Lover and His Lass."
1. Describe how sixteenth notes work, then sing a part of the lesson to demonstrate how well you can perform them.
2. Sing the Vocal Warm-Up to show your ability to sing scalewise patterns with flexibility. Tell what you learned in this lesson to help sing these patterns.

3. Discuss the stylistic characteristics of a song composed in madrigal style. Referring to measure numbers, describe where madrigal characteristics are found in "It Was a Lover and His Lass."
4. Tell what you have learned about singing in madrigal style.

Vocal Warm-Up
This Vocal Warm-Up is designed to prepare students to:
• Read and sing scalewise passages and sixteenth notes.
• Sing scale passages and sixteenth notes with flexibility.
Have students:
• Read through the Vocal Warm-Up directions.
• Sing, following your demonstration.

Sight-Singing
This Sight-Singing exercise is designed to prepare students to:
• Practice sight-singing in two parts.
• Sing with a light, lively, quick style.
Have students:
• Read through the Sight-Singing exercise directions.
• Read each voice part rhythmically, using rhythm syllables.
• Sight-sing through each part separately using solfége and hand signs or numbers.
• Sing all parts together.

Singing: "It Was a Lover and His Lass"

Match style to text.
Have students:
• Read the text on page 61.
• Imagine what they would wear to the different events, then discuss whether they would be appropriately dressed for the event.
• Describe the mood of the Sight-Singing exercise (fun-loving), and what style to use. (If necessary, give a choice—slow and sustained, like a march, or light and bouncy.)
• Read the text of "A Lover and His Lass," determining that it has the same style as the Sight-Singing exercise.

1. Review Movement Warm-Up.
Prepare for singing by stretching the body. Have students:
- Review the Movement Warm-Up on page 60.
- Discuss relaxation techniques of bending and stretching.

2. Review Vocal Warm-Up.
Develop good resonance. Sing octave leaps. Have students:
- Sing the Vocal Warm-Up on page 60 in the style established—light, lively, and quick.
- Use Blackline Master 9, *Mad About Madrigals,* to identify the characteristics of a madrigal, and compare the exercise to the characteristics.

3. Review Sight-Singing.
Identify and practice a light, bouncy style. Have students:
- Review the Sight-Singing exercise on page 60 using solfège and hand signs or numbers, then the text.
- Describe the characteristics that make this exercise like a madrigal, then sing in madrigal style.

4. Sight-sing "It Was a Lover and His Lass" using solfège and hand signs or numbers.
Have students:
- Speak the text in measures 4–15 in rhythm.
- Discuss why this text is in the style of a madrigal.
- Divide in voice sections (SATB) and read each part rhythmically, using rhythm syllables.
- Still in sections, sing with solfège and hand signs or numbers, identifying and working on problem areas.

It Was a Lover and His Lass

Music by Michael Larkin
Text by William Shakespeare (1564–1616)

SATB, Accompanied

The Madrigal Style

Madrigals were composed mostly in Italy and England, and were secular vocal pieces, often with a theme of unrequited love. Many madrigals were polyphonic, with intricately interwoven melodic lines which had many scalewise passages and fast-moving rhythms. The English madrigals often had couplets of rhymes, interspersed with refrains of *fa la* or the like. Madrigals were usually composed for individual voices on each part, to be sung with a light, quick style that enhanced the intricate weaving of the lines, and quick rhythms. The dominant line was sung stronger, and each line came forward or receded to accommodate the most important melodic part.

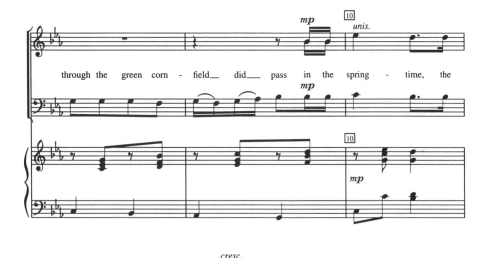

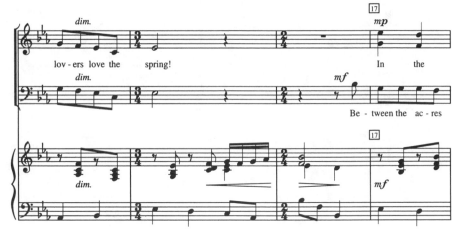

through the green corn-field did pass in the spring-time, the
only pret-ty ring-time when birds do sing hey ding-a-ding ding, sweet
ding, ding, ding, sweet
lov-ers love the spring!
In the
Be - tween the ac-res

- Sing the piece through, using solfège and hand signs or numbers, with full ensemble.
- Divide into sections and recite the text rhythmically for each voice part.
- Sing the piece through with text as a full ensemble.

5. Emphasize an important melody.

Have students:

- Sing the bass part (in appropriate registers), measures 16–22.
- Sing the soprano/alto parts, measures 16–22.
- Decide which should be sung louder and why. (Bass line has the melody and poem text.)
- Sing measures 16–22 with the full ensemble, bringing out the primary melodies.

6. Sing with the text in a madrigal style.

Have students:

- Sing through the piece, using the words of the text, and bringing out important melodies.
- Review the madrigal style—light and quick.
- Discuss some of the challenges of singing in this style, including dynamics, phrasing, and pitch accuracy.
- Sing the piece through with the text, using a madrigal-type style.

CURRICULUM CONNECTIONS
Writing

Guide students in writing a poem, using Shakespeare's poem as a model.
Have students:

- Write the text of "It Was a Lover and His Lass" on the board or on paper, making a new line for each phrase.
- Underline all repeated phrases.

- Circle all rhyming words.
- Discuss the form based on the highlighting just done.
- Create a poem, using the form of the Shakespeare poem.
- Optional: Create a madrigal-type melody for their poem.

VOCAL DEVELOPMENT

To encourage vocal development, have students:

- Demonstrate good vocal tone by singing tall vowels and altering (or modifying) the vowel sounds in a Shakespearean English accent style when necessary, such as *lover* (*lawh* instead of *uh*), *pass* (*pawh* instead of *pehs*), *and*, *country*, and *love*.
- Energize sustained tones by increasing the breath support and dynamic level.
- Sustain phrases by staggering the breathing and moving forward through the phrases.
- Demonstrate the correct singing of the *r* consonant after a vowel. It should be almost silent as in *lover*, *cornfield*, *birds*, and *flow'r*.
- The *r* before a vowel can be flipped once. Try it on the words such as *spring*, *rye*, and *springtime*, to get a Shakespearean English effect.
- Balance the chords between the parts by listening to them. Encourage students to try adding more weight to one part to determine the effect on the chord.
- Articulate the different rhythmic patterns by conducting and speaking the rhythms, then conducting and speaking the text in rhythms. Clearly enunciate the words, thinking Shakespearean English while speaking the text.
- Keep a light head tone quality to reflect the character of the song and to be able to execute the fast rhythms quickly and precisely.

TEACHING STRATEGY
Relaxation Techniques for Singers

Pulling together many singers whose minds and bodies are diverted to many different places is a real challenge for the choral music director! A common focus and clearing of tension from body and mind needs to occur before effective music making can take place. Use natural body movements and vivid imagery to develop a central focus.

- Imagine waking up in the morning, stretching, and yawning. Stretch in all different directions.
- Roll the shoulders forward and backward; lift the shoulders to the ears, pressing hard. Drop the shoulders back and down.
- Turn sideways in a line and massage the back of the person in front of you.

Informal Assessment

During this lesson, students showed the ability to:

- Read and sing sixteenth notes and scalewise patterns in the Vocal Warm-Up exercise.
- Sing with a light, quick style in the Vocal Warm-Up exercise.
- Read and sing using madrigal style in the Sight-Singing exercise.
- Sing in madrigal style, bringing out important melody lines, in "It Was a Lover and His Lass."

Student Self-Assessment

Have students:

- Evaluate their performance with the How Did You Do? section on page 61.
- Answer the questions individually. Discuss them in pairs or small groups and/or write their responses on a sheet of paper.

Individual Performance Assessment

To further demonstrate accomplishment, have each student:

- In small groups, sing sections of this piece selected by you, demonstrating appropriate style.
- Sing through the whole piece in ensemble, signaling with raised fingers the part that should be brought out the most: 1=soprano, 2=alto, 3=tenor, and 4=bass.

It Was a Lover and His Lass **65**

Reverse and have your back massaged.

- Imagine rushing or jogging to school. Grab your school books and dance away to school. Skip or jog while waving to friends. Stop to pick up dropped items from the ground—imagine any active scenario.

- Close eyes and imagine picking up a penny by the toes—feel only that sensation, concentrating on it intently. (Use any kind of imagery to focus the mind.)
- Bring singers back to reality with easy respiration and phonation exercises.

Extension

Compare the Madrigal to Today's Pop Music

The madrigal was the pop music of its day.
Have students:
- Compare the characteristics of a madrigal with songs they listen to today. Ask: What is the same? What is different?

Comparing Madrigals

Have students:
- Listen to a recording of a madrigal. Some examples are "As Vesta Was Descending" by Weelkes, performed by Chanticleer, and "Au Joli Jeu" by Janequin, performed by The King's Singers.
- Identify the characteristics of a madrigal heard in each piece.
- Discuss the differences and similarities between the two pieces and the performing groups.
- Compare the characteristics of the madrigal with "A Lover and His Lass," determining how the piece is, and is not, like a madrigal.

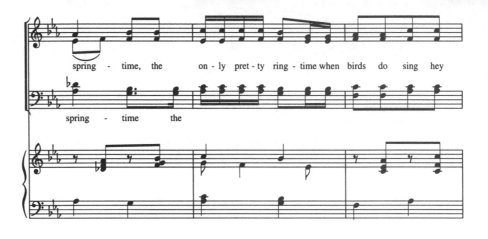

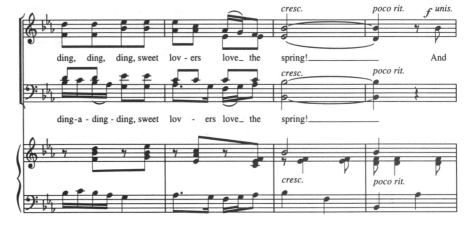

National Standards

The following National Standards are addressed through the Extension and bottom-page activities:

1. Singing, alone and with others, a varied repertoire of music. **(b)**
6. Listening to, analyzing, and describing music. **(a, c)**
7. Evaluating music and music performances. **(a)**
8. Understanding relationships between music, the other arts, and disciplines outside the arts. **(c, d)**
9. Understanding music in relation to history and culture. **(a, c)**

CURRICULUM CONNECTIONS
History

Have students:
- Research more about the madrigal. Students should be encouraged to describe the historical period and what the society was like at the time, where this form of music was performed, who are the great madrigal performers of today, and what famous madrigals are exemplary.

- Attend a concert during which madrigals are performed.
- Prepare a lecture with visual and aural examples, and present the lecture to the class.

WARNER BROS. PUBLICATIONS
15800 N.W. 48th Avenue • Miami, Florida 33014
A Warner Music Group Company

I Hear a Sky-Born Music

LESSON 9

I Hear a Sky-Born Music

CHORAL MUSIC TERMS
analogy
articulation
dynamics
line
vocal tone color

COMPOSER: *Lois Land*
TEXT: *Ralph Waldo Emerson (1803–1882)*

VOICING
SATB

PERFORMANCE STYLE
Moderate
A cappella

FOCUS
• Identify and select correct vocal tone colors for different songs.
• Demonstrate various combinations of articulation, dynamics, and volume as choices in vocal tone color.
• Describe an analogy between painting a picture and composing, arranging, or performing a piece of music.

Warming Up

Vocal Warm-Up
Sing this exercise on the text provided. Move up or down by a half step on each repeat. Loosen the upper torso of your body as you sing, so it is free of tension. This exercise will help you focus the tone and produce unified vowels. How would you create a purple tone color? light blue? crimson red?

Neh nee nah noh, neh nee nah noh, neh nee nah noh   noo ____

etc.

Sight-Singing
Divide into voice part sections and sight-sing your line on page 70, using solfège and hand signs or numbers. Then sing the piece with full ensemble. Discuss places that present problems, and repeat until the pitches are correct. Once you know the pitches, sing the exercise with different dynamics and/or articulation.

TEACHER'S RESOURCE BINDER

National Standards
1. Singing, alone and with others, a varied repertoire of music. **(a, b, c)**

4. Composing and arranging music within specified guidelines. **(a)**
5. Reading and notating music. **(e)**
6. Listening to, analyzing, and describing music. **(c)**
7. Evaluating music and music performances. **(a, b, c)**
8. Understanding relationships between music, the other arts, and disciplines outside the arts. **(a)**

I Hear a Sky-Born Music

COMPOSER: Lois B. Land
TEXT: Ralph Waldo Emerson (1803–1882)

Focus

OVERVIEW
Vocal tone color; tone painting.

OBJECTIVES
After completing this lesson, students will be able to:
• Identify and select correct vocal tone colors for different songs.
• Demonstrate various combinations of articulation, dynamics, and volume as choices in vocal tone color.
• Describe an analogy between painting a picture and composing, arranging, or performing a piece of music.

CHORAL MUSIC TERMS
Define the Choral Music Terms for students, giving pronunciation, and answering any questions that may arise.

Warming Up

Vocal Warm-Up
(This warm-up should be used toward the end of your warm-up session to help students focus the tone.)
This Vocal Warm-Up is designed to prepare students to:
• Sing with a focused tone.
• Loosen the upper torso of the body.
• Produce unified vowels.
• Explore tone colors.

(continued on page 70)

Have students:
- Read through the Vocal Warm-Up directions.
- Sing, following your demonstration.

Sight-Singing

This Sight-Singing exercise is designed to prepare students to:
- Read rhythms in 3/4 meter.
- Sing independently in four parts.
- Sight-sing using solfège and hand signs or numbers.
- Experiment with tone color, dynamics, and articulation.

Have students:
- Read through the Sight-Singing exercise directions.
- Read each voice part rhythmically, using rhythm syllables.
- Sight-sing through each part separately using solfège and hand signs or numbers.
- Sing all parts together.

Singing: "I Hear a Sky-Born Music"

Construct an analogy between painting a picture and creating a tone painting.

Have students:
- Read the text on student page 70.
- In small groups, construct an analogy between the painting and tone painting.
- Share these ideas with the full ensemble, discussing how close each analogy comes to the ideas of other groups.
- Discuss how tone color, line, dynamics, and articulation might fit into this analogy.

Suggested Teaching Sequence

1. Review Vocal Warm-Up.

Have students:
- Review the Vocal Warm-Up on page 69.
- Loosen the upper torso for a relaxed tone.
- Listen to each other as they

70

 Singing: "I Hear a Sky-Born Music"

If you were going to paint a picture, you would need paint, a brush, and canvas. The paint supplies the color, the brush applies the line and color, and the canvas displays the art.

Construct an analogy for the information above that begins this way:

If you were going to compose, arrange, or perform a tone painting, you would need . . .

You will have the chance to paint with sound in "I Hear a Sky-Born Music," by making decisions about color, line, dynamics, and articulation.

Now turn to the music for "I Hear a Sky-Born Music" on page 71.

HOW DID YOU DO? ? ?

Just as a painting comes to life color by color and line by line, you have constructed your performance of "I Hear a Sky-Born Music" day by day.

Think about your preparation and performance of "I Hear a Sky-Born Music."
1. Describe vocal tone color, and the process you went through to choose the correct tone color for this piece.

2. What musical elements did you try out in preparing your performance, and how did you make decisions about what was correct?
3. Describe the supplies an artist uses to create a painting, then construct an analogy for these supplies that applies to the process you and the ensemble went through to "paint" your performance of "I Hear a Sky-Born Music."

70 *Choral Connections   Level 3 Mixed Voices*

 "I Hear a Sky-Born Music"

"I Hear a Sky-Born Music" was commissioned by the Texas University Interscholastic League for Sightreading Contest, 1988, Class AAAA.

 Composer Lois B. Land

Presently the organist and director of music at an Episcopal church in Garland, Texas, Lois B. Land is also adjunct professor at Texas Christian University. She has published choral compositions and textbooks in music education. Her background also includes teaching music at both the high school and elementary levels.

I Hear a Sky-Born Music

Music by Lois Land
Words by Ralph Waldo Emerson

International copyright secured. Printed in U.S.A. All rights reserved.

I Hear a Sky-Born Music **71**

Ralph Waldo Emerson

Born in Boston, Massachusetts, in 1803 into a family that included many members of the clergy, Ralph Waldo Emerson seemed destined to become a minister. He graduated from Harvard University at age 18, taught school, then became a minister. Finally, determined that his calling was to reach people through his written and spoken words, he wrote essays and poems and became an outspoken orator on subjects ranging from religion to abolition. His criticism of organized religion led to an idealism known as Transcendentalism. Some of the titles in his first volume of *Essays* (1841) convey topics that were important to Emerson: self-reliance, spiritual law, love, friendship, and prudence. Scholars frequently credit Emerson as a major influence on other American writers.

sing the vowels, being sure they match the group. (See the Teaching Strategy at the bottom of pages 72 and 73.)
- Look at crayons or objects of the three colors suggested—purple, light blue, and crimson red—and discuss what vocal tone color might be appropriate. For example: purple—a dark tone; light blue—a hazy tone, perhaps breathier; crimson red—a brilliant tone.
- Demonstrate these vocal tone colors, one at a time. Then have one voice section sing purple while another sings light blue to demonstrate the importance of uniform vowel production.

2. Review Sight-Singing.
Have students:
- Review the Sight-Singing exercise on page 69 using solfège and hand signs or numbers, first in voice sections (SATB), then as a full ensemble.
- Look at or think about a display of large, medium, and small paint brushes.
- Discuss the lines that would be created by each, and find an analogy in tone painting. For example: large brush—thick line, full sound; medium brush—medium line, medium sound; thin brush—thin line, small sound; very small brush—less paint, more intricate tonal application.
- Demonstrate each of these vocal painting styles with the Sight-Singing exercise.
- Discuss ways the paint can be applied in a painting, and then find an analogy in tone painting. For example: dab with large brush—marcato; stroke with large brush—legato; dab with a small brush—staccato; stroke with a medium brush—slight separation.
- Demonstrate each of these vocal painting styles with the Sight-Singing exercise.

71

3. Sight-sing "I Hear a Sky-Born Music" using solfège and hand signs or numbers.

Have students:

- Notice that the piece is homophonic.
- Divide into voice sections (SATB) and read each part rhythmically, using rhythm syllables.
- Still in sections, sing with solfège and hand signs or numbers, identifying and working on problem areas.
- Sing the piece through, using solfège and hand signs or numbers, with full ensemble.
- Divide into sections and recite the text rhythmically for each voice part.
- Sing the piece through with text as a full ensemble.

4. Practice tone painting.

Have students:

- Analyze the song, considering the colors and brush techniques to be administered.
- By voice section, sing isolated phrases of the song, trying out ideas, revising, and determining the correct interpretation.
- Practice, then perform the piece as decided.

Assessment

Informal Assessment

During this lesson, students showed the ability to:

- Construct analogies between painting a picture and tone painting throughout the lesson.
- Identify and explore vocal tone color in the Vocal Warm-Up exercise.
- Identify and explore dynamics and articulation in the Sight-Singing exercise.
- Explore tone painting, creating an interpretation using vocal tone color, dynamics, articulation, and volume variation, in "I Hear a Sky-Born Music."

TEACHING STRATEGY
Unified Vowels

Description: Vowels are the fundamental building blocks of tone production, intonation, and blend. A pure vowel is one that does not change when sung. When the pure vowels *ee, ay, ah, oh,* and *oo* are sung identically by all singers, there is a magical musical resonance and blend that can occur, seemingly an amplified sound without mechanical amplification.

Why is it important? The unity of vowels when sung by a chorus is the key to resonance and blend. The choral instrument should sound as one voice, and even one voice in a hundred singing a different sounding vowel can destroy the resonance and blend of the artistic choral tone. Try singing identical vowels and have one or more singers sing the same vowel slightly differently. Ask: Can you hear the difference?

Student Self-Assessment

Have students:

- Evaluate their performance with the How Did You Do? section on page 70.
- Answer the questions individually. Discuss them in pairs or small groups and/or write their responses.

Individual Performance Assessment

To further demonstrate accomplishment, have each student:

- Select and describe the appropriate tone color for any piece performed previously, giving the rationale for the choice, and providing other options that were considered, in writing.
- In a small group (not more than eight students), decide on, practice, describe, and perform an interpretation for the Sight-Singing exercise, either videotaped or assessed by the class in writing.

VOCAL DEVELOPMENT

To encourage vocal development, have students:

- Energize sustained tones by increasing the breath support and intensity.
- Listen for tall vowels and alter (modify) the vowel sounds when necessary as in *from* and *young*.
- Create a ringing resonance with *oo* and *oh* vowel sounds on words such as *go* and *music*.
- Demonstrate the correct singing of the *r* consonant after a vowel, as in *sky-born, fair, cheerful, darkest, where-e'er*, and *hear*.
- Listen for diphthongs in *sounds, foul*, and *out*.
- Articulate the text and its meaning with careful diction on vowels and consonants. Sing the consonants at the ends of words such as *will, still, old*, and *foul*.
- Balance the unison and part sections by listening carefully.

How to do it. Each vowel has a different shape in the mouth. Warm-ups and vocal exercises should focus on the shape and sound of each individual vowel and change from one vowel to another. The key is listening carefully to the vocal model and to the surrounding singers to adjust and blend the vowel tone. Connecting the vowel to breath support is another crucial feature of unified vowels. Lowered larynx, raised soft palate, and open throat also contribute to the unity of the vowel sounds.

Extension

Using Analogy

Constructing analogies requires analysis, synthesis, and evaluation skills—the higher level thinking skills that are so important for students to develop. Give students the opportunity to think out loud, and discuss the various options that emerge, evaluating their correctness. Try not to provide answers, but rather wait for the students to think it out for themselves.

Extending the Analogy

Have students:

- List the analogies they have found between visual art and music in this lesson.
- Extend each analogy to drama and movement as best they can.

Interpretation

The "correct" interpretation of a phrase, line, or section can be controversial.

Have students:

- Discuss whether one interpretation should be considered more correct than another. (It depends on who is making the decision and for what purpose.)
- Discuss why some people consider stylistic characteristics more or less correct for any given piece. (expectations based on style, period, text, musical elements, and so on)
- Identify times when it might be appropriate to use "incorrect" interpretation. (PDQ Bach does this with great success and humor, but only because he understands the appropriate style so well that he can make these decisions.)
- Select a few students in the ensemble to create a stylistically incorrect performance that has humor as its purpose.

National Standards

The following National Standards are addressed through the Extension and bottom-page activities:

1. Singing, alone and with others, a varied repertoire of music. **(f)**
3. Improvising melodies, variations, and accompaniments. **(a, d, e)**
7. Evaluating music and music performances. **(c)**
8. Understanding relationships between music, the other arts, and disciplines outside the arts. **(d)**
9. Understanding music in relation to history and culture. **(c)**

Four Spanish Christmas Carols

CHORAL MUSIC TERMS
meter
Spanish
style

Traditional Carols
ARRANGER: *Noe Sanchez*

VOICING
| SATB

PERFORMANCE STYLE
| Varied
| A cappella

FOCUS
• Sing, using correct Spanish pronunciation.
• Identify and perform characteristic styles of Spanish songs.

Warming Up

Vocal Warm-Up
Sing this warm-up using solfège and hand signs or numbers. Next, sing it once, using a smooth legato *loo*, maintaining accurate, precise rhythms. Then sing it at a faster tempo, using a staccato *deet*. Finally sing it as a four-part canon, starting at two-measure intervals, working for harmonic precision.

Sight-Singing
Sight-sing through all three parts in unison using solfège and hand signs or numbers. Then divide into groups and sing the parts in different combinations, finally singing all three at the same time. Notice the beginning incomplete measures in parts I and II, and the one-beat measure at the end to create a complete measure.

Lesson 10: Four Spanish Christmas Carols **75**

TEACHERS RESOURCE BINDER
Blackline Master 10, *Translation Guide for "Alegria, Alegria, Alegria,"* page 87
Blackline Master 11, *Translation Guide for "El desembre congelat,"* page 88
Blackline Master 12, *Translation Guide for "Soy un pobre pastorcito,"* page 89
Blackline Master 13, *Translation Guide for "Vamos todos a Belén,"* page 90

National Standards
1. Singing, alone and with others, a varied repertoire of music. **(a, b, c)**
5. Reading and notating music. **(b)**
6. Listening to, analyzing, and describing music. **(a)**
8. Understanding relationships between music, the other arts, and disciplines outside the arts. **(c)**
9. Understanding music in relation to history and culture. **(a, d)**

LESSON 10

Four Spanish Christmas Carols

Traditional Carols
ARRANGER: Noe Sanchez

Focus

OVERVIEW
Characteristic style of Spanish music; Spanish pronunciation.

OBJECTIVES
After completing this lesson, students will be able to:
• Sing, using correct Spanish pronunciation.
• Identify and perform characteristic styles of Spanish songs.

CHORAL MUSIC TERMS
Define the Choral Music Terms for students, giving pronunciation, and answering any questions that may arise.

Warming Up

Vocal Warm-Up
This Vocal Warm-Up is designed to prepare students to:
• Read and sing in 6/8 meter using solfège and hand signs or numbers.
• Sing harmony in imitative style.
• Sing with rhythmic and harmonic precision.
• Use staccato and legato articulation.
Have students:
• Read through the Vocal Warm-Up directions.
• Sing, following your demonstration.

Sight-Singing

The Sight-Singing exercise on page 75 is designed to prepare students to:

- Read rhythms in 3/4 meter.
- Sight-sing using solfège and hand signs or numbers.
- Sing independently in two or three parts.
- Hear the relationship of chord tones when parts are sung in different ranges.
- Hear and sing characteristics of Spanish music from the first carol.

Have students:

- Read through the Sight-Singing exercise directions.
- Read each voice part rhythmically, using rhythm syllables.
- Sight-sing through each part separately using solfège and hand signs or numbers.
- Sing all parts together.

Singing: "Four Spanish Christmas Carols"

Identify characteristics of Spanish music.

Have students:

- Read the text on page 76.
- Tell what they know about Spanish musical style from their own experience.
- Listen to a selection of flamingo guitar music that you play.
- Identify characteristics they heard, compare them to their original ideas, and come up with a revised definition of the characteristics of Spanish music.

Singing: "Four Spanish Christmas Carols"

These four carols come from Puerto Rico, Spain, and Catalonia (a region of northeastern Spain). They all reflect the Spanish musical style.

Based on your current knowledge of Spanish musical style, predict what musical characteristics you think will make a song sound like it reflects this style.

Listen to "Alegria, Alegria, Alegria," and check it against your predictions. Listen again to add some new ideas based on what you have heard. Then compare your predictions, and the new information, as you listen to "El desembre congelat," "Soy un pobre pastorcito," and "Vamos todos a Belén."

Now turn to the music for "Four Spanish Christmas Carols" on page 77.

HOW DID YOU DO?

? ? ?

To learn about the characteristics of any style of music, you begin with your own knowledge, collect more ideas through listening and reading, and then adjust your original idea based on new information.

Think about your preparation and performance of "Four Spanish Christmas Carols."

1. Is it easy or difficult to sing in Spanish? What is the most difficult? What do you do well?

2. Give a broad definition of characteristics of Spanish musical style, then compare the characteristics of each of the "Four Spanish Christmas Carols," telling how they match the characteristics, and how they are unique to themselves.

3. How would you know if a new song was in a Spanish musical style?

4. Do you think it is appropriate to make general characteristics for the songs of a whole culture? Why? Why not? Give specific examples to support your argument.

CULTURAL CONNECTIONS
The Roots of Folk Songs

Have students:

- Identify the cultures they each have as roots.
- Collect folk songs or stories from their cultures through interviews, reading, or other research.
- Research the musical characteristics of the culture, including vocal tone color, performance style, and harmonies.

- Arrange one or several of these pieces, using their knowledge of the style to set tempo, determine texture and harmonies, and recommend vocal tone color, articulation, and dynamics.
- Practice and perform their pieces as a celebration of the cultures they represent.

Four Spanish Christmas Carols

Alegria, Alegria, Alegria

Traditional Puerto Rican Carol
Arranged by Noe Sanchez

SATB Voices, A cappella

1. Pas - tor - cil - llos, _____ va - mos to - dos _____ al por - tal _____ de Be - lén.
2. En cuan - to a Be - lén lle - ga - ron _____ po - sa - dal pun - to pi - die - ron,
3. Los pa - ja - ri - llos del bos - que _____ al ver pa - sar los es - po - sos,

Va - mos to - dos _____ a Be - lén _____ a dar glo - ria _____ al E - den.
Na - die les qui - so ho - spe - dar _____ Por - que tan po - bres les vie - ron.
Le can - ta - ban _____ mel - o - dí - as _____ con sus tri - nos ar - mo - nio - sos.

Copyright © 1995, AMC Publications
A Division of Alliance Music Publications, Inc.
Houston, Texas
International Copyright Secured   All Rights Reserved

Four Spanish Christmas Carols **77**

TEACHING STRATEGY

Spanish Pronunciation

Have students:
- Listen to and echo a native Spanish speaker if at all possible, to recognize the nuances of the language.
- Learn the Spanish text for each song thoroughly in a conversational manner before attempting to add it to the music.

(It will help if students practice it in the rhythm of the piece, slowly at first, then gradually getting faster as they are more confident.)
- Speak the Spanish text in rhythm at the tempo of the piece before singing it.

Suggested Teaching Sequence

1. Review Vocal Warm-Up.
Sing legato and staccato, slow and fast. Sing in canon.
Have students:
- Review the Vocal Warm-Up on page 75.
- Review the terms *legato* and *staccato,* and discuss maintaining rhythmic accuracy when using staccato articulation.
- Sing in canon, tuning the harmonic intervals carefully.
- Identify the 6/8 meter as a characteristic meter for Spanish music, and see which pieces of the four carols are in 6/8 meter. ("Soy un pobre pastorcito" and "Vamos todos a Belén")

2. Review Sight-Singing.
Sight-sing in three parts, in 3/4 meter. Combine parts in different ways.
Have students:
- Review the Sight-Singing exercise on page 75 using solfège and hand signs or numbers.
- Combine the parts in different ways.
- Listen for the different harmonic relationships, depending upon which part is sung by the tenor/bass sections.
- Notice the upbeats and 3/4 meter, identify them as characteristic of Spanish music, and look through the four carols for examples of these characteristics. ("Alegria, Alegria, Alegria" is in 3/4 meter. "Alegria, Alegria, Alegria" and "Soy un pobre pastorcito" begin with upbeats.)

3. Sight-sing "Alegria, Alegria, Alegria" using solfège and hand signs or numbers.

Have students:

- In voice sections (SATB), read each part rhythmically, using rhythm syllables.
- Still in sections, sing with solfège and hand signs or numbers, identifying and working on problem areas.
- Sing their voice part on *doo* with crisp style and precise tuning, adding dynamics to shape phrases.
- Discuss where the accents fall. (on the first beat of measures 2, 4, 6, 8, and so on)
- Understand that the downbeats of odd-numbered measures are negated by the tied quarter notes.
- Learn the Spanish text using Blackline Master 10, *Translation Guide for "Alegria, Alegria, Alegria."*
- Read through the piece using *doo,* with full ensemble.
- Read through the piece, using correct Spanish pronunciation, in full ensemble.

VOCAL DEVELOPMENT

To encourage vocal development, have students:

- Sing the Spanish text of "Alegria, Alegria, Alegria" with tall, pure vowels, articulating the consonants.
- Feel the swinging rhythm by conducting in a circular one beat while speaking the text.
- Articulate the rhythm patterns, especially the triplet pattern.
- Tune the chords with solfège and hand signs or numbers, hearing the parallel thirds in the upper voices.
- Balance the chords by listening carefully to each part. Notice the effect if one voice is louder than the other voices.

TEACHING STRATEGY

Creating Accompaniment and Movement

To create accompaniment, have students:

- Select instruments that would be appropriate to accompany the carols. (guitar, marimba, any chordal instruments)
- Analyze the chord structure of one or all of the pieces.
- Improvise or write simple chordal accompaniments for any or all of the pieces.
- Determine the style of accompaniment—chordal tremolos (xylophones or marimbas), block chords with a rhythmic ostinato (guitar, marimbas, or keyboard), broken chords (guitar, marimba, keyboard).

El desembre congelat

Traditional Catalonian Carol
Arranged by Noe Sanchez

SATB Voices, A cappella

1. El de-sem-bre con-ge-lat, con-fús es re-
2. El pri-mer pa-re cau-sà la nit te-ne-
3. El més de maig ha flo-rit, sen-se ser en-

ti (ti) ra. A-bril de flors co-ro-nat,
bro (ro) sa; que a tot el món o-fus-cà,
ca (ca) ra; un lli-ri blanc y po-lit,

*In this carol each verse should be sung slower with the last verse in 4 rather than in 2.

Four Spanish Christmas Carols **79**

4. Sight-sing "El desembre congelat" using solfège and hand signs or numbers.

Have students:

- Divide into voice sections (SATB) and read each part rhythmically, using rhythm syllables.
- Still in sections, sing with solfège and hand signs or numbers, identifying and working on problem areas.
- Sing their part line staccato on *deet,* being careful of style and phrasing.
- Identify similarities in phrases of the piece. (measures 1–4, 5–8 = same; 9–10, 11–12 = similar; 13–16 = similar rhythms; 18–19 = same as 3–4)
- Compare "Alegria, Alegria, Alegria" and "El desembre congelat" for differences. (tempo, meter, style)
- Learn the Spanish text using Blackline Master 11, *Translation Guide for "El desembre congelat."*
- Read through the piece using *deet,* with full ensemble.
- Read through the piece, using correct Spanish pronunciation, in full ensemble.

VOCAL DEVELOPMENT

To encourage vocal development, have students:

- Sing the Spanish text of "El desembre congrelat" with tall, pure vowels, articulating the consonants.
- Feel *alla breve* meter by conducting in two while speaking the text.
- Articulate the bass line by energizing on repeated notes.
- Tune the chords with solfège and hand signs or numbers, hearing the consonant and dissonant chords.
- Balance the chords by listening carefully to each part.

- Practice, then perform the pieces.

To create movement, have students:

- Discuss the form of each carol.
- In small groups, explore and create movement that shows the form and mood of the piece.
- Share and critique each group's movement.

- Revise the movement according to suggestions discussed above.
- Learn the final versions of the movements, and then perform the pieces with movement.

5. Sight-sing "Soy un pobre pastorcito" using solfège and hand signs or numbers.

Have students:

- Divide into voice sections (SATB) and read each voice part rhythmically, using rhythm syllables.
- Still in sections, sing with solfège and hand signs or numbers, identifying and working on problem areas.
- Sing their part line on *lee,* with rounded mouth to prevent the vowel from spreading, adding dynamics to shape phrases.
- Compare the form of this carol to the first two. (two-phrase verse with refrain that is patterned after the verse)
- Learn the Spanish text using Blackline Master 12, *Translation Guide for "Soy un pobre pastorcito."*
- Read through the piece using *lee* with full ensemble.
- Read through the piece, using correct Spanish pronunciation, in full ensemble.

VOCAL DEVELOPMENT

To encourage vocal development, have students:

- Sing the Spanish text of "Soy un pobre pastorcito" with tall, pure vowels, articulating the consonants.
- Feel the swing of 6/8 meter by conducting in 2 while speaking the text.
- Articulate the text by energizing on repeated notes in all parts.
- Tune the chords with solfège and hand signs or numbers, hearing the consonant and dissonant chords.
- Balance the chords by listening carefully to each part. Notice the effect if one voice is louder than the other voices.

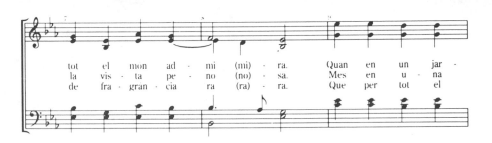

tot el mon ad - mi (mi) - ra. Quan en un jar -
la vis - ta pe - no (no) - sa. Mes en u - na
de fra - gran - cia ra (ra) - ra. Que per tot el

di d'a - mor neix u - na di - vi - na flor.
mit - ja nit bri - lla el sol que n'és___ eix - it.
mon se - sent, de lle - vant fins a___ po - nent.

D'u - na ro ro ro, d'u - na sa sa sa, d'u - na ro, d'u - na
D'u - na bel bel bel, d'u - na la la la, d'u - na bel, d'u - na
To - ta sa sa sa, to - ta dul dul dul, to - ta sa, to - ta

sa, d'u - na ro - sa be - lla, fe - cun da i pon - ce (ce) - lla.
la, d'u - na be - lla au - ro - ra, que el cel en - a - mo (mo) - ra.
dul, to - ta sa dul - çu - ra, l'o - lor, amb ven - tu (tu) - ra.

MORE ABOUT... Noé Sánchez

Noé Sánchez teaches music at Christa McAuliffe Middle School in San Antonio, Texas. His graduate studies have been in the area of ethnomusicology, with a concentration on Spanish folk songs. His goal is to preserve folk songs in their original harmonic and melodic settings.

Soy un pobre pastorcito

SATB Voices, A cappella

Traditional Spanish Carol
Arranged by Noe Sanchez

*If this carol is sung alone (not as part of a set), please end in g minor. If sung in tandem with the following "Vamos todos a Belén," please end in G major.

Four Spanish Christmas Carols **81**

National Standards

The following National Standards are addressed through the bottom-page activities:

2. Performing on instruments, alone and with others, a varied repertoire of music. **(b)**

3. Improvising melodies, variations, and accompaniments. **(a, d)**

4. Composing and arranging music within specified guidelines. **(b, c)**

7. Evaluating music and music performances. **(a)**

8. Understanding relationships between music, the other arts, and disciplines outside the arts. **(b)**

9. Understanding music in relation to history and culture. **(a, d, e)**

---

6. Sight-sing "Vamos todos a Belén" using solfège and hand signs or numbers.

Have students:

- Divide into voice sections (SATB) and read each part on page 82 rhythmically, using rhythm syllables.

- Still in sections, sing with solfège and hand signs or numbers, identifying and working on problem areas.

- Sing their part line lightly on *dee,* with rounded mouth to prevent the vowel from spreading, adding dynamics to shape phrases.

- Discuss the form of the carol. (refrain first, then verses with refrain in between and again at the end)

- Compare the musical elements of "Vamos todos a Belén" to the other three carols.

- Learn the Spanish text using Blackline Master 13, *Translation Guide for "Vamos todos a Belén."*

- Read through the piece using *dee* with full ensemble.

- Read through the piece, using correct Spanish pronunciation, in full ensemble.

7. Identify characteristics of Spanish music.

Have students:

- Review their list of characteristics of Spanish music from the beginning of the lesson.

- Compare each of the four pieces in the lesson for similarities and differences, and then add to the list of general characteristics of Spanish music.

- Determine that there are general characteristics which can be attributed to any type of music, but each piece also has its own unique combination of characteristics. To the extent that the two overlap the specific piece is or is not representative of the style.

Assessment

Informal Assessment

During this lesson, students showed the ability to:

- Identify and use staccato and legato articulation in the Vocal Warm-Up.
- Identify and sing in 6/8 meter in the Vocal Warm-Up.
- Identify and sing upbeats and 3/4 meter in the Sight-Singing exercise.
- Sing using correct Spanish pronunciation and style, in "Four Spanish Christmas Carols."
- Identify characteristics of Spanish music throughout the lesson.

Student Self-Assessment

Have students:

- Evaluate their performance with the How Did You Do? section on page 76.
- Answer the questions individually. Discuss them in pairs or small groups and/or write their responses on a sheet of paper.

Individual Performance Assessment

To further demonstrate accomplishment, have each student:

- Sing their voice part line in measures 1–8 from any one of the Spanish carols to demonstrate correct Spanish pronunciation.
- In a small ensemble, sing one verse and refrain, demonstrating stylistic accuracy.

Vamos todos a Belén

Traditional Spanish Carol
Arranged by Noe Sanchez

82 *Choral Connections   Level 3 Mixed Voices*

 VOCAL DEVELOPMENT

To encourage vocal development, have students:

- Sing the Spanish text of "Vamos todos a Belén" with tall, pure vowels, articulating the consonants.
- Feel the swing of 6/8 meter by conducting in 2 while speaking the text.
- Articulate the text by energizing on repeated notes in all parts. The bass line

sings the tonic and dominant throughout, as a foundation for the harmony.

- Tune the chords with solfège and hand signs or numbers, hearing the consonant and dissonant chords.
- Identify broken chord patterns with solfège and hand signs or numbers.
- Balance the chords by listening carefully to each part.

Alleluía

COMPOSER: *Will James*

CHORAL MUSIC TERMS
beginning
dynamic shading
end
evaluation
peak
phrase
rhythmic motif

VOICING
SATB

PERFORMANCE STYLE
Moderate
A cappella

FOCUS
- Identify rhythmic motifs.
- Identify and sing musical phrases, using dynamic shading.
- Listen to and evaluate group performance.

Warming Up

 Vocal Warm-Up 1
When you take a proper breath, your lungs should expand your waist. Place your hands just above your waist, on your back—thumbs forward. As you inhale, feel your hands separate. As you exhale, feel your hands move back toward each other. Now you know you are breathing properly for singing.

 Vocal Warm-Up 2
Sing the exercise below, using the breathing described above. Follow the dynamic markings. Move a half step up on each repeat.

Do the same exercise using the following rhythms. How will you change the dynamics? Should you change from *loo*? What will you change to? Why?

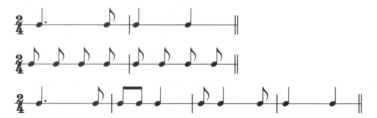

Lesson 11: Alleluía **83**

TEACHER'S RESOURCE BINDER

 National Standards
1. Singing, alone and with others, a varied repertoire of music. **(a, b, c)**
5. Reading and notating music. **(b)**
6. Listening to, analyzing, and describing music. **(a, c, f)**
7. Evaluating music and music performances. **(a)**
8. Understanding relationships between music, the other arts, and disciplines outside the arts. **(c)**

LESSON 11

Alleluía

COMPOSER: Will James

Focus

OVERVIEW
Rhythmic motif; phrase; performance evaluation.

OBJECTIVES
After completing this lesson, students will be able to:
- Identify rhythmic motifs.
- Identify and sing musical phrases, using dynamic shading.
- Listen to and evaluate group performance.

CHORAL MUSIC TERMS
Define the Choral Music Terms for students, giving pronunciation, and answering any questions that may arise.

Warming Up

Vocal Warm-Ups
These Vocal Warm-Ups are designed to prepare students to:
- Breathe properly, expanding the waist.
- Read and sing rhythmic motifs.
- Sing, using dynamic shading.
- Consider how consonant/vowel combinations affect articulation.
Have students:
- Read through the set of Vocal Warm-Up directions.
- Sing, following your demonstration.

Sight-Singing

The Sight-Singing exercise on page 83 is designed to prepare students to:

- Read and sing in 2/4 meter, using solfège and hand signs or numbers.
- Use dynamic shading on motifs and phrases.
- Identify complete phrases and phrase segments.

Have students:

- Read through the Sight-Singing exercise directions.
- Read each voice part rhythmically, using rhythm syllables.
- Sight-sing through each part separately using solfège and hand signs or numbers.
- Sing all parts together.

Singing: "Alleluia"

Identify motif.
Have students:

- Read the text on page 84.
- Read each of the short thoughts, then combine them in different ways.
- Notice that some combinations make more sense than others.
- Define motif, and notice the rhythmic motifs used in the Vocal Warm-Up and Sight-Singing exercises.
- Look at "Alleluia," clapping and speaking the rhythm, and identifying the rhythmic motifs in the soprano part, measures 1–20.

 Sight-Singing

Sight-sing each of the following using solfège and hand signs or numbers. Do you find any rhythm patterns that are repeated? Where do you think the phrases begin, peak, and end? Try them as two-measure, four-measure, and eight-measure phrases, using dynamics to shade them. Which feels the best to you?

 Singing: "Alleluia"

Sometimes you hear a short pattern that has meaning, for example:

> "Here we go . . ."
> ". . . gathering at the lake"
> " . . . studying for the test"
> "Got to stay home . . ."
> "I can't believe it . . ."
> ". . . 99 and 44/100 percent pure"

These catchy little sound bites can be repeated over and over, or combined to create longer ideas. Try each one out, then combine them. (Some combinations make more sense than others.)

A motif is a short musical idea. It can be rhythmic, melodic, or both.

Now turn to the music for "Alleluia" on page 85. Can you find the rhythmic motifs, the patterns that are repeated, in "Alleluia"?

HOW DID YOU DO? Think about your preparation and performance of "Alleluia."
1. Describe rhythmic motif, then sing a part of this lesson that will demonstrate one.
2. With three classmates, choose a phrase to perform from "Alleluia," then sing it with correct dynamics.

3. What is the difference between a motif and a phrase?
4. How would you assess your ensemble's performance of "Alleluia"? What do you do especially well? What do you need to work on?

 Composer Will James

Will James was born in Shelbyville, Illinois, and was known as "Mr. Music" in the city of Springfield, Illinois. Recognized as a composer of religious anthems, his pieces have been favorites of church congregations across the nation.

To Horatio M. Farrar and the
Southwest Missouri State College Choir, Springfield, MO

Alleluía

Will James
(ASCAP)

Four-part Chorus SATB A cappella

Used by Permission.

Alleluia **85**

TEACHING STRATEGY
Subtle Shadings

Have students:
* Read the text so that they hear the two-note slurs on *lu* of *Alleluia.*
* Speak examples so that the dynamics will be:

* Sing examples of two-note (and sometimes three-note) phrases that occur when two or more notes use only one syllable.

Suggested Teaching Sequence

1. Review Vocal Warm-Ups.
Breathe properly. Sing rhythmic motifs, shading with dynamics. Have students:
* Review the Vocal Warm-Ups on page 83.
* Identify the rhythms as motifs.
* Describe the changes in dynamic shading necessary for the different rhythms.
* Try out different syllables— *doo, doot, nah,* and so on, continuing to focus on dynamic shading.
* Review or find the rhythms from the Vocal Warm-Ups in "Alleluia," and clap the rhythm of the piece.

2. Review Sight-Singing.
Sing using solfège and hand signs or numbers. Identify phrases and motifs.
Have students:
* Review the Sight-Singing exercise on page 83 using solfège and hand signs or numbers.
* Identify the rhythmic motifs.
* Try different phrase lengths, shaping the phrases with dynamics.
* Decide which phrase structures feel best.
* Distinguish between motif and phrases, noticing that motifs provide "mini-phrases" within longer complete phrases, both of which require dynamic shading.

3. Sight-sing "Alleluia" using solfège and hand signs or numbers.

Have students:

- Divide into voice sections (SATB), and speak and clap the rhythm, adding dynamics to shape the motifs and phrases.
- Speak the rhythm of the piece as a full ensemble, noticing any differences in phrasing, and deciding on one interpretation for all. (Especially notice measures 31–34, where there is a longer segment.)
- In sections, sight-sing the piece first using solfège and hand signs or numbers, then text.
- Sing the piece with full ensemble, first using solfège and hand signs or numbers, then text, using correct dynamic shading throughout.

4. Evaluate a performance.

Have students:

- Discuss what a good performance of "Alleluia" would sound like, listing their criteria on the board.
- Listen as you add your criteria to theirs.
- Listen to a tape of their performance of "Alleluia."
- Discuss how well their performance met their criteria, what was well done, and what needs more work.

TEACHING STRATEGY
Motifs and Phrases

In music analysis there are often different interpretations of pieces, but none so often debated as phrasing. What is most important is that the performers are all performing with an agreed-upon interpretation. Both motifs and phrases require dynamic shading, and it is a subtle but crucial distinction. The shading of motifs, although building and releasing tension, needs to build across motifs to the peak of the phrase. It is this complex relationship of tensions and releases within and across that provides the emotional drama of phrasing. By experimenting with different phrasings in this lesson, the students will come to their own conclusions and interpretations based on phrase.

Alleluia **87**

MORE ABOUT... Motifs

Motifs (patterns) are found everywhere. Have students:

- Think about music/word motifs used in commercials.
- Listen to Beethoven's Fifth Symphony, First Movement, or Wagner's *Flying Dutchman* Overture for motifs. Beethoven's is abstract; Wagner's motifs represent characters in the story.

- Find examples of visual motifs in patterns that are repeated over and over.
- Discuss how any of these motifs might be represented in one of the other art forms; for example: the motion of a wave could be represented in painting through repeated line, or in music by an upward and downward melodic line repeated in canon by different sections.

Assessment

Informal Assessment

During this lesson, students showed the ability to:

- Identify rhythmic motifs in "Alleluia."
- Identify, practice, and shape rhythmic motifs using dynamic shading in the Vocal Warm-Ups.
- Identify and sing phrases using dynamic shading in the Sight-Singing exercise.
- Distinguish between a rhythmic motif and a phrase in the Sight-Singing exercise.
- Sing, using correct phrasing and dynamic shading in "Alleluia."
- Establish criteria and evaluate their performance of "Alleluia."

Student Self-Assessment

Have students:

- Evaluate their performance with the How Did You Do? section on page 84.
- Answer the questions individually. Discuss them in pairs or small groups and/or write their responses on a sheet of paper.

Individual Performance Assessment

To further demonstrate accomplishment, have each student:

- In a small group, sing measures 35–58, demonstrating appropriate dynamic shading of the phrases.
- Choose and sing a segment of "Alleluia" that illustrates the concept of rhythmic motif, and then clap the motif that was demonstrated.
- Write a critique of the taped performance of "Alleluia," giving specific criteria for assessment, and stating specific recommendations for improvement.

Al - le - lu - ia, Al - le - lu - ia,

Al - le - lu - ia, Al - le - lu - ia,

Al - le - lu - ia, Al - le - lu - ia,   Al - le - lu - ia,

Al - le - lu - ia, Al - le - lu - ia,   Al - le - lu - ia,

Al - le - lu - ia, Al - le - lu - ia,   Al - le - lu - ia,

Al - le - lu - ia, Al - le - lu - ia,   Al - le - lu - ia,   Al - le - lu - ia,

Al - le - lu - ia   Al - le - lu - ia,   Al - le - lu - ia,   Al - le - lu - ia,

Al - le - lu - ia,   Al - le - lu - ia,

Extension

Melodic Sequence

This piece has many examples of melodic sequencing, where a rhythmic motif is repeated, beginning at different pitches, but keeping the same melodic contour in each repetition.

Have students:

- Listen to the description of melodic sequencing above.
- Write some examples on the board.
- Find examples in the piece, for instance: measures 1–2, 3–4, 13–14, and 15–16.

Composing Using Motif and Sequence

Have students:

- Create a rhythmic motif.
- Choose a tone set. (major scale, minor scale, pentatonic scale, whole tone scale)
- Write a short piece by creating a melody for the motif, then repeating it several times, beginning the melody on different pitches of the scale.
- Decide when a release is needed from the continuing sequence of motifs, and write a short contrasting ending for the phrase. (Notice measures 1–8 of "Alleluia" as an example.)
- Share the short motific pieces with one another, and combine a few into a piece with ABA form.

Alleluia **89**

National Standards

The following National Standards are addressed through the Extension and bottom-page activities:

1. Singing, alone and with others, a varied repertoire of music. **(a, b)**

4. Composing and arranging music within specified guidelines. **(a, d)**

6. Listening to, analyzing, and describing music. **(a, c)**

8. Understanding relationships between music, the other arts, and disciplines outside the arts. **(a, c)**

Flow Gently, Sweet Afton

CHORAL MUSIC TERMS
conducting pattern
legato singing
3/4 meter

Scottish Folk Song
ARRANGER: *John Leavitt*

VOICING

SATB

PERFORMANCE STYLE

Freely
Accompanied

FOCUS

- Read and sing in 3/4 meter.
- Conduct in 3/4 meter.
- Sing, using a legato style.

Warming Up

 Vocal Warm-Up

Sing this exercise, moving up by a half step on each repeat. Now try this challenge:
- March in place with light steps on each beat as you sing.
- Add these arm movements: fists down on beat 1, chest level on beat 2, straight overhead on 3, back to chest on 4. How well coordinated are you?

Hoo hoo hoo hoo hoo hoo hoo hoo   hoo hoo hoo hoo hoo.

Continue up by half steps.

If you were going to sing this exercise in a legato style, what would you need to change? Give it a try!

 Sight-Singing

Sight-sing each part on solfège and hand signs or numbers, using legato articulation. Combine the parts in different ways. Create an arrangement using unison and combination singing of the parts.

Lesson 12: Flow Gently, Sweet Afton **91**

 TEACHER'S RESOURCE BINDER

National Standards

1. Singing a varied repertoire of music. **(a, b, c)**
5. Reading and notating music. **(a)**
6. Listening to, analyzing, and describing music. **(b)**
7. Evaluating music and music performances. **(a)**
9. Understanding music in relation to history and culture. **(a, c, d)**

LESSON 12

Flow Gently, Sweet Afton

Scottish Folk Song
ARRANGER: John Leavitt

Focus

OVERVIEW
3/4 meter; legato style.

OBJECTIVES
After completing this lesson, students will be able to:
- Read and sing in 3/4 meter.
- Conduct in 3/4 meter.
- Sing, using a legato style.

CHORAL MUSIC TERMS
Define the Choral Music Terms for students, giving pronunciation, and answering any questions that may arise.

Warming Up

Vocal Warm-Up
This Vocal Warm-Up is designed to prepare students to:
- Prepare to sing.
- Be ready to work with attention.
- Distinguish between staccato and legato style.
Have students:
- Read through the Vocal Warm-Up directions.
- Sing, following your demonstration.

Sight-Singing

The Sight-Singing exercise on page 91 is designed to prepare students to:

- Sight-sing in 3/4 meter using solfège and hand signs or numbers.
- Sing, using legato articulation.
- Sing independently in more than one part.
- Read in treble and bass clefs.

Have students:

- Read through the Sight-Singing directions.
- Read each voice part rhythmically, using rhythm syllables.
- Sight-sing through each part separately using solfège and hand signs or numbers.
- Sing all parts together.

Singing: "Flow Gently, Sweet Afton"

Conduct in 3/4 meter.
Have students:

- Read the text on page 92.
- Perform the movement of a wheel as directed.
- Practice conducting in 3/4 meter, first alone, then with "Flow Gently, Sweet Afton."

 ## Singing: "Flow Gently, Sweet Afton"

Trace the shape of a large wheel in front of you with both hands, fingers relaxed and palms down. You are making the shape of a circle in the air. Now add weight at the bottom of the circle. Feel the weight at the bottom, and the release on the movement up and around.

In 3/4 meter, the first beat of each measure has the weight, and beats 2 and 3 receive less stress. Try conducting in 3/4 meter.

Following the diagram at the right, conduct in 3/4 as you listen to "Flow Gently, Sweet Afton."

Now turn to the music for "Flow Gently, Sweet Afton" on page 93.

HOW DID YOU DO?

A peaceful song can be a source of inspiration and learning. Think about your preparation and performance of "Flow Gently, Sweet Afton."

1. Sing "Flow Gently, Sweet Afton," conducting in 3/4 meter.

2. Choose a phrase to sing that will demonstrate your ability to sing in legato style.

3. What is the message of "Flow Gently, Sweet Afton"? Do you know any other songs that communicate this mood or message? Would you consider this a good song? Why or why not?

Flow Gently, Sweet Afton

Scottish Folk Song
Setting by John Leavitt

SATB, Accompanied

Flow Gently, Sweet Afton **93**

Suggested Teaching Sequence

1. Review Vocal Warm-Up.
Stimulate the body and diaphragm for singing.
Have students:
* Review the Vocal Warm-Up on page 91, with the movement. (Be careful that students use small steps, so they are not out of breath at the end.)
* Decide how to change the drill so they can sing legato. (slow tempo, separate repeated pitches a bit)
* Sing the drill legato.

2. Review Sight-Singing.
Read in 3/4 meter. Sing legato style. Sing parts independently.
Have students:
* Review the Sight-Singing exercise on page 91 using solfège and hand signs or numbers, reading each part separately then combining them.
* Identify legato style as smooth and connected.
* Create an arrangement of the parts, and perform their creation.

3. Sight-sing "Flow Gently, Sweet Afton" using solfège and hand signs or numbers.
Have students:
* Divide into voice sections (SATB) and read each part rhythmically, using rhythm syllables.
* Still in sections, sing with solfège syllables or numbers, identifying and working on problem areas.
* Sing the piece through using solfège syllables or numbers with full ensemble.
* Review legato singing, and discuss phrasing and dynamics, then sing again, attending to the articulation and phrasing.
* Sing the piece through with text as a full ensemble.

(continued on page 94)

TEACHING STRATEGY
Phrasing

Have students:
* Speak the text in rhythm, pausing where it seems natural to breathe.
* Identify these spots as the phrase markers in this piece—it follows the natural flow of the text.

4. Evaluate a performance.

Have students:
- Discuss what a good performance of "Flow Gently, Sweet Afton" would sound like, listing their criteria on the board.
- Listen as you add your criteria to theirs.
- Listen to a tape of their performance of "Flow Gently, Sweet Afton."
- Discuss how well their performance met their criteria, what was well done, and what needs more work.

5. Conduct in 3/4 meter.

Have students:
- Perform "Flow Gently, Sweet Afton" as classmates conduct in 3/4 meter.

TEACHING STRATEGY
Sight-Singing

This piece is fairly straightforward and should be easy for students to read, making it a good assessment piece for sight-singing skill. It is also in a comfortable range, and fairly short, so it can be used as an assessment for individual singing (in quartets).

* Although the optional accompaniment is provided here, it is preferred that this section be a cappella.

Flow Gently, Sweet Afton **95**

VOCAL DEVELOPMENT

To encourage vocal development, have students:

- Demonstrate good vocal tone by singing tall vowels and alter (or modify) the vowel sounds in a Shakespearean English accent style when necessary, as in *Afton* (*awh* instead of *eh*).
- Energize sustained tones by increasing the breath support and dynamic level.
- Sustain phrases by staggering the breathing and moving forward through the phrases.
- Demonstrate the correct singing of the *r* consonant after a vowel; it should be almost silent, as in *river, Mary, murmuring, disturb, her, where, there, over,* and *birk*.
- Listen for diphthongs (two vowel sounds when one vowel is written) in words such as *praise, braes,* and *wild*. Sing or sustain the first vowel sound and barely sing the second vowel sound with the next syllable.
- Balance the chords between the parts by listening to them. Encourage students to try adding more weight to one part to determine the effect on the chord.
- Articulate the two-note phrases by pressing or emphasizing the first note and tapering off on the second note.
- Energize the last three chords to allow the harmonic cadence to be realized.

Assessment

Informal Assessment

During this lesson, students showed the ability to:

- Sing legato in the Vocal Warm-Up.
- Read in 3/4 meter with legato articulation in the Sight-Singing exercise.
- Conduct in 3/4 with "Flow Gently, Sweet Afton."
- Sing independently in parts, using legato articulation and correct phrasing in "Flow Gently, Sweet Afton."

Student Self-Assessment

Have students:

- Evaluate their performance with the How Did You Do? section on page 92.
- Answer the questions individually. Discuss them in pairs or small groups and/or write their responses on a sheet of paper.

Individual Performance Assessment

To further demonstrate accomplishment, have each student:

- Perform "Flow Gently, Sweet Afton," conducting while singing.
- Sing the song in an ensemble of no more than eight students, two on a part, as others listen and critique their performance.
- Write a critique of the taped performance of "Flow Gently, Sweet Afton," giving specific criteria for assessment, and stating specific recommendations for improvement.

TEACHING STRATEGY
Folk Songs

One of the reasons this piece is so easy to sing is because it is a folk song. Folk songs tend to feel almost second nature, and have characteristics that make them easy to sing, such as following the natural rhythm of the text and moving mostly stepwise, with easy rhythms.

Have students:

- Identify characteristics of folk songs.

- Listen and watch as you add any others that you think are important.
- Improvise a folk tune that is four measures long in 3/4 meter, with the ensemble echoing each improvisation. (Use the key of F, and limit the pitches if necessary, but usually F major works fine.)

Extension

Arranging Folk Tunes
Have students:
- Find a folk tune from your region.
- Using the characteristics of the setting of "Flow Gently, Sweet Afton," arrange the folk song for at least two parts.

Flow Gently, Sweet Afton **97**

National Standards
The following National Standards are addressed through the Extension and bottom-page activities:
3. Improvising melodies, variations, and accompaniments. **(c)**
4. Composing and arranging music within specified guidelines. **(c)**
8. Understanding relationships between music, the other arts, and disciplines outside the arts. **(c)**

Jesu Dulcis Memoria

COMPOSER: Tomás Luis de Victoria (c. 1548–1611)

Focus

OVERVIEW
Text; tonality; tone color; and mood.

OBJECTIVES
After completing this lesson, students will be able to:
- Read and sing in C major and C minor.
- Explore the relationship between text, tonality, and tone color to create mood.

CHORAL MUSIC TERMS
Define the Choral Music Terms for students, giving pronunciation, and answering any questions that may arise.

Warming Up

Vocal Warm-Up
This Vocal Warm-Up is designed to prepare students to:
- Sing independently in four parts using solfège and hand signs or numbers.
- Distinguish between major and minor tonality.
- Explore vocal tone colors.
- Identify mood and respond with movement or expression while singing.

Have students:
- Read through the Vocal Warm-Up directions.
- Sing, following your directions.

98

LESSON 13

Jesu Dulcis Memoria

COMPOSER: Tomás Luis de Victoria (c. 1548–1611)

CHORAL MUSIC TERMS
major
minor
text
tonality
tone color

VOICING
SATB

PERFORMANCE STYLE
Slowly
A cappella

FOCUS
- Read and sing in C major and C minor.
- Explore the relationship between text, tonality, and tone color to create mood.

Warming Up

Vocal Warm-Up

Sing this exercise using solfège and hand signs or numbers. Notice the different tonalities. Do they evoke different moods? How are A, B, and C different?

Try singing in these vocal tone colors: bright, dull, hazy, glaring, hot, cool, muted, foggy (think of some more by yourself). Let your body respond naturally to the tone color you sing, showing the mood through your posture and expression. You might choose consonant/vowel combinations that fit the mood you are singing, for example: *bah* for dull, and *doot* for bright.

TEACHER'S RESOURCE BINDER
Blackline Master 14, *Translation and Pronunciation Guide for "Jesu Dulcis Memoria,"* page 91

National Standards
1. Singing a varied repertoire of music. **(a, b, c)**
3. Improvising. **(b)**
5. Reading and notating music. **(a, b)**
6. Listening to, analyzing, and describing music. **(f)**
7. Evaluating music and performances. **(a, b)**
8. Understanding relationships between music, the other arts, and disciplines outside the arts. **(c)**

98

 Sight-Singing
Sight-sing this melody using solfège and hand signs or numbers.

 Singing: "Jesu Dulcis Memoria"

The mood of a song is communicated through many elements. Three of these are tonality, text, and tone color.

- *Tonality* is the key in which the music is written. Most Western art music is written in major or minor tonalities.

- *Text* is the words, usually set in a poetic style to express a central thought, idea, moral, or narrative.

- *Tone color* is the unique quality of sound produced by a voice or an instrument.

Read the text of "Jesu Dulcis Memoria," and tell what tonality and tone color you would choose if you were going to write a musical setting.

Now turn to the music for "Jesu Dulcis Memoria" on page 100.

HOW DID YOU DO?

? ?

What mood expresses your opinion about your own learning in this lesson? Think about your preparation and performance of "Jesu Dulcis Memoria."
1. What three elements did you explore in this lesson that contribute to mood? Describe each in one sentence.
2. Tell what choices the composer made about these three elements. What choices did

you make as a performing group? What mood were you trying to convey, and how effective would this combination be for an audience?
3. In a small group, sing a segment of this lesson to illustrate your understanding of the relationship of these three elements.

Sight-Singing
This Sight-Singing exercise is designed to prepare students to:
- Sight-sing in a minor tonality.
- Sing, phrasing correctly.
Have students:
- Read through the Sight-Singing exercise directions.
- Read each voice rhythmically, using rhythm syllables.
- Sight-sing through each part separately using solfège and hand signs or numbers.
- Sing all parts together.

Singing: "Jesu Dulcis Memoria"

Identify tonality, text, and tone color as three elements that communicate mood.
Have students:
- Read the text on page 99.
- Share any additional details that they know about tonality, text, and tone color; for example: information about the relationship of major and minor scales—parallel or relative.
- Listen to examples and remember the tone color exploration in the Vocal Warm-Up.
- Read the translation of the text of "Jesu Dulcis Memoria," identify the mood, and speculate about what mode and vocal tone color the composer might choose.

Suggested Teaching Sequence

1. Review Vocal Warm-Up.
Have students:
- Review the Vocal Warm-Up on page 98, first with solfège and hand signs or numbers, and then with different vocal tone colors.
- Move their bodies or use expressions as they naturally occur.
- Discuss the tonalities of the C major and A minor scales, listening to both scales on the piano. Identify any moods that seem to be associated with each; for example: minor is sometimes associated with sad and somber moods, while major is associated with joyful and excited moods.
- Improvise a joyful A minor tune, or a somber C major one, over a drone bass.

2. Review Sight-Singing.
Sight-sing in minor. Identify phrase. Sing text. Explore vocal tone color.
Have students:
- Review the Sight-Singing exercise on page 99 using solfège and hand signs or numbers.
- Identify phrases, and then sing them expressively.
- Discuss what tone color would be effective with this melody, and try out suggestions, evaluating their effectiveness.

3. Sight-sing "Jesu Dulcis Memoria" using solfège and hand signs or numbers.
Have students:
- Divide into voice sections (SATB), and speak and clap the rhythm, adding dynamics to shape the phrases.
- Still in sections, sing with solfège and hand signs or numbers, identifying and working on problem areas.
- Sing the piece through, using solfège and hand signs or numbers, with full ensemble.

100

Copyright 1959 by BELWIN, Inc.
International Copyright Secured
c/o CPP/BELWIN, INC., Miami, Florida 33014

 "Jesu Dulcis Memoria"

"Jesu Dulcis Memoria" is the Vesper hymn for the Feast of the Holy Name of Jesus, which is celebrated on the Sunday between the feast of the Circumcision (January 1) and Epiphany (January 6). The earliest musical setting of this text that can be traced is found in Gregorian chant. This chant can be found on page 452 of the *Liber Usualis,* an ancient Catholic book of Gregorian chant.

- Review text, tonality, and tone color, and then determine the appropriate tone color. (rich, deep, dark, sad, somber)
- Sing again, attending to accurate pitches in minor and effective tone color.

4. Add Latin text.
Have students:
- Use Blackline Master 14, *Translation and Pronunciation Guide for "Jesu Dulcis Memoria."*
- Read or echo the text slowly.
- Speak the text from the manuscript in rhythm, first slowly, then at performance tempo.
- Sing the piece using correct Latin pronunciation.

 VOCAL DEVELOPMENT

To encourage vocal development, have students:
- Create a mystical feeling by singing softly with great intensity.
- Energize sustained tones by increasing the breath support and intensity.
- Sustain phrases by staggering the breathing and moving forward through the phrases.
- Balance the chords between the parts by listening to them. Encourage students to try adding more weight to one part to determine the effect of uneven weight on the sound of the chord.
- Articulate the rhythms by emphasizing the moving parts in each of the voices.
- Emphasize the two-note phrases by pressing on the first note with added intensity or accent and sliding to the second note.

 Tomás Luis de Victoria

Tomás Luis de Victoria (da Vittoria) was born in Avila, Spain, c. 1548. He received his preliminary musical training in his native city, where he served as a boy chorister in the Cathedral. His friendship with Palestrina, and a probable period of study with that master, inspired him to pursue a career in music. Although of Spanish birth, the influence of the Italian composer Palestrina made Victoria a permanent staple of the Roman school of polyphony.

Victoria firmly believed that music should be directed only to "the praise and glory of God." Consequently, all of his almost two hundred compositions are for the church and place him at the side of Palestrina as a leading composer of the Counter-Reformation. Victoria died in Madrid in 1611.

Assessment

Informal Assessment

During this lesson, students showed the ability to:

- Read, sing, and compare major and minor tonalities in the Vocal Warm-Up.
- Improvise in major and minor in the Vocal Warm-Up.
- Sing a melody with correct phrasing in the Sight-Singing exercise.
- Explore vocal tone color in the Vocal Warm-Up and Sight-Singing exercises.
- Sing independently in parts, in minor, using correct phrasing, vocal tone color, and Latin pronunciation in "Jesu Dulcis Memoria."

Student Self-Assessment

Have students:

- Evaluate their performance with the How Did You Do? section on page 99.
- Answer the questions individually. Discuss them in pairs or small groups and/or write their responses on a sheet of paper.

Individual Performance Assessment

To further demonstrate accomplishment, have each student:

- In a small ensemble of four to eight, perform "Jesu Dulcis Memoria," demonstrating correct phrasing, vocal tone color, and Latin pronunciation, with or without taping.
- Critique the performance of other groups, giving feedback on criteria established from the goals of this lesson.
- Read an English text (poem or short story), and then plan a composition that suggests tonality and tone color based on the mood of the text.

CONNECTING THE ARTS
Color and Mood

The term *vocal tone color* begs a connection with visual art color. Some say this is a good analogy, and some think it is not worthy. Try this experiment to see if your students can establish any consistent connection between visual color and mood.

Have students:

- Look at different, contrasting colors of construction paper.

- Think about what mood each conveys, write down a list of words that describe the mood, but don't share their responses yet.
- Compare responses to see if there is any agreement between how students associate moods with each color.

Extension

Setting a Text for Its Interpretive Qualities

Have students:

- Choose a text (preferably a lyric poem) that they are fond of or one that they are studying in a Language Arts class. (Encourage students to find works by writers who represent a range of cultural and gender groups, and perhaps a secular text for the sake of variety.)
- Read the text, and then discuss the textual mood.
- Determine the tonality that would be appropriate, and create a melody for the text.
- Determine the vocal tone color to be used and indicate how it would be incorporated into the melody.
- Work on phrasing, interpretive dynamics, and other additions and revisions.
- Perform their piece for the class or in a concert setting.

Phrasing

Have students:

- Look through "Jesu Dulcis Memoria" and identify dynamic markings and breath marks.
- Sing through the piece with careful attention to these phrase indicators.

Sight-Singing with Independence

This piece is fairly straightforward, and should be easy to read. However, the parts are a bit polyphonic, and require secure learning of individual parts before they are put together.

Have students:

- Look through the piece to determine when their part moves with other parts, and when it moves all by itself.
- Be brave about reading the rhythm for themselves, since all parts move independently.
- Practice their part as a section until it is very secure before putting the four parts together.

National Standards

The following National Standards are addressed through the Extension and bottom-page activities:

1. Singing, alone and with others, a varied repertoire of music. **(a, b, c)**
4. Composing and arranging music within specified guidelines. **(a, d)**
5. Reading and notating music. **(a, b)**
8. Understanding relationships between music, the other arts, and disciplines outside the arts. **(c)**

May the Road Rise to Meet You

Irish Blessing
COMPOSER: David Hamilton

Focus

OVERVIEW
Ascending melodic skips; legato style.

OBJECTIVES
After completing this lesson, students will be able to:
- Read and sing ascending melodic skips.
- Sing in legato style.

CHORAL MUSIC TERMS
Define the Choral Music Terms for students, giving pronunciation, and answering any questions that may arise.

Warming Up

Vocal Warm-Up
This Vocal Warm-Up is designed to prepare students to:
- Sing in four-part harmony.
- Move up or down by half steps, maintaining the same harmonic scheme.
- Tune chord tones carefully.
- Sing in legato style.
Have students:
- Read through the Vocal Warm-Up directions.
- Sing, following your demonstration.

LESSON 14

May the Road Rise to Meet You

CHORAL MUSIC TERMS
ascending intervals
chord progression
legato style

Irish Blessing
COMPOSER: *David Hamilton*

VOICING
SATB

PERFORMANCE STYLE
Slowly, legato
Accompanied by organ (or piano may be substituted)

FOCUS
- Read and sing ascending melodic skips.
- Sing in legato style.

Warming Up

Vocal Warm-Up
Sing these two four-part exercises. As you end each chord progression, move up by a half step. Pay sharp attention to tuning and legato style, and challenge yourself to see how accurately you can tune with the ensemble.

Sight-Singing
Sight-sing this folk song–like exercise using solfège and hand signs or numbers. Move from chord to chord carefully, tuning each pitch. Then sing on *loo*, shaping the phrases, with legato style. Notice the ascending skips of more than a third, and practice them carefully.

104 *Choral Connections   Level 3 Mixed Voices*

TEACHER'S RESOURCE BINDER

National Standards
In this lesson, students should develop the following skills and concepts:
1. Singing, alone and with others, a varied repertoire of music. **(a, b, c)**
5. Reading and notating music. **(b)**
7. Evaluating music and music performances. **(a)**
8. Understanding relationships between music, the other arts, and disciplines outside the arts. **(c)**

 Singing: "May the Road Rise to Meet You"

Sometimes music is used to enhance an already powerful message. Read this Irish Blessing aloud.

> May the road rise to meet you.
> May the wind be always at your back,
> the sun shine warm upon your face,
> the rain fall soft upon your fields,
> and until we meet again,
> may God hold you in His hand,
> may God hold you in the hollow of His hand.
> Amen.

How are the images in the poem related to real-life situations? What musical elements would you use to enhance this message?

Now turn to the music for "May the Road Rise to Meet You" on page 106.

 HOW DID YOU DO?

Did the images in the poem help you learn this piece? Think about your preparation and performance of "May the Road Rise to Meet You."

1. What was easy for you in learning this piece? What was a challenge?

2. Describe an ascending melodic skip, and tell which skips are difficult for you. Choose a phrase of the piece to sing that was a challenge you overcame.

3. Why is legato style appropriate for this piece? Choose three classmates and sing a phrase, demonstrating it with and without legato style singing.

4. Do you think the composer enhanced the text with his music? Give specific musical examples to support your answer.

Lesson 14: May the Road Rise to Meet You **105**

Composer David Hamilton

David Hamilton is a choral director from New Zealand. Having published well over 60 choral pieces, he is recognized as one of the country's leading composers.

"May the Road Rise to Meet You"

There are many settings of this familiar text, which is most often called the "Irish Blessing." This selection can easily be performed a cappella or accompanied by guitar or piano. A guitar accompaniment is available in the four-part treble arrangement.

Sight-Singing

This Sight-Singing exercise is designed to prepare students to:
- Read and sing in harmony using solfège and hand signs or numbers.
- Sing phrases in legato style.
- Identify and sing ascending melodic skips.
- Experience anacrusis.

Have students:
- Read through the Sight-Singing exercise directions.
- Read through each voice part rhythmically, using rhythm syllables.
- Sight-sing through each part separately using solfège and hand signs or numbers.
- Sing all parts together.

Singing: "May the Road Rise to Meet You"

Identify the message of the text. Have students:
- Read the text on page 105.
- Discuss the images and how they might symbolize events in everyday life.
- Predict what musical elements will be used to enhance the message.

Suggested Teaching Sequence

1. Review Vocal Warm-Up.
Sing in four parts in legato style. Have students:
- Review the Vocal Warm-Up on page 104.
- Identify legato style, then repeat.
- Stay in tune while all parts are singing.

2. Review Sight-Singing.
Sing in parts using solfège and hand signs or numbers. Identify ascending melodic skips. Have students:
- Review the Sight-Singing exercise on pages 104–105 using solfège and hand signs or numbers.
- Sing the exercise on *loo.* (open mouth/throat, tall vowel shape, fully extended lips)
- Identify phrases, and the dynamic arch of each phrase that occurs with legato singing.
- Sing the exercise again on *loo,* demonstrating legato style.
- Identify ascending intervals of more than a third. Sing the intervals out of context, discussing which are hard to master.
- Explore their parts in "May the Road Rise to Meet You" for ascending melodic leaps and practice them out of context.

May the Road Rise to Meet You

Irish Blessing
Music by David Hamilton

SATB, with Organ Accompaniment

106 *Choral Connections   Level 3 Mixed Voices*

CONNECTING THE ARTS
Visual Arts
Have students:
- Interpret the Irish Blessing through visual representations in any medium they choose.
- Avoid the literal or stereotypical interpretations, and work for an original and more abstract interpretation that works for the same mood as the piece.
- Photograph selected art interpretations, and make slides or transparencies to show on a screen as students perform the musical piece.
- Apply this same activity to dance, constructing a creative dance to go with the piece.

3. Sight-sing "May the Road Rise to Meet You" using solfège and hand signs or numbers.

Have students:

- Divide into voice sections (SATB) and read each part rhythmically, using rhythm syllables. Identify when the rhythms are the same in all parts, and when they are different from one another.
- Still in sections, sing with solfège and hand signs or numbers, identifying and working on problem areas.
- Sing the piece through using solfège and hand signs or numbers with full ensemble.
- Divide into sections and recite the text rhythmically for each voice part.
- Sing the piece through with text as a full ensemble.

May the Road Rise to Meet You **107**

Assessment

Informal Assessment

During this lesson, students showed the ability to:

- Sing using legato style in the Vocal Warm-Up exercise.
- Identify and practice singing legato style in the Sight-Singing exercise.
- Identify ascending melodic intervals and practice them in the Sight-Singing exercise.
- Identify ascending melodic intervals in "May the Road Rise to Meet You."
- Sing independently in parts in legato style, singing intervals accurately, in "May the Road Rise to Meet You."

Student Self-Assessment

Have students:

- Evaluate their performance with the How Did You Do? section on page 105.
- Answer the questions individually. Discuss them in pairs or small groups and/or write their responses on a sheet of paper.

Individual Performance Assessment

To further demonstrate accomplishment, have each student:

- Sing various specified ascending intervals from a pitch that you play.
- In a double quartet, sing the piece, demonstrating legato style.

til we meet a - gain, may God hold you, hold___

til we meet a - gain, may God hold you, hold___

til we meet a - gain, may God hold you,

til we meet a - gain, may God hold you,

poco rit. p a tempo

— you in His hand, may God hold you in the hol - low of His hand,

— you in His hand, may God hold you in the hol - low of His hand,

hold you in His hand, may God hold you in the hol - low of His hand,

hold you in His hand, may God hold you in the hol - low of His hand,

Extension

Creating a Gospel/Pop Improvisation to Replace the Tenor-Bass "Echo" Phrases

Have students:

* Identify the echo phrases in the piece; for example, measures 8 and 12.
* Create new versions of these phrases with original style and new words.
* Sing their new improvisations in place of the originals, matching the style and harmony of the piece.
* Compare the effectiveness of the original and the newly improvised versions.

Transcribing the Piece for an Instrumental Ensemble

Have students:

* Discuss the mood and style of the piece, and decide which instruments would be their choice for interpretation. (suggestions: string ensemble, wind quartet or quintet, handbells/tone chimes, percussion ensemble, electronic keyboard/ MIDI)
* Learn about any transpositions or difficulties there may be for those instruments with certain pitches or leaps.
* Transcribe the piece.
* Rehearse the piece, and then share it.
* Discuss the effectiveness of the transcription, and how well the piece can be enjoyed without text.

May the Road Rise to Meet You **109**

National Standards

The following National Standards are addressed through the Extension and bottom-page activities:

1. Singing, alone and with others, a varied repertoire of music. **(a, b, c)**
3. Improvising melodies, variations, and accompaniments. **(a)**
4. Composing and arranging music within specified guidelines. **(b)**
7. Evaluating music and music performances. **(a, b, c)**
8. Understanding relationships between music, the other arts, and disciplines outside the arts. **(c, d, e)**

LESSON 15

In Memoria Aeterna

Psalm 112
COMPOSER: *Antonio Vivaldi (1678–1741)*
ENGLISH TEXT: *Douglas R. McEwen*

CHORAL MUSIC TERMS
fugue
round

VOICING
SATB

PERFORMANCE STYLE
Andante molto
Accompanied by keyboard

FOCUS
- Identify round and fugal form.
- Distinguish between round and fugal form.
- Sing in fugal form.

Warming Up

Vocal Warm-Up
    Sing this warm-up exercise with a lot of energy. Repeat moving up or down by half steps. Bend from the waist and touch your toes on the top pitch on each repetition—and don't bend your knees! Stretch and strengthen your range.

Sight-Singing
    Sight-sing this exercise using solfège and hand signs or numbers. Divide into two groups, then sing it as a round, with group II beginning in measure 2.

Lesson 15: In Memoria Aeterna **111**

TEACHER'S RESOURCE BINDER
Blackline Master 15, *Translation and Pronunciation Guide for "In Memoria Aeterna,"* page 92

National Standards
1. Singing, alone and with others, a varied repertoire of music. **(a, b, c)**
5. Reading and notating music. **(e)**
6. Listening to, analyzing, and describing music. **(a, b)**
7. Evaluating music and music performances. **(a)**
8. Understanding relationships between music, the other arts, and disciplines outside the arts. **(c)**

LESSON 15

In Memoria Aeterna

Psalm 112
COMPOSER: Antonio Vivaldi (1678–1741)
ENGLISH TEXT: Douglas R. McEwen

Focus

OVERVIEW
Round and fugal forms.

OBJECTIVES
After completing this lesson, students will be able to:
- Identify round and fugal forms.
- Distinguish between round and fugal forms.
- Sing in fugal form.

CHORAL MUSIC TERMS
Define the Choral Music Terms for students, giving pronunciation, and answering any questions that may arise.

Warming Up

Vocal Warm-Up
This Vocal Warm-Up is designed to prepare students to:
- Sing while performing physical exercises, loosening the entire body to prepare for rehearsal.
- Strengthen and extend their vocal range.
Have students:
- Read through the Vocal Warm-Up directions.
- Sing, following your demonstration.

111

Sight-Singing

The Sight-Singing exercise on page 111 is designed to prepare students to:

- Read tonic chord tones using solfège and hand signs or numbers.
- Read and sing in 3/4 meter.
- Identify and sing a round.
- Experience anacrusis.

Have students:

- Read through the Sight-Singing exercise directions.
- Read through each voice part rhythmically, using rhythm syllables.
- Sight-sing through each part separately using solfège and hand signs or numbers.
- Sing all parts together.

Singing: "In Memoria Aeterna"

Distinguish between a round and fugue form.

Have students:

- Read the text on page 112.
- Identify familiar rounds, including the Sight-Singing exercise in this lesson.
- Define round as an imitative style in which the perpetual theme begins in one group and is strictly imitated in other groups in an overlapping fashion.
- Predict differences between a round and a fugue, and then compare their answers with the following definition: A fugue is a form similar to the round because it is based on the principle of imitation. It is a compositional form in which the subject (tune) is begun in one group and later imitated by another group. However, the imitation is at a different pitch level from the original subject. Some of the melodic and rhythmic material in a fugue is not imitated, but extends the specific melodic line, and provides harmonic material for other entrances of the subject.

Singing: "In Memoria Aeterna"

You know how to sing a round, but do you know the difference between a round and a fugue? Sing some rounds you know, then create a definition of round. A fugue is similar to a round, but there are some important differences. Like a round, a fugue is based on the principle of imitation. What else might be different?

Now turn to the music for "In Memoria Aeterna" on page 113.

HOW DID YOU DO?

Think about your preparation and performance of "In Memoria Aeterna."

1. Describe a round and a fugue, and the differences and similarities. Is it easier to sing a round or a fugue? Is it more enjoyable to sing a round or a fugue?

2. In a group, find a way to demonstrate a round and a fugue, using materials from this lesson.

3. How would you rate the ensemble's performance of "In Memoria Aeterna"? What criteria will you use other than the ability to correctly perform the fugue form? What was the most challenging aspect for you? What was the most challenging aspect for the group?

"In Memoria Aeterna"

"In Memoria Aeterna" is the seventh part of the larger work *Beatus Vir*, which is taken from the Book of Psalms (111–112). Vivaldi set the entire liturgical text to music written for orchestra, chorus, and soli. The *Beatus Vir* is one of the five Lucernal or Vesper psalms; it is sung after the antiphon at Sunday Vespers.

In Memoria Aeterna

(For the Righteous Shall be Remembered)

Antonio Vivaldi (1678–1741)
Edited by Douglas R. McEwen
Psalm 112 from *Beatus Vir*
English text by Douglas R. McEwen

Mixed Voices* SATB, Accompanied

*Altos and Sopranos may sing if a soft balance can be maintained.
**Softly "floated" tone should be sung clearly and actively.

In Memoria Aeterna **113**

Composer Antonio Vivaldi

Antonio Vivaldi was born in Venice, Italy, in 1678. Early in his life, he received intensive music instruction from his father and from Giovanni Legrenzi. However, his primary interest during his formative years was to become a priest, and in 1703 he received Holy Orders in the Catholic church, all the while perfecting his skills on the violin. In 1703 he became a teacher of the violin, and after 1709 he served as Maestro di Concerti at the Ospedale della Pieta in Venice.

Vivaldi wrote some 40 operas, a hundred or so major choral works, 400 concertos, approximately 25 secular cantatas, 73 sonatas, and various other musical forms. During the last years of his life, Vivaldi suffered from extreme poverty and neglect. He died in Vienna in July 1741.

Suggested Teaching Sequence

1. Review Vocal Warm-Up.
Sing and exercise. Warm up the body and voice.
Have students:
- Review the Vocal Warm-Up on page 111.
- Add the exercise to loosen the whole body and get the brain and voice ready to work.

2. Review Sight-Singing.
Read using solfège and hand signs or numbers. Sing a round.
Have students:
- Review the Sight-Singing exercise on page 111 using solfège and hand signs or numbers.
- Sing the exercise as a three-part round.
- Review the difference between a round and fugue style, identifying what they sang in the exercise as a round.
- Look at the music for "In Memoria Aeterna," finding places that look like a subject or imitation of a subject; for example, measure 17 is the subject, with imitation at measures 20 and 23. Identify the piece as being in fugal form.

3. Sight-sing "In Memoria Aeterna" using solfège and hand signs or numbers.

Have students:

- Divide into voice sections (SATB) and read each part rhythmically, using rhythm syllables. Identify where they see imitative segments relating to other parts.
- Still in sections, sing with solfège and hand signs or numbers, identifying and working on problem areas.
- Sing the piece through using solfège and hand signs or numbers with full ensemble.

4. Learn the Latin text pronunciation.

Have students:

- Using Blackline Master 15, *Translation and Pronunciation Guide for "In Memoria Aeterna,"* practice the pronunciation of the Latin text.
- Echo the phrases in rhythm.
- Speak the text of the piece slowly in rhythm using correct pronunciation. Practice difficult parts.
- Sing the piece at tempo, using correct Latin pronunciation.

VOCAL DEVELOPMENT

To encourage vocal development, have students:

- Speak and sing the Latin text with tall, open vowels and stressed consonants.
- Use plenty of breath support to carry the *f* dynamics and sustained notes through the entire phrase.
- Identify the vertical and linear chord structures. Use solfège and hand signs or numbers to sing and tune the chords.
- Balance the chords by listening to each voice in the chords. Demonstrate the effect of balancing chords by giving more weight to one voice. Ask: How does it change the music?
- Articulate the rhythm by emphasizing any interesting rhythm patterns.
- Clap and speak the rhythm; conduct and speak the text in rhythm. Be precise on attacks and releases of phrases.
- Notice the musical road signs such as the slurs, dashes (*tenuto* means hold or press it slightly), and dynamics.

TEACHING STRATEGY

More Interpretation

The hushed serenity and simplicity expressed by the three choral parts of "In Memoria Aeterna" are deeply moving. The linear line and horizontal lyricism form the underlying texture of the piece. Phrases should be shaped over the persistently constant eighth-note inner pulsation in the accompaniment, maintaining a constant tempo.

Have students:

- Look through the piece to identify dynamic markings and breath marks.
- Notice the constant eighth-note accompaniment pattern.
- Describe the mood of the piece as hushed and reverent.
- Perform with increasing sensitivity to the intricacies of the composition.

Assessment

Informal Assessment

During this lesson, students showed the ability to:

- Distinguish between a round and a fugue in the Sight-Singing exercise.
- Sing in fugal style in "In Memoria Aeterna."
- Sing using correct Latin pronunciation in "In Memoria Aeterna."

Student Self-Assessment

Have students:

- Evaluate their performance with the How Did You Do? section on page 112.
- Answer the questions individually. Discuss them in pairs or small groups and/or write their responses on a sheet of paper.

Individual Performance Assessment

To further demonstrate accomplishment, have each student:

- In writing, analyze measures 1–7 of "In Memoria Aeterna" and identify the compositional form of the piano introduction (round), describing the characteristics that lead to this conclusion.
- In writing, analyze measures 17–28 of "In Memoria Aeterna" and identify the compositional form of this section (fugue), describing the characteristics that lead to this conclusion.
- In a double quartet, sing a self-selected segment from "In Memoria Aeterna" that demonstrates fugal form.

Extension

Composing a Fugue
Have students:
- Write a fugue of not more than 20 measures.
- First write a short melodic and rhythmic motif, using only a few pitches.
- Next, try to add one more part, deciding when to have it enter, and at what pitch, in order to establish some harmonies vertically.
- Add more to the first part to keep it going as the motif is stated by the second part.
- Now add a third part. Ask: When will it begin, and on what pitch? What will the other two parts do? When will part I return to the theme, or will it?
- Discuss the difficulties and intricacies of writing fugues.

Listening to a Recorded Fugue
Have students:
- Listen to a recording of a fugue.
- Discuss those characteristics of a fugue that they recognize in the recording.
- Identify other musical elements they heard in the listening selection.

National Standards
The following National Standards are addressed through the Extension and bottom-page activities:
1. Singing, alone and with others, a varied repertoire of music. **(d)**
4. Composing and arranging music within specified guidelines. **(a)**
6. Listening to, analyzing, and describing music. **(a, c)**
9. Understanding music in relation to history and culture. **(a, c, d)**

Making Historical Connections

Renaissance Period

Focus

OVERVIEW
Understanding the development of choral music during the Renaissance period.

OBJECTIVES
After completing this lesson, students will be able to:
- Describe characteristics of architecture, fine art, and music during the Renaissance period.
- Identify several musical forms of the Renaissance period.
- Define *a cappella, madrigal, motet,* and *polyphony.*
- Identify some of the key musical composers of the Renaissance.

CHORAL MUSIC TERMS
Define the Choral Music Terms for students, giving pronunciation, and answering any questions that may arise.

Introducing the Lesson

Introduce the Renaissance through visual art.
Analyze the artwork on pages 124 and 127 of the text.
Have students:
- Study the painting and basilica, describing features in as much detail as possible.
- Discuss the information about each illustration provided at the bottom of pages 125 and 127 in your Teacher's Wraparound Edition.

The Adoration of the Magi by Sandro Botticelli (1445–1510) reflects the Renaissance interest in religious subjects. Framing the central figures within the strong geometric pillars emphasized those subjects over others. Similar organizational principles are apparent in the Renaissance composers' ability to create intricate polyphonic works.

c. 1481. Sandro Botticelli. *The Adoration of the Magi.* (Detail.) Tempera on wood. 70 x 104 cm (27⅝ x 41"). National Gallery of Art, Washington, D.C. Andrew W. Mellon Collection.

124 *Choral Connections   Level 3 Mixed Voices*

TEACHER'S RESOURCE BINDER
Fine Art Transparency 1, *The Adoration of the Magi,* by Botticelli

Optional Listening Selections:
Music: An Appreciation, 6th edition
"As Vesta Was Descending": CD 1, Track 77
Ricercar in the Twelfth Mode: CD 1, Track 79

National Standards
This historical lesson addresses the following National Standards:
6. Listening to, analyzing, and describing music. **(a)**
8. Understanding relationships between music, the other arts, and disciplines outside the arts. **(a, b, c, d, e)**
9. Understanding music in relation to history and culture. **(a, c, d)**

Renaissance Period

After completing this lesson, you will be able to:

- Describe some of the major developments of the Renaissance period.
- Explain the difference between sacred music and secular music.
- Discuss the major musical forms of the Renaissance period.
- Identify at least three major composers of the Renaissance period.

In the history of Western Europe, the period from around 1430 until 1600 is called the Renaissance. This name comes from a French word meaning "rebirth," and the period was in many ways a time of rebirth or renewal. The scholars and artists of the Renaissance made a conscious effort to reestablish the standards of intellectual and cultural greatness they saw in the accomplishments of the ancient Greeks and Romans. Although the great figures of the Renaissance may have been looking back to earlier cultures, they were not moving back; instead, they were moving radically ahead into modern times.

A Time of Discovery

The Renaissance was a time of discovery in many fields. Modern science and scientific methods began to develop. Scholars no longer simply accepted what they read. Rather, they realized that careful observation and experimentation could help them draw new conclusions about the world around them. The results of this approach were a series of important advancements in science, mathematics, and technology. Better clocks and navigating instruments became available; scientists began to develop better lenses for instruments such as telescopes and microscopes. Astronomers established that the Earth and other planets revolved around the sun, and the positions of many stars were accurately calculated.

In part because of the technological advances of the period, the Renaissance was an era of increasing exploration and trade. For the first time, European sailing ships reached the southern coast of Africa, the Americas, and India. In 1519, the first successful round-the-world voyage was undertaken. These journeys brought a new, expanding sense of the world and an influx of new ideas—as well as new opportunities for trade—to the people of Renaissance Europe.

One technological advancement of the Renaissance had an impact on many aspects of life: the invention of the printing press with movable type, usually credited to Johann Gutenberg. Until this development, books had been copied by hand. The development of the printing press meant that books could be produced much more quickly and easily, and much less expensively. More and more people had access to books and the ideas they communicated, and thus prepared themselves to take advantage of this opportunity by learning to read both words and music. Books—of facts, of new ideas, and of music—were no longer the property of only the privileged.

COMPOSERS

John Dunstable (c. 1390–1453)
Guillaume Dufay (1400–1474)
Josquin Desprez (c. 1440–1521)
Heinrich Isaac (c. 1450–1517)
Clement Janequin (c. 1485–1560)
Adrian Willaert (1490–1562)
Christopher Tye (c. 1500–c. 1572)
Thomas Tallis (1505–1585)
Andrea Gabrieli (1520–1586)
Giovanni Pierluigi da Palestrina (c. 1525–1594)
Orlande de Lassus (1532–1594)
William Byrd (1543–1623)
Thomas Morley (c. 1557–c. 1603)
Michael Praetorius (c. 1571–1621)
Thomas Weelkes (1575–1623)

ARTISTS

Donatello (1386–1466)
Sandro Botticelli (1445–1510)
Leonardo da Vinci (1452–1519)
Albrecht Dürer (1471–1528)
Michelangelo (1475–1564)
Raphael (1483–1520)
Titian (c. 1488–1576)

AUTHORS

Sir Thomas More (1478–1536)
Martin Luther (1483–1546)
Miguel de Cervantes (1547–1616)
Sir Walter Raleigh (c. 1552–1618)
Sir Philip Sidney (1554–1586)
William Shakespeare (1564–1616)

CHORAL MUSIC TERMS

a cappella
Gregorian chant
madrigal
mass
motet
polyphony
sacred music
secular music

Renaissance Period **125**

Suggested Teaching Sequence

1. Examine the Renaissance period.
Have students:
- Read the text on pages 125–129.
- Share what they know about the composers, artists, and authors listed on this page.
- Read, discuss, and answer the review questions individually, in pairs, or in small groups.
- Discuss their answers with the whole group, clarifying misunderstandings.

2. Examine the Renaissance in historical perspective.
Have students:
- Turn to the time line on pages 126–129 and read the citations.
- Discuss why these people and events are considered important to the Renaissance period.
- Compare each of these events to what they know occurred before and after the Renaissance.
- Write a statement of one or two sentences in length that describes the Renaissance, based on one of the events in the time line. (The Renaissance spirit prospered as a result of the invention of the printing press. Because of the press, more people were exposed to new ideas and could write down their ideas.)

MORE ABOUT... The Adoration of the Magi

During the Renaissance, there was a renewed focus back to the ancient culture of the Roman empire and the classical spirit. In visual art this was represented by a shift from sacred symbolism to realistic art. Perspective was explored as a result of interest in geometry, and the flat canvas now represented three-dimensional perspective from one point of view outside the plane of the art.

The human form was celebrated, and the ideal was a realistic representation. *The Adoration of the Magi* illustrates some of the characteristic changes in Renaissance art, including the humanizing of figures, the use of light and shadow, the use of perspective, and the idealization of the Roman classical form, indicated by the columns and ruins.

3. Define the musical aspects of the Renaissance period.

Have students:

- Review the changes in music during the Renaissance period.
- Define *a cappella, madrigal, motet,* and *polyphony,* telling how they reflected the development of choral music during the Renaissance.
- Describe the contributions of Renaissance composers such as John Dunstable, Josquin Desprez, Adrian Willaert, and Martin Luther.
- Identify musicians who contributed to the popularity of the madrigal. (Clement Jonequin, Heinrick Isaac, Thomas Tallis, William Byrd, Thomas Morley, and Thomas Weelkes)

Gutenberg press; beginning of modern printing   Copenhagen becomes Danish capital   First printed music appears

▼ c. 1435   ▼ 1445   ▼ 1465

▲ 1441   ▲ 1453
Eton College and King's College,   Ottoman Turks capture Constantinople, marking end
Cambridge, founded   of Byzantine Empire

During the Renaissance, the Catholic church gradually lost some of the influence it had exerted as a center of learning, a formidable political power, and an important force in the daily lives of nearly all Europeans. Rejecting the absolute laws set down by the Church, though not necessarily rejecting any faith in God, Renaissance scholars accepted humanism, a belief in the dignity and value of individual human beings. In addition, the first Protestant churches were established, in opposition to the rule of the Catholic hierarchy.

A Renaissance of the Visual Arts

The developments and discoveries of the Renaissance were reflected in the arts of the period. The works of painters and sculptors became more lifelike and realistic. Painters gave new depth to their work by using perspective and by manipulating light and shadow; they also began using oil paints, which allowed them to revise and refine their work. Sculptors created more individualized human figures, and sculpture began to be considered a true art, rather than a craft.

Many paintings and sculptures of the Renaissance depicted religious subjects, especially scenes from the Bible. However, artists increasingly crafted works with non-religious subjects, often taken from Greek and Roman mythology.

Careful observation and an intense interest in the natural world helped Renaissance artists develop more realistic and individualized paintings and sculptures. Some of the most notable artists worked in several media and delved deeply into science as well. Leonardo da Vinci, one of the foremost painters and sculptors of the Renaissance, was also an architect, a scientist, an engineer, and a musician.

The Influence of the Catholic Church on Music

In the centuries preceding the Renaissance—a time usually called the Middle Ages—most composed music was for the Catholic church and performed as part of religious services. The most important musical form of the period was the **Gregorian chant,** *a melody sung in unison by male voices.* The chants were sung **a cappella,** *without instrumental accompaniment.* All the chants were composed in Latin, the language of all Church services at that time, and were based on sacred texts, often from the Book of Psalms in the Old Testament.

Although the earliest Gregorian chants consisted of a single melodic line, a second melodic line was added to most chants during the Middle Ages. This was the beginning of **polyphony,** *the simultaneous performance of two or more melodic lines.* In polyphonic music, each part begins at a different place, and each part is independent and important. The use of various kinds of polyphony has continued through the centuries; in fact, polyphony is a significant feature in some modern jazz compositions.

da Vinci sketches an early helicopter design
1483

Columbus lands in West Indies/Americas
1492

1473–1480
Sistine Chapel built

1488
Diaz sails around the Cape of Good Hope

1498
da Gama sails around Africa and lands in India

The artists and architects of the Renaissance rediscovered Classical antiquity and were inspired by what they found. In 1547, Michelangelo (1475–1564) became chief architect for the replacement of the original basilica of Old St. Peter's. Architect Giacomo della Porta finished the dome 26 years after Michelangelo's death.

1546–64. Michelangelo. Exterior view, St. Peter's. St. Peter's Basilica, Vatican State, Rome, Italy. (Dome completed by Giacomo della Porta, 1590.)

Sacred Music of the Renaissance

During the Renaissance, the Catholic church continued to exert a strong influence on daily life and on the arts. Much of the important music composed during the Renaissance was **sacred music**, *music used in religious services.*

The two most important forms of sacred Renaissance music were the **mass**—*a long musical composition that includes the five major sections of the Catholic worship service*—and the **motet**—*a shorter choral work, set to Latin texts and used in religious services, but not part of the regular mass.* In the early years of the Renaissance, one of the most influential composers

Renaissance Period **127**

St. Peter's Basilica

When Michelangelo assumed responsibility for the design and construction of the basilica at Old St. Peter's, he applied his belief that architecture, like the human body, should be symmetrical. He established this sense of balance and unity in the dome of the basilica. Although della Porta later altered Michelangelo's plans, when the dome is viewed from the west (apse) end, one sees how it unifies the building from the base to the summit. Such unity harkens back to the classical symmetry of Roman architecture.

Sistine Chapel ceiling painted by Michelangelo	Cortez conquers Mexico	Women seen for the first time on Italian stages	Council of Trent meets to discuss Reformation and Counter Reformation
▼ 1508	▼ 1519	▼ 1529	▼ 1545

▲ 1517	▲ 1531
Protestant Reformation begins in Germany with Luther's 95 Theses	Henry VIII declared head of the Church of England

▲ 1519
Magellan begins voyage around the world

Extension

Notation

Musical notation had its beginnings in the churches during the Middle Ages. Notation continued to develop throughout the Renaissance, spurred by the invention of the printing press. Have students:

- Research the development of musical notation from the Middle Ages through the Renaissance period, including how and when the following became used: one line staff, five line staff, *do* clef, treble clef, bass clef, key signatures, rhythmic stem notation, note heads (diamond, triangle, circular), meter signatures, bar lines, dynamics, and markings for tempo.

Networking with Your Community

Renaissance music is performed today by madrigal groups and small chamber choirs or orchestras. Many use early instruments to achieve an authentic representation of the sound. Renaissance dancing is also an area of interest for local groups. Have students check with their local arts council and neighboring universities to discover groups who might be willing to perform for the students, and discuss the unique pleasures and challenges of performing Renaissance music and dance.

of both masses and motets was John Dunstable. Dunstable developed a new harmonic structure of polyphony; his music helped establish the Renaissance as the "golden age of polyphony."

Later in the period, Josquin Desprez began to change the sound of Renaissance choral music. He believed that music should be structured to make the words of the text understandable, and he also thought that all the voices in a choral setting could be equal in importance. Desprez is considered one of the founders of Renaissance music, because he introduced three new musical concepts:

1. Homophonic harmonies, produced by chords that support a melody;
2. Motive imitation, short repeating melodies between voice parts;
3. A more natural cadence, or sense of conclusion.

During the Renaissance, instruments were added to accompany and echo the voices used in sacred music. Adrian Willaert was one of the first composers to combine voices, pipe organs, and other instruments. He also began to use dynamics and was among the first to compose for two imitative voices.

The first music for Protestant religious services was written during this period. Here, sacred music was sung not in Latin but in the languages of the worshipers. One of the most important leaders of the Protestant Reformation, Martin Luther, wrote German hymns that are still sung in Protestant churches today.

The Evolution of Secular Music

Secular music, *any music that is not sacred*, changed in quality and quantity during the Renaissance period. Secular music became increasingly important as the center of musical activity began to shift from churches to castles and towns. Many court and town musicians traveled throughout Europe, so new styles and musical ideas spread relatively rapidly.

The **madrigal**, *a secular form of music written in several imitative parts*, became popular during the Renaissance. Madrigals were composed by such musicians as Clement Janequin, Heinrich Isaac, Thomas Tallis, William Byrd, Thomas Morley, and Thomas Weelkes, to be sung by everyday people. Whole collections of songs in the madrigal form were printed in part books. A family might purchase a set of part books (one for soprano, one for alto, and so on); then family members and friends would gather around these part books and sing.

Most madrigals were composed for three or more voices. Typically, a madrigal was based on a secular poem and incorporated the expression of strong emotions, usually about love. The polyphony within madrigals was often quite challenging, even though the songs were intended primarily for home entertainment. Europeans of the noble and emerging middle classes placed an increased importance on the education of the individual; reading music and singing were considered essential aspects of that education.

128 *Choral Connections   Level 3 Mixed Voices*

Elizabeth I crowned Queen of England
(died 1603)

1558

Portuguese colonize Angola
and found São Paulo

1574

William Shakespeare begins play writing

c. 1590

1564

First violins made by Andrea Amati

1584

Sir Walter Raleigh discovers Virginia

1599

Globe Theatre built in London

Check Your Understanding

Recall

1. What were the most important differences between the music of the Middle Ages and the music of the Renaissance?

2. What is a cappella music?

3. What is polyphony?

4. What is the difference between a mass and a motet?

5. What is the difference between sacred music and secular music?

6. How are motets and madrigals alike? How are they different?

Thinking It Through

1. The word *polyphony* comes from two roots: poly, meaning *many*, and phony, meaning *sounds*. Explain the relationship between these roots and polyphonic music.

2. If you listened to a piece of unidentified music, what clues could help you decide whether it was a Renaissance composition?

Renaissance Period **129**

ANSWERS TO RECALL QUESTIONS

1. During the Middle Ages, most music was composed in Latin for religious services and vocal parts were equal.
2. Without instrumental accompaniment.
3. The simultaneous performance of two or more melodic lines.
4. The mass is a long musical composition that includes the five major sections of the Catholic worship service; the motet is a shorter choral work, set to Latin texts and used in religious services, but not part of the regular mass.
5. Sacred music is used in religious services; secular music is any music that is not sacred.
6. Both are short choral works. Madrigals are secular while motets are sacred.

Enrichment Projects

The Renaissance is an exciting theme for a unit of study. Have students research possible approaches to the period by making a chart with columns for "What We Know," "What We'd Like to Know," and "How We Can Find Out." Using the information in this textbook, and quick research in encyclopedias, on-line services, or other resources, fill out the columns, and then determine what projects each individual or group will work on. These projects can take many forms, ranging from reviewing a performance to performing a madrigal.

One popular and exciting all-school event is the creation of a Renaissance fair, including food preparation, costumes, music, games (chess, log wrestling), and so on. Each student should be encouraged to choose some task where learning and rigor will be required. Students should also be aware of all other projects going on, and link ideas together whenever possible.

Native American, Asian, and African Cultures and the Renaissance

Have students:

• Explore the music that was being performed and created in other cultures from 1430 to 1600, using the following questions as guides: Was there music occurring in the culture during this time period? What was the music like? Was there any influence from European Renaissance music? If so, how did these music types change each other, if at all?

Listening to..
Renaissance Music

This feature is designed to expand students' appreciation of choral and instrumental music of the Renaissance period.

CHORAL SELECTION: "As Vesta Was Descending" by Weelkes

Have students:

- Read the information on this page to learn more about "As Vesta Was Descending."
- Watch as you follow a transparency of Blackline Master, Listening Map 1.

Using the Listening Map

Begin at the top left and follow the text. The key is at the bottom of the map.

Have students:

- Read the English text and the translation in contemporary jargon.
- Listen as you explain that each picture on the map represents the text painting on that line.
- Identify examples of text painting. See if students can identify how many times "Fair Oriana" is sung. (The score states 68 times.)
- Listen to the selection as you point to the transparency.

Listening to . . .
Renaissance Music

CHORAL SELECTION

Thomas Weelkes — "As Vesta Was Descending"

Thomas Weelkes (1575–1623), an organist and church composer, was one of England's best madrigalists. "As Vesta Was Descending" is in a collection of madrigals called *The Triumphes of Oriana*, published in 1601. This is a six-voice madrigal that uses text painting.

In the song "As Vesta Was Descending," Vesta is portrayed as the Roman goddess of the hearth fire coming down the hill with her servants, "Diana's darlings." (Diana is the protector of servants.) At the same time, Oriana (Queen Elizabeth I) is climbing the hill with her shepherd followers. When Vesta's attendants see the Queen, they desert Vesta and hurry down the hill to join Oriana, whereupon everyone sings the Queen's praises.

INSTRUMENTAL SELECTION

Andrea Gabrieli — Ricercar in the Twelfth Mode

Andrea Gabrieli (1520–1586) was the organist at St. Mark's Cathedral in Venice, Italy, from 1564 until his death. He composed instrumental as well as sacred and secular vocal music.

A *ricercar* is a polyphonic instrumental composition that uses imitation. "In the Twelfth Mode" means that it is based on a scale corresponding to C major.

TEACHER'S RESOURCE BINDER
Blackline Master, Listening Map 1
Blackline Master, Listening Map 2

Optional Listening Selections:
Music: An Appreciation, 6th edition
"As Vesta Was Descending": CD 1, Track 77
Ricercar in the Twelfth Mode: CD 1, Track 79

National Standards
This lesson addresses the following National Standard:
6. Listening to, analyzing, and describing music. **(a)**

♪♪ RENAISSANCE CONNECTIONS

Introducing...
"O Domine Jesu Christe"

Giovanni Pierluigi da Palestrina

Setting the Stage

As you sing "O Domine Jesu Christe," you will perform the musical elements of which you have read: the feeling of central key (tonality) and the flow of the individual part lines resulting in chords (harmony), which are very pleasant to hear. Listen carefully for the interplay of rhythm between two parts as the piece is performed (for example, in measures 5 and 6, between the alto, tenor, and bass lines). Palestrina's techniques of composition lived long after his death, forming a solid basis for the music of the future beyond the Renaissance period. You can appreciate his contributions to our music today because most of our songs are written in major or minor keys. This musical theory was one that Palestrina helped solidify.

Meeting the Composer
Giovanni Pierluigi da Palestrina (c. 1525–1594)

Giovanni Pierluigi da Palestrina is considered to be the master of Renaissance church music. He refined the motet and the mass partly in an effort to honor the Roman Catholic Church's request that music consider the text as the primary factor of composition, keeping the music objective, rational, logical, emotionally restrained, balanced, and ordered. As one sings Palestrina's music, the linear motion of and logical voice leadings in each part line results in harmonies that are recognizable and pleasing to our "modern" ears.

Renaissance Connections **131**

INSTRUMENTAL SELECTION: Ricercar in the Twelfth Mode by Andrea Gabrieli
Have students:
- Read the information on page 130 to learn more about Ricercar in the Twelfth Mode.
- Watch as you follow a transparency of Blackline Master, Listening Map 2.

Using the Listening Map
Begin at the first jester hat at the top left. Each icon is one strong beat. Note the meter change from B to C. At the castle, point to the dot in the window and then to each dot on the wall. Point to the knight when the meter changes.
Have students:
- Understand that this ricercar is played by four recorders. (soprano, alto, tenor, and bass)
- Listen as you go over the motive and theme key at the bottom of the listening map. Explain that the icons represent the entrance of an imitative motive or theme in the different recorder voices.
- Listen as you play the listening selection and point to the transparency.

INTRODUCING . . .
"O Domine Jesu Christe"
This feature is designed to introduce students to the Renaissance Lesson on the following pages.
Have students:
- Read Setting the Stage on this page to learn more about "O Domine Jesu Christe."
- Read Meeting the Composer to learn more about Giovanni Pierluigi da Palestrina.
- Turn the page and begin the Renaissance Lesson.

ASSESSMENT
Individual Performance Assessment
To further demonstrate understanding of Renaissance music, have each student:
- Listen again to "As Vesta Was Descending" and circle other examples of text painting.
- Try to identify all 68 times that "Fair Oriana" is sung.

- Listen again to Ricercar in the Twelfth Mode and circle where the motive is heard in the A section. For the B section, tap the strong beat. For the C section, notice the phrase marks when the theme is imitated.

O Domine Jesu Christe

Latin Text

COMPOSER: Giovanni Pierluigi da Palestrina (c. 1525–1594)

Focus

OVERVIEW
Homophonic texture.

OBJECTIVES
After completing this lesson, students will be able to:
- Visually and aurally identify homophonic texture.
- Sing homophonic texture.
- Sing a Renaissance piece a cappella.

CHORAL MUSIC TERMS
Define the Choral Music Terms for students, giving pronunciation, and answering any questions that may arise.

Warming Up

Vocal Warm-Up
This Vocal Warm-Up is designed to prepare students to:
- Read and sing traditional harmonic movement of voice parts.
- Identify homophonic texture visually and aurally.
- Tune while singing four-part harmony.

Have students:
- Read through the Vocal Warm-Up directions.
- Sing, following your demonstration.

RENAISSANCE LESSON

O Domine Jesu Christe

Latin Text

COMPOSER: Giovanni Pierluigi da Palestrina (c. 1525–1594)

ARRANGER: Gerald Knight

CHORAL MUSIC TERMS
a cappella
homophonic
imitation
polyphonic
Renaissance

VOICING
SATB

PERFORMANCE STYLE
Andante
A cappella

FOCUS
- Visually and aurally identify homophonic texture.
- Sing homophonic texture.
- Sing a Renaissance piece a cappella.

Warming Up

 Vocal Warm-Up

Sing the following exercise using solfège and hand signs or numbers, then on *loo*. Move down by a half step on each repeat. Is this an example of *homophonic* or *polyphonic* texture? How do you know?

 Sight-Singing

Sight-sing this exercise using solfège and hand signs or numbers. Although this is written in homophonic style, there are a few interesting places where voices move independently. Watch and listen carefully, tuning your own voice part to those around you. When you sing with no accompaniment, it is called *a cappella*.

TEACHER'S RESOURCE BINDER

Blackline Master 16, *Translation and Pronunciation Guide for "O Domine Jesu Christe,"* page 93

National Standards

In this lesson, students should develop the following skills and concepts:
1. Singing, alone and with others, a varied repertoire of music. **(a, b, c)**
5. Reading and notating music. **(b)**
6. Listening to, analyzing, and describing music. **(a)**
8. Understanding relationships between music, the other arts, and disciplines outside the arts. **(a, c)**

Singing: "O Domine Jesu Christe"

Imagine that you have a set of square blocks on a desk. How would you arrange them so they represented polyphony, several voice parts supporting each other but moving independently?

How would you arrange them differently to represent homophony, several voice parts moving together in block chords?

Now turn to the music for "O Domine Jesu Christe" on page 134.

HOW DID YOU DO?

?

Just like block chords have pitches supporting one another, your ensemble provides support for you as a singer.

Think about your preparation and performance of "O Domine Jesu Christe."

1. Describe the difference between polyphony and homophony, and apply these descriptions to "O Domine Jesu Christe."

2. How can you identify homophony visually? aurally?

3. How can you tell that this is a Renaissance period piece? What clues can be found in the notation? What clues can be found in the sound?

O Domine Jesu Christe **133**

This Sight-Singing exercise is designed to prepare students to:

- Read and sing in four parts using solfège and hand signs or numbers.
- Sing with independent voice leading, intonation, and phrasing.
- Sing dissonances through passing tones (measures 1, 2, and 7) and suspensions (measures 2–3 and 3).
- Sing a cappella.

Have students:

- Read through the Sight-Singing exercise directions.
- Read each voice part rhythmically, using rhythm syllables.
- Sight-sing through each part separately.
- Sing all parts together.

Singing: "O Domine Jesu Christe"

Use the analogy of blocks to distinguish between polyphony and homophony.

Have students:

- Read the text on page 133.
- Discuss or construct these representations of polyphony and homophony. (Polyphony would be represented by blocks in horizontal lines, each line with a similar pattern, but beginning at different places on the desk to represent independence and focus on the horizontal structure. Homophony would be represented by vertical block piles of three or four in each pile, to represent the vertical structure.)
- Look at "O Domine Jesu Christe," visually identifying the homophonic texture created by all voices moving at the same time.
- Discuss the visual differences between polyphonic and homophonic notation. (Homophonic is aligned; polyphonic zigzags vertically.)

Suggested Teaching Sequence

1. Review Vocal Warm-Up.
Sing and identify homophonic texture.
Have students:
- Review the Vocal Warm-Up on page 132.
- Identify this exercise as being homophonic.

2. Review Sight-Singing.
Read and sing a cappella in homophonic style.
Have students:
- Review the Sight-Singing exercise on page 132, using solfège and hand signs or numbers.
- Identify the homophonic texture, and define a cappella singing.
- Identify places where dissonance occurs as voice parts move.
- Sing again, tuning carefully and listening for the dissonances.

3. Sight-sing "O Domine Jesu Christe" using solfège and hand signs or numbers.
Have students:
- Divide into voice sections (SATB) and read each part rhythmically, using rhythm syllables, adding dynamic shape to the phrases.
- Still in sections, sight-sing the pitches using solfège and hand signs or numbers, working on problem areas.
- Sing the piece through, using solfège and hand signs or numbers, with full ensemble.

4. Strengthen chordal alignment.
Have students:
- Sing the piece legato on *loo*.
- Listen for accuracy in chordal alignment.
- Listen for rhythmic accuracy in the polyphonic sections.

O Domine Jesu Christe
(O Lord Jesus Christ)

Giovanni Pierluigi da Palestrina (c. 1525–1594)
Edited and Arranged by Gerald Knight
(English text by Gerald Knight)
(ASCAP)

A cappella Chorus of Mixed Voices

Duration
1 min. 15 sec.

134 *Choral Connections   Level 3 Mixed Voices*

VOCAL DEVELOPMENT

To encourage vocal development, have students:
- Sing tall, open vowels for the Latin text.
- Enunciate the consonants clearly.
- Energize and sustain the phrases with breath support and the feeling of moving forward. Sing forward to the climax of each phrase and carry to the end of the phrase.
- Use movement to illustrate the forward feeling of the music.
- Balance the chords by listening to each voice in the chords.
- Create intensity in soft singing with the same breath support used in loud singing.
- Articulate the moving parts in each voice to add contrast to the chordal style.

Have students:
- Using Blackline Master 16, *Translation and Pronunciation Guide for "O Domine Jesu Christe,"* say the words phonetically in a conversational manner.
- Read the words rhythmically from the notation.
- Sing, using correct Latin pronunciation.

Assessment

Informal Assessment

During this lesson, students showed the ability to:
- Read and sing four parts homophonically in the Vocal Warm-Up.
- Distinguish between homophony and polyphony in the Sight-Singing exercise.
- Define a cappella singing in the Sight-Singing exercise.
- Read, identify, and sing homophonic texture in "O Domine Jesu Christe."

Student Self-Assessment

Have students:
- Evaluate their performance with the How Did You Do? section on page 133.
- Answer the questions individually. Discuss them in pairs or small groups and/or write their responses on a sheet of paper.

Individual Performance Assessment

Have each student:
- Visually identify examples of homophonic texture in "O Domine Jesu Christe."
- Identify homophonic texture aurally by signaling while listening to a recording of the "Hallelujah" chorus from the *Messiah.*

TEACHING STRATEGY
Renaissance Characteristics

Have students:
- Describe the musical characteristics of "O Domine Jesu Christe."
- Recall characteristics of Renaissance music.
- Construct a Venn diagram, demonstrating the overlapping characteristics of the two that define the piece as an example of Renaissance music.

Extension

Shifting Meters
Have students:
- Listen for a shift from duple groupings to triple within the homophonic texture at measures 2–4 (*Domini Jesu*), and measures 9 and 10 (*te in cruce*). Some analysts suggest that this shift to threes is word painting that represents the Trinity, and possible word painting for the cruelty of the cross.

Composing in Homophonic Style
Have students:
- In groups with at least one singer from each voice part, construct and notate four-part homophonic phrases.
- At first, write any four pitches for each chord.
- Sing the chords, noticing the dissonance and voice leadings.
- Revise the original until it satisfies the group. (It does not need to use traditional harmonies, but will be easier to sing if it does.)

TEACHING STRATEGY
Evaluating the Piece and a Performance

Have students:
- Discuss what evaluation criteria they would consider important when assessing a performance of "O Domine Jesu Christe."
- Construct a rubric, describing what characteristics would constitute an adequate, good, and excellent performance.
- Listen to a recording of their performance of "O Domine Jesu Christe," assessing the performance according to the criteria on their rubric.

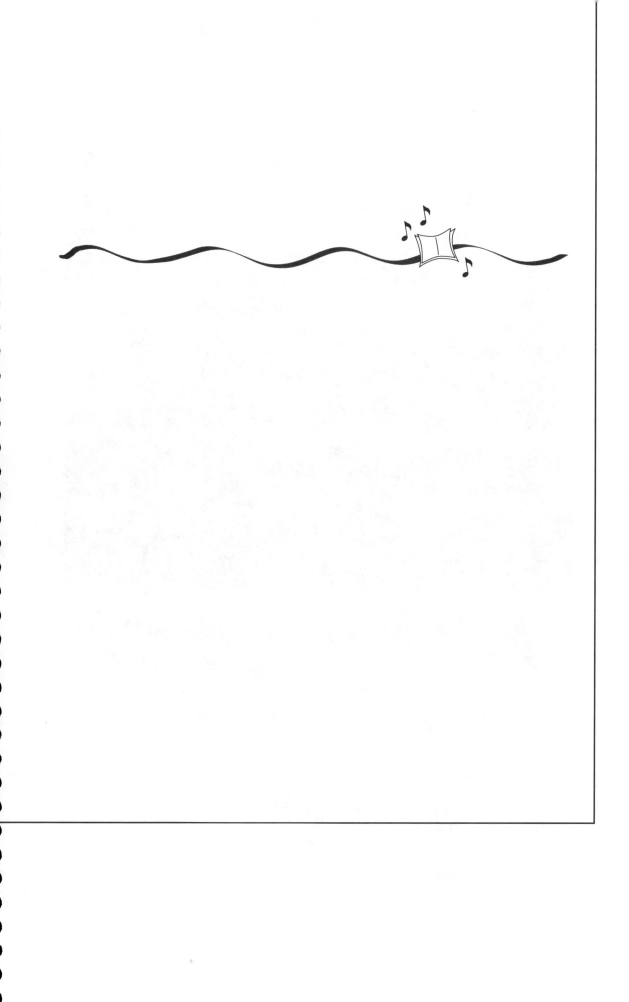

Baroque Period

Focus

OVERVIEW
Understanding the development of choral music during the Baroque period.

OBJECTIVES
After completing this lesson, students will be able to:
- Describe characteristics of architecture, fine art, and music during the Baroque period.
- Identify several musical forms of the Baroque period.
- Define *aria, cantata, chorale, concerto grosso, continuo, opera, oratorio,* and *recitative.* Explain how each of these terms is related to the Baroque period.
- Identify some of the key musical figures of the Baroque.

CHORAL MUSIC TERMS
Define the Choral Music Terms for students, giving pronunciation, and answering any questions that may arise.

Introducing the Lesson

Introduce the Baroque period through visual art.
Analyze the artwork on pages 138 and 140.
Have students:
- Study the painting and architecture.
- Discuss the information about each illustration provided at the bottom of pages 139 and 140 in your Teacher's Wraparound Edition.

▲ Attention to detail, particularly in direct and reflected light in mirrors and doorways, characterizes this work of Diego Velázquez (1599–1660). The challenge to the viewer to find all the images in *Las Meninas* equals the challenge to comprehend the intricacies in a Bach fugue or concerto, representative musical works of the same period.

1656. Diego Velázquez. *Las Meninas.* Oil on canvas. 3.20 x 2.76 m (10'5" x 9'). Museo del Prado, Madrid, Spain.

138 *Choral Connections   Level 3 Mixed Voices*

TEACHER'S RESOURCE BINDER
Fine Art Transparency 2, *Las Meninas,* by Velázquez

Optional Listening Selections:
Music: An Appreciation, 6th edition
"Hallelujah" Chorus: CD 2, Track 43
Organ Fugue in G Minor (*Little Fugue*):
    CD 2, Track 11

National Standards
This historical lesson addresses the following National Standards:
6. Listening to, analyzing, and describing music. **(a)**
8. Understanding relationships between music, the other arts, and disciplines outside the arts. **(a, b, c, d, e)**
9. Understanding music in relation to history and culture. **(a, c, d)**

Baroque Period

After completing this lesson, you will be able to:

- Describe the general characteristics of Baroque visual arts.
- Discuss the most important differences between Renaissance music and Baroque music.
- Identify at least five new musical forms of the Baroque period.
- Identify at least four major composers of the Baroque period.

The artworks of the Renaissance reflect the ideas and ideals of the period. They are balanced and restrained; they communicate a sense of calm. The next period of European history—the Baroque period, which lasted from about 1600 until around 1750—was an age of reaction against the restraint and balance of the Renaissance. Baroque artists expressed the ideals of their own time by adding emotion, decoration, and opulence to their works.

A Time of Continued Development

The explorations and developments of the Renaissance continued into the Baroque period. European trade with distant lands increased, and European kingdoms sought to expand their power by establishing empires. The first European settlers left their homes and sailed to the Americas. People had a growing sense of possibility and excitement.

The study of science and mathematics continued to advance, and new technological developments were made. The basis of modern chemistry was established, and medical research, as well as medical practices, improved. The study of science became a more complex and consuming endeavor, one that no longer attracted the special interests of artists.

During the Baroque period, aristocrats—including emperors, kings, princes, and other nobles—seemed intent on displaying their wealth and power. Part of this display involved attracting great artists, including musicians, to their courts. Both the aristocracy and the Catholic church were generous patrons of the arts throughout the Baroque period. The artworks created during the Baroque period are typically large in scale and dramatic in effect. Painters and sculptors of the time built upon the forms established by Renaissance artists and added their own complex details and dramatic elaborations.

Baroque Music

Baroque music reflected the same style exhibited in the visual arts of the time; it was written on a grand scale, full of vitality and emotion. Compositions typically had a strong sense of movement, often including a **continuo**, *a continually moving bass line.* Usually the melody was highly ornamental. In many compositions, additional ornamentations were improvised, or invented on the spur of the moment during performances.

COMPOSERS

Claudio Monteverdi (1567–1643)
Arcangelo Corelli (1643–1713)
Henry Purcell (1659–1695)
Antonio Vivaldi (1678–1741)
Georg Philipp Telemann (1681–1767)
Johann Sebastian Bach (1685–1750)
George Frideric Handel (1685–1759)

ARTISTS

El Greco (1541–1614)
Michelangelo da Caravaggio (c. 1565–1609)
Peter Paul Rubens (1577–1640)
Frans Hals (1580–1666)
Artemisia Gentileschi (1593–1653)
Gianlorenzo Bernini (1598–1680)
Diego Velázquez (1599–1660)
Rembrandt van Rijn (1606–1669)
Judith Leyser (1609–1660)

AUTHORS

John Donne (c. 1573–1631)
Rene Descartes (1596–1650)
John Milton (1608–1674)
Molière (1622–1673)

CHORAL MUSIC TERMS

arias
cantata
chorale
concerto grosso
continuo
movements
opera
oratorio
recitative
suite

Baroque Period **139**

Las Meninas

The Baroque period was a time of opulence and ornamentation. Using similar forms as the Renaissance, Baroque artists decorated each element. The distinction between the aristocracy and the common people was highly defined during this period, with the wealthy involved in the arts for their own pleasure and in an effort to represent their status in society.

Las Meninas, by Velázquez, is representative of the visual art of the period. The wealthy are represented in their finery. Notice the elaboration and ornamentation of the artist's style.

Suggested Teaching Sequence

1. Examine the Baroque period.

Have students:

- Read the text on pages 139–141.
- Share what they know about the composers, artists, and authors listed on this page.
- Read, discuss, and answer the review questions individually, in pairs, or in groups.
- Discuss their answers with the whole group.

2. Examine the Baroque period in historical perspective.

Have students:

- Turn to the time line on pages 140–141 and read the citations.
- Discuss why these events and people are important to the Baroque period.
- Compare each of these events to what occurred before and after the Baroque period.
- Write a statement of one or two sentences in length that describes the Baroque period based on one of the events in the time line. (Louis XIV's building of Versailles was characteristic of the Baroque period, during which the rich taxed the general population in order to maintain their opulent lifestyle and impress one another.)
- Write one additional sentence which tells how this Baroque event is related to the student's world. (Today, many people complain that the middle class and poor are taxed to benefit the rich in much the same way.)

3. Define the musical aspects of the Baroque period.

Have students:

- Review the changes in music during the Baroque period.
- Define *aria, cantata, chorale, concerto grosso, continuo, opera, oratorio,* and *recitative.*

Galileo	Henry Hudson explores the Hudson River	Pilgrims land in America	Isaac Newton	Quakers arrive in Massachusetts
1564–1642	1609	1620	1642–1727	1656

1607	1618–1648	1636	1643–1715
Jamestown, Virginia, established settlement	Thirty Years' War	Harvard College founded	Reign of Louis XIV as King of France

1608
Telescope invented in Holland

Assessment

Informal Assessment
In this lesson, students showed the ability to:
- Identify characteristics of the Baroque period and music of the Baroque.
- Compare music in the Baroque period to today's world.
- Define concerto grosso, chorale, cantata, oratorio, and opera; explain how each of these terms is related to the Baroque period.

Student Self-Assessment
Have students:
- Return to page 141 and answer the Check Your Understanding questions.
- Write a paragraph describing how much they understand about the development of music during the Baroque period.

Individual Performance Assessment
To further demonstrate accomplishment, have each student:
- Learn more about one aspect of the music during the Baroque period.
- Share information with the class in a creative way, such as in a poster, demonstration, CD or video design contest, and so on.

Extension

Networking with Your Community
Baroque music is performed today frequently by chamber, vocal, and instrumental groups. Large orchestras have many Baroque pieces in their repertoire, and simply dismiss parts of the larger orchestra for the specific piece. Baroque music is likewise performed in many church concerts. Check with your local arts council, performing groups, and neighboring universities to discover locations and times of Baroque performances for students to attend.

During this period, instrumental music gained in importance, both in the church and as music commissioned for the entertainment of the courts of Europe. Vocal music also underwent changes. Instrumental accompaniments were increasingly added to both sacred and secular vocal works, and several new musical forms developed.

▲ **The ornate interior decor is reflected endlessly in the Hall of Mirrors, designed by François de Cuvilliés (1696–1768). Musical embellishment and ornamentation of the Baroque period provide similar stylistic elements in compositions by Johann Sebastian Bach and his contemporaries.**

1734–39. François de Cuvilliés. Hall of Mirrors, Amalienburg, Munich, Germany.

Instrumental Forms
As instrumental music grew more important, the musical instruments themselves were refined and their uses changed. The violin, previously a solo instrument, was added to ensemble groups. The harpsichord and the organ became the most important keyboard instruments.

Longer instrumental works were composed during the Baroque period. Often, these compositions consisted of several **movements**, *individual pieces that sound fairly complete within themselves but are part of a longer work.*

One of the new instrumental forms of the Baroque period was the **concerto grosso**. This *composition for a small chamber orchestra consists of several movements and features a moving bass line and an elaborate melody.* Most of the major Baroque composers wrote concerti grossi. Among the best known are *The Four Seasons* by Antonio Vivaldi and the set of six *Brandenburg Concertos* by Johann Sebastian Bach.

Another instrumental form that developed was the **suite**, *a set of musical movements, usually inspired by dances, of contrasting tempos and styles.* Suites and suite-related compositions were very popular during this time; the most famous suites were those composed by Bach.

Vocal and Mixed Forms
Vocal music became more varied and notably more dramatic during the Baroque period. Sacred music continued to be predominantly choral, but new instrumental accompaniment added greater variety and strength to many compositions. One of the new forms of the Baroque period was the **chorale**, or *hymn tune*. Chorales were

140 *Choral Connections   Level 3 Mixed Voices*

The Hall of Mirrors

Call students' attention to the opulence of the Hall of Mirrors. Have them notice how the mirrors tease the eye at every curve. The use of mirrors was new in the Baroque period, and allowed images to be produced in multiples. In a sense, they decorated the decoration.

	Johann Sebastian Bach	First American newspaper established, *Boston News Letter*	Handel comes to England
	▼ **1685–1750**	▼ **1704**	▼ **1710**

▼ **1682**
LaSalle explores the Mississippi

▼ **1685–1759**
George Frideric Handel

▼ **1706–1790**
Benjamin Franklin

▼ **1687**
Publication of Newton's *Mathematical Principles*

composed for Lutheran services, using German texts. They were easy to sing and to remember, so all members of a church congregation could join in.

A related Baroque form was the **cantata**, *a collection of compositions with instrumental accompaniment consisting of several movements based on related secular or sacred text segments.* The fact that this form could be composed as either a sacred or a secular work itself marks a new development of the period. Music directors at important Protestant churches were required to compose cantatas for weekly services. Bach, who served as a music director in Leipzig for 25 years, composed nearly 300 sacred cantatas.

Another mixed form from the Baroque period is the **oratorio**, *a composition for solo voices, chorus, and orchestra, that was an extended dramatic work on a literary or religious theme presented without theatrical action.* Like a cantata, an oratorio was composed to be performed in a concert setting, without costumes and scenery. However, the oratorio was written on a larger scale and told a story, usually religious, with plot and resolution. The oratorio was typically performed by a small chorus, an orchestra, and four vocal soloists.

Of all the new musical forms that developed during the Baroque period, perhaps the most characteristic is the **opera**, *a combination of singing, instrumental music, dancing, and drama that tells a story.* Opera combined many art forms, including drama, dance, architecture, and visual art, with music. And, in the true sense of Baroque style, opera was emotional and lavish. The best known composers of Baroque opera were Claudio Monteverdi, who wrote *Orfeo*, the first important opera, in 1607, and Henry Purcell.

The highlights of most operas are the **arias**, *dramatic songs for solo voices with orchestral accompaniment.* Another important feature of an opera is the **recitative**, *a vocal line that imitates the rhythm of speech.*

Check Your Understanding

Recall

1. What is a continuo?

2. What is a concerto grosso? Which Baroque composers are particularly remembered for this kind of composition?

3. What is a cantata?

4. What is the difference between an oratorio and an opera?

5. How are an aria and a recitative alike? How are they different?

6. List at least three adjectives you would use to describe the music of the Baroque period.

Thinking It Through

1. Identify one Baroque composition you have listened to. What characteristics mark that composition as a Baroque work?

2. For whom was Baroque music written? Who were the intended performers and the intended audience?

Baroque Period **141**

Notation and Improvisation

In the character of the Baroque period, melodic lines and harmonies became more and more fancy, but not all the decorations were written down. During the Baroque period, one measure of good musicianship was the ability to improvise around the original melody, remaining stylistically and harmonically correct.
Have students:

• Take a well-known, simple melody.

• Sing it over and over, adding more and more ornamentation through passing tones, sustaining tones longer than written, adding chord tones between pitches, and adding grace notes and melismas.

• Avoid any judgmental behaviors for as long as possible, getting more and more frivolous, to get the feel of Baroque-style improvisation.

North America and the Baroque

What was going on in North America during the Baroque period?
Have students:

• Look at the time line and discover any citations that relate to North America.

• Research what music was being sung, played, and created in North America. Was there any contact between Europe and North America that affected music? Did the Baroque spirit foster any new musical inventions in North America?

• What non-European music was being performed and created in North America?

ANSWERS TO RECALL QUESTIONS

1. A continually moving bass line.
2. A composition for a small chamber orchestra that consists of several movements and features a moving bass line and an elaborate melody. Antonio Vivaldi and Johann Sebastian Bach.
3. A collection of compositions with instrumental accompaniment consisting of several movements based on related secular or sacred text segments.

4. The opera included theatrical action, while the oratorio does not.
5. Both are part of an opera. The aria is a song; the recitative is a vocal line that imitates speech.
6. Answers will vary, but should indicate that students recognize the elaborate, decorative style of the Baroque period.

**BAROQUE
CONNECTIONS**

Listening to . . .
Baroque Music

This feature is designed to expand students' appreciation of choral and instrumental music of the Baroque period.

CHORAL SELECTION:
"Hallelujah" Chorus from the *Messiah* by Handel
Have students:
- Read the information on this page to learn more about the "Hallelujah" Chorus.
- Watch as you follow a transparency of Blackline Master, Listening Map 3.

Using the Listening Map
Using the key provided on the map, follow the symbols as you listen to the words.
Have students:
- Review characteristics of the Baroque style.
- Listen as you point out the polyphonic section at box 4. Explain that these imitative sections fit together in chord structure unlike the imitative polyphony of the Renaissance period.
- Listen to the recording as you point to the transparency.
- Compare the musical elements of this selection to "As Vesta Was Descending," on page 130. (The strong bass line that defines the harmony in the Handel selection demonstrates a Baroque characteristic, missing from the Renaissance piece. The Renaissance piece has polyphony where each voice is independent, while the Baroque piece has polyphony that is harmonically compatible with the other parts.)

Listening to . . .
Baroque Music

CHORAL SELECTION | **Handel — *Messiah*, "Hallelujah" Chorus**

George Frideric Handel (1685–1759) was a contemporary of Johann Sebastian Bach. Handel's compositions, great in number, were mostly English oratorios and Italian operas. Of all of his works, *Messiah* is the most well known. It is also exceptional in that it has no plot and is based on Old and New Testament passages of the Bible. *Messiah* was written in less than a month and was first performed in Ireland in 1741. It did not gain favor in England until a decade after its first performance in 1742. However, since that time it has grown to have tremendous popularity, being one of the favorite musical works of the Christmas and Easter holiday seasons.

INSTRUMENTAL SELECTION | **Bach — Organ Fugue in G Minor (*Little Fugue*)**

Johann Sebastian Bach (1685–1750) was born into a family of musicians. Through his lifetime, he held many positions as organist and church musician, the longest standing being at Weimar, Cothen, and Leipzig. During his employment at Cothen, Bach composed mostly secular works (at the request of the prince, his benefactor). For nearly all of his career as a composer he wrote music for the organ. His organ music has a characteristic use of the obbligato pedals, contributing yet again to the elaborate style that we associate with music from the Baroque period.

TEACHER'S RESOURCE BINDER
Blackline Master, Listening Map 3
Blackline Master, Listening Map 4
Optional Listening Selections:
Music: An Appreciation, 6th edition
"Hallelujah" Chorus: CD 2, Track 43
Organ Fugue in G Minor (*Little Fugue*):
    CD 2, Track 11

National Standards
This lesson addresses the following National Standard:
9. Understanding music in relation to history and culture. **(a)**

♪ BAROQUE CONNECTIONS

Introducing...

"Werfet Panier Auf Im Lande"

Georg Philipp Telemann

Setting the Stage

"Werfet Panier Auf Im Lande," attributed to Georg Philipp Telemann, is based on Jeremiah's prophecy in the Bible predicting the destruction of Babylon because of its sinful ways. Keep this theme in mind so that you don't become carried away with the dancelike quality of the music. If Telemann meant for there to be any joy in the music, it is in troops marching to war accompanied by the stirring music of a military band with its trumpet calls.

Meeting the Composer

Georg Philipp Telemann

In his own time, Georg Philipp Telemann (1681–1767) was one of the most highly esteemed of all German musicians. Although he was one of the most prolific composers of all time, he composed in the shadows of Bach and Handel. Perhaps for this reason, this great Baroque composer is hardly more than a name in the twentieth century.

Telemann's vast output of music includes some 40 operas, 700 church cantatas, 44 Passions, 600 French overtures, and innumerable other orchestral, chamber, and harpsichord compositions.

Baroque Connections **143**

BAROQUE LESSON

Werfet Panier Auf Im Lande

COMPOSER: Georg Philipp
Telemann (1681–1767)

TEXT: Jeremiah 51:27–29

FOCUS

OVERVIEW
6/8 meter; mood.

OBJECTIVES
After completing this lesson,
students will be able to:
- Read and sing in 6/8 meter.
- Interpret a piece to convey a
  specific mood.

CHORAL MUSIC TERMS
Define the Choral Music Terms
for students, giving pronunciation, and answering any questions that may arise.

Warming Up

Vocal Warm-Up
This Vocal Warm-Up is designed
to prepare students to:
- Relax jaw muscles and
  surrounding muscles.
- Produce resonant vowel
  sounds.
- Articulate to separate
  repeated tones.
Have students:
- Read through the Vocal
  Warm-Up directions.
- Sing, following your
  demonstration.

BAROQUE LESSON

Werfet Panier Auf Im Lande

COMPOSER: *Georg Philipp Telemann* (1681–1767)
TEXT: *Jeremiah* 51:27–29

CHORAL MUSIC TERMS
articulation
Baroque
interpretation
mood
motet
6/8 meter

VOICING
SATB

PERFORMANCE STYLE
Rhythmically, like a march
A cappella

FOCUS
- Read and sing in 6/8 meter.
- Interpret a piece to convey a specific mood.

Warming Up

Vocal Warm-Up

Before you begin singing, concentrate on relaxing the jaw and muscles that surround the jaw
area, including your neck muscles. Roll your shoulders forward and backward, shake out your
arms, move your head/neck area forward, back, and from side to side.

Now, sing this exercise on *mah* or *nah* to develop a resonant tone. Separate the repeated tones
for clarity. Move up or down by half steps on each repeat.

Sight-Singing
Before singing this exercise out loud, sing it in your mind. Look at the key signature, meter
signature, rhythms, and melodic leaps. Where will you need to really work for accuracy? Now
sight-sing this exercise using solfège and hand signs or numbers. What mood does it convey?
What can you do to help your singing enhance this mood?

TEACHER'S RESOURCE BINDER
Skill Master 6, *Rhythm Challenge in 6/8
Meter,"* page 28
Blackline Master 17, *Translation and
Pronunciation Guide for "Werfet Panier
Auf Im Lande,"* page 94

National Standards
In this lesson, students should develop the
following skills and concepts:
1. Singing, alone and with others, a varied
   repertoire of music. **(a, b, c)**
5. Reading and notating music. **(b)**
6. Listening to, analyzing, and describing
   music. **(a)**
8. Understanding relationships between
   music, the other arts, and disciplines
   outside the arts. **(a, c)**

Singing: "Werfet Panier Auf Im Lande"

Music is often played when people gather for special events. Describe the music you would expect to hear at a football game. What kind of music would you expect to hear at a wedding? Describe the music you would expect to hear at a funeral. If selected appropriately, music can enhance the mood of any occasion.

Now turn to the music for "Werfet Panier Auf Im Lande" on page 146.

HOW DID YOU DO?	Think about your preparation and performance of "Werfet Panier Auf Im Lande." **1.** Describe how you perform 6/8 meter. Choose a phrase to sing to demonstrate your ability to perform in 6/8 meter. **2.** Describe the mood of "Werfet Panier Auf Im Lande," and tell how you performed the music to enhance the mood.	**3.** Where might you suggest that this piece be performed? **4.** Tell why this piece is considered an exemplary model of Baroque vocal music. Give specific musical characteristics.

Sight-Singing

This Sight-Singing exercise is designed to prepare students to:
- Analyze notation before reading it to prepare mentally for singing.
- Sight-sing in 6/8 meter.
- Identify and sing to convey mood.

Have students:
- Read through the Sight-Singing exercise directions.
- Read through the exercise rhythmically, using rhythm syllables.
- Sight-sing through the exercise.

Singing: "Werfet Panier Auf Im Lande"

Identify the ability of music to establish or enhance mood.
Have students:
- Read the text on page 145.
- Discuss the questions, suggesting adjectives which describe the music they would expect to hear at the various events.
- Identify music's ability to establish or enhance mood.
- Read the translation of "Werfet Panier Auf Im Lande," discussing the mood.
- Follow "Werfet Panier Auf Im Lande," as it is played by you, identifying the mood. (a fight song or march to battle)

Suggested Teaching Sequence

1. Review Vocal Warm-Up.
Warm up muscles. Sing with resonant tone.
Have students:
- Review the Vocal Warm-Up on page 144.
- Separate the tones for clarity.
- Sing with a relaxed, resonant tone.

2. Review Sight-Singing.
Analyze before reading. Sight-sing in 6/8 meter. Determine mood.
Have students:
- Review the Sight-Singing exercise on pages 144–145 using solfège and hand signs or numbers.
- Discuss any difficulties and whether or not they anticipated these specific problems.
- Discuss any problems with 6/8 meter, clarifying misunderstandings.
- Discuss the mood (energetic, like a fight song, stately, majestic, steady, profound, bold), and discuss how to enhance the mood in their singing. (strong vocal production, clear sharp diction, lively steady tempo)

Werfet Panier Auf Im Lande
(Wave All the Flags in the Country)

Georg Philipp Telemann (1681–1767)
Edited by Abraham Kaplan
Jeremiah 51: 27–29
English version by Joseph Boonin

Motet for Four-part Chorus of Mixed Voices, A cappella

 German Pronunciation

When working with the German text, several letters and combinations of letters give particular problems. When two dots appear over a vowel, they alter its sound; the dots are called an "umlaut" (oohm'-lout). Certain consonants change sounds as well; pay close attention to the phonetic spellings of the words.

3. Sight-sing "Werfet Panier Auf Im Lande" using solfège and hand signs or numbers.

Have students:

- Establish the fundamental pulsation of ♩. = 66 by repeatedly vocalizing on eighth notes while a metronome is sounding the beat and maintaining a constant tempo.
- Divide into voice sections (SATB) and read each part rhythmically, using rhythm syllables.
- Still in sections, sing with solfège and hand signs or numbers, identifying and working on problem areas.
- Sing the piece through, using solfège and hand signs or numbers, with full ensemble.

4. Learn German text.

Have students:

- Using Blackline Master 17, *Translation and Pronunciation Guide for "Werfet Panier Auf Im Lande,"* say the words phonetically in a conversational manner.
- Speak the words rhythmically from the notation.
- Sing, using correct German pronunciation.

MUSIC LITERACY

To help students expand their music literacy, have them:

- Listen to the text of the piece, and then look and listen to see what choices of musical elements the composer made, and whether they were appropriate.
- Notice the tempo and meter.
- Notice the leaps and trumpetlike melody.
- Notice the staggered entrances, sustained tones, downward stepwise melody, repeated tones, and melodic elaborations—match them with the text to see if they fit.

VOCAL DEVELOPMENT

To encourage vocal development, have students:

- Use plenty of breath support to carry the *f* dynamics and rhythmic intensity of the notes.
- Energize sustained notes with breath support and increased intensity by making a crescendo on the long note.
- Balance the chords by listening to each voice in the chords. Demonstrate the effect of balancing chords by giving more weight to one voice. Ask: How does it change the music?
- Contrast the homophonic and polyphonic textures by emphasizing the multiple imitative entrances of all voice parts.
- Articulate the repeated note melisma by increasing the intensity and loudness.
- Notice the musical road signs such as the slurs, dashes (*tenuto* means hold or press it slightly), and dynamics. Press or emphasize the first note of a two- or four-note "phrase."
- Practice the German text in rhythm, tapping the beat and conducting.

CURRICULUM CONNECTIONS
Visual Art

Have students:

- Create a visual representation of the text of "Werfet Panier Auf Im Lande" that evokes the same steady, battlelike mood, in Baroque style.

Assessment

Informal Assessment
During this lesson, students showed the ability to:
- Sing in 6/8 meter with a relaxed and resonant tone in the Vocal Warm-Up.
- Analyze and sight-sing in 6/8 meter in the Sight-Singing exercise.
- Identify and enhance mood in the Sight-Singing exercise.
- Read, identify, and sing in 6/8 meter with the appropriate mood in "Werfet Panier Auf Im Lande."

Student Self-Assessment
Have students:
- Evaluate their performance with the How Did You Do? section on page 145.
- Answer the questions individually. Discuss them in pairs or small groups and/or write their responses on a sheet of paper.

Individual Performance Assessment
To further demonstrate accomplishment, have each student:
- In small groups, sing excerpts of familiar songs they have been assigned, establishing the mood of the song through performance decisions.
- Read and clap assigned lines of 6/8 meter shown on an overhead projector. (See Skill Master 6 in the TRB.)

Werfet Panier Auf Im Lande **149**

Extension

Evaluating the Piece and Performance

Have students:

- Discuss what evaluation criteria they would consider important in assessing a performance of "Werfet Panier Auf Im Lande."
- Construct a rubric, describing what characteristics would constitute an adequate, good, and excellent performance.
- Listen to a recording of their performance of "Werfet Panier Auf Im Lande," assessing the performance according to the rubric criteria.

Identifying Baroque Characteristics

Have students:

- Describe the musical characteristics of "Werfet Panier Auf Im Lande."
- Recall characteristics of Baroque music.
- Construct a Venn diagram, demonstrating the overlapping characteristics of the two that define the piece as an example of Baroque music.

National Standards

The following National Standards are addressed through the Extension and bottom-page activities:

4. Composing and arranging music within specified guidelines. **(a)**
5. Reading and notating music. **(a)**
6. Listening to, analyzing, and describing music. **(a, c, f)**

7. Evaluating music and music performances. **(a)**
8. Understanding relationships between music, the other arts, and disciplines outside the arts. **(c, d)**
9. Understanding music in relation to history and culture. **(a, c, d)**

Classical Period

Focus

OVERVIEW
Understanding the development of choral and instrumental music during the Classical period.

OBJECTIVES
After completing this lesson, students will be able to:
- Describe characteristics of architecture, fine art, and music during the Classical period.
- Identify several musical forms of the Classical period.
- Define *chamber music, sonata-allegro form,* and *symphony;* explain how each of these terms is related to the Classical period.
- Identify some of the key musical figures of the Classical period.

CHORAL MUSIC TERMS
Define the Choral Music Terms for students, giving pronunciation, and answering any questions that may arise.

Introducing the Lesson

Introduce the Classical period through visual art.
Analyze the artwork on pages 154 and 156.
Have students:
- Study the painting and library, describing features in as much detail as possible.
- Discuss the information about each artwork provided at the bottom of pages 155 and 156 in your Teacher's Wraparound Edition.

▲ **Anne Louis Girodet-Trioson, (1767–1824) through this portrait of *Jean-Baptiste Bellay, Deputy of Santo Domingo,* expressed the interest of Europeans in revolution for the rights of the individual. As visual artists worked with such themes, composers were also influenced by similar revolutionary thought. The *Eroica Symphony in E-Flat* by Beethoven is one of many examples of music inspired by revolution.**

1797. Anne Louis Girodet-Trioson. *Jean-Baptiste Bellay, Deputy of Santo Domingo.* Oil on canvas. 160 x 114 cm (63 x 45"). Musée National du Château de Versailles, Versailles, France.

154 *Choral Connections Level 3 Mixed Voices*

TEACHER'S RESOURCE BINDER
Fine Art Transparency 3, *Jean-Baptiste Bellay, Deputy of Santo Domingo,* by Anne Louis Girodet-Trioson

Optional Listening Selections:
Music: An Appreciation, 6th edition
"Lá Ci Darem la Mano": CD 3, Track 61
Symphony No. 40 in G Minor, First Movement: CD 3, Track 5

National Standards
This historical lesson addresses the following National Standards:
6. Listening to, analyzing, and describing music. **(a, b, c)**
7. Evaluating music. **(a)**
8. Understanding relationships between music, the other arts, and disciplines outside the arts. **(a, b, c, d, e)**
9. Understanding music in relation to history and culture. **(a, c, d, e)**

Classical Period
1750–1820

After completing this lesson, you will be able to:

- Discuss the major changes that took place during the Classical period.
- Identify the ideals of the Classical arts.
- Discuss the most important musical forms of the Classical period.
- Identify the two most important Classical composers.

The emotion and drama of the Baroque period were followed by the clarity and simplicity of the Classical period. The word *Classical* has many meanings. It refers to the works and ideas of ancient Greece and Rome. It also refers to the period of European art and music that lasted from about 1750 until around 1820. During this time, artists "looked back" to the standards of balance and unity they saw in ancient Greek and Roman artworks.

The Age of Enlightenment

The Classical period is often called the Age of Enlightenment. It was a time when people put their faith in reason and thought, not in tradition and emotion. It was also a time of great faith in "progress." Members of the growing middle classes believed that their rights could and would be established and that the power and privilege of the aristocracy would be curtailed.

The attitudes of the Classical period were reflected in the major political events of the era. The American colonists revolted against their British rulers and established an independent United States. Thirteen years after the signing of the Declaration of Independence, the French Revolution began; this uprising established a new government and a new societal structure in France.

During the Classical period, the Catholic church's support of the arts declined sharply. However, noble and wealthy individuals and families commissioned artworks of all kinds in increasing numbers. In spite of this patronage, some important visual artists created works that poked subtle fun at the activities and attitudes of the aristocracy.

The paintings, sculpture, and architecture of this period are usually referred to as Neoclassical. (The prefix *neo-* adds the meaning "new"; this term distinguishes Neoclassical artworks from the Classical artworks created in ancient Greece and Rome.) Neoclassical works stress the balance and grandeur that artists saw in the ancient Classical works. Painters such as Jacques Louis David used ancient Roman settings and emphasized firm lines and clear structures. The simpler and grand styles developed in painting, sculpture, and architecture were both an evocation of Classical balance and a reaction against the emotional excesses of late Baroque art.

COMPOSERS

Franz Joseph Haydn (1732–1809)
Wolfgang Amadeus Mozart (1756–1791)
Luigi Cherubini (1760–1842)
Ludwig van Beethoven (1770–1827)
Vincento Bellini (1801–1835)

ARTISTS

Antoine Watteau (1684–1721)
Francois Boucher (1703–1770)
Jean-Honoré Fragonard (1732–1806)
Francisco Gôya (1746–1828)
Jacques Louis David (1748–1825)
Anne Louis Girodet-Trioson (1767–1824)

AUTHORS

Jonathan Swift (1667–1745)
Samuel Richardson (1689–1761)
Voltaire (1694–1778)
Henry Fielding (1707–1754)
Wolfgang Goethe (1749–1832)
Friedrich von Schiller (1759–1805)
Jane Austen (1775–1817)

CHORAL MUSIC TERMS

chamber music

sonata form

string quartets

symphony

Suggested Teaching Sequence

1. Examine the Classical period.

Have students:

- Read the text on pages 155–157.
- Share what they know about the composers, artists, and authors listed on this page.
- Read, discuss, and answer the review questions individually, in pairs, or in small groups.
- Discuss their answers with the whole group, clarifying misunderstandings.

2. Examine the Classical period in historical perspective.

Have students:

- Turn to the time line on pages 156–157 and read the citations.
- Discuss why these events and people are considered important to the Classical period.
- Compare each of these events to what they know happened before and after the Classical period.
- Write a one- or two-sentence statement that describes the Classical period based on one of the events in the time line. (The excavation of Pompeii rekindled interest in the Classical simplicity that had previously occurred in the Renaissance period.)
- Write one additional sentence that tells how this event of the Classical period is related to the student's world. (Today, many people suggest that a return to the "good old days" when life was more simple would help resolve the troubles of our society.)

Jean-Baptiste Bellay, Deputy of Santo Domingo

The Classical period was highlighted by a return to the ideal of Greek and Roman simplicity and balance. Likewise, social development seemed to swing like a pendulum along a continuum from excess to control. When the Baroque period was at its most opulent, there began to be an upsurge of indignant rebellion from the common people, leading to a return to more sensible, clean and symmetrical artistic representations. The painting of Jean-Baptiste Bellay, by Anne Louis Girodet-Trioson, is a symmetrical, balanced, uncluttered, natural representation of Bellay. It is interesting that the bust of the philosopher Abbe Raynal, whose writings inspired the black revolt in Haiti leading to Bellay's trip as representative to Paris, is watching closely in the background.

Swift's *Gulliver's Travels* published	George Washington	Thomas Jefferson	American Revolutionary War fought
1726	**1732–1799**	**1743–1826**	**1775–1783**

1732–1757
Franklin writes *Poor Richard's Almanac*

1775
James Watt invents the steam engine

3. Define the musical aspects of the Classical period.

Have students:

• Review the changes in music during the Classical period.

• Define *chamber music, sonata-allegro form,* and *symphony,* explaining how they reflected the changes of the Classical period.

Assessment

Informal Assessment

In this lesson, students showed the ability to:

• Identify characteristics of the Classical period and music of the Classical period.

• Compare music in the Classical period to today's world.

• Define *chamber music, sonata-allegro form,* and *symphony,* and explain how each of these terms is related to the Classical period.

Student Self-Assessment

Have students:

• Return to page 157 and answer the Check Your Understanding questions.

• Write a paragraph describing how much they understand abut the development of music during the Classical period.

Individual Performance Assessment

To further demonstrate accomplishment, have each student:

• Learn more about one aspect of music during the Classical period.

• Share information with the class in a creative way, such as in a poster, demonstration, design for the cover of a CD or video, and so on.

Music of the Classical Period

Like Neoclassical paintings, sculpture, and architecture, Classical music left behind the extreme drama and emotion of the Baroque period. Exaggerated embellishments and improvisations had no place in Classical compositions. Instead, Classical music emphasized precision and balance. An essential characteristic of the period was a careful balance between the content of the music and the form in which it was expressed.

During this period, middle-class people took an increasing interest in music. Composers responded by writing works that were accessible to the general public. Comic operas began to replace the serious operas of Baroque times. Dance music, including familiar folk tunes, were included in many compositions. Music, like other art forms, gradually became available to a wider range of the population.

Vocal and mixed forms, especially the opera and the oratorio, continued to develop during the Classical period. However, the most important Classical developments came in instrumental music, which gained in importance during this time.

Chamber music—*music for a small group of instruments designed to be played in a room (or chamber) rather than in a public concert hall*—became significant during the Classical period. Such compositions are generally light and entertaining, both for the performers and for the listeners. The most popular Classical chamber music compositions were **string quartets**, *pieces composed for two violins, a viola, and a cello.*

Another important instrumental form of the Classical period was the **sonata form**, *a movement written in A A′ B A form.* The sonata form begins with a theme (A), which is then repeated with elaboration (A′). Then comes a contrasting development (B), and the form closes with a return to the original theme (A).

The concerto also changed and developed during the Classical period. The Baroque concerto featured an instrumental group supported by an orchestra. The Classical concerto, by contrast, became a work for an instrumental soloist—often a pianist, but also a violinist, trumpeter, clarinetist, bassoonist, or cellist—and orchestra.

▲ **Interest in archeology, particularly Greek and Roman models, resulted in the design of the library at Kenwood House by Robert Adam. This room combines Roman stucco ornamentation with the symmetry and geometric precision of the Classical period. Symmetry and precision are vital elements in musical compositions of the Classical period along with formal design and structure.**

Begun in 1767. Robert Adam. Library at Kenwood House. London, England.

156 *Choral Connections Level 3 Mixed Voices*

Library at Kenwood House

The library at Kenwood House, by Robert Adam, begun in 1767, likewise reflects a return to a more clean, symmetrical, Roman style of architecture. However, signs of the Baroque and Rococo are evident here and there, as each period leaves a trace of influence on the next.

Notice the open space in both the painting and architecture, and the controlled use of design as an accent rather than as the complete style. Notice, also, the natural use of light and shadow, developed much more clearly during this period.

In a Classical concerto, the soloist and the orchestra are equals—another example of the Classical emphasis on balance.

Perhaps the most important instrumental development of the period was the **symphony**, *a large-scale piece for orchestra in three or more movements*. A Classical symphony usually consisted of four movements in this order: 1) A dramatic, fast movement; 2) A slow movement, often in sonata form; 3) A dance-style movement; 4) An exciting, fast movement.

Major Classical Composers

The Classical period was dominated by two composers, Franz Joseph Haydn and Wolfgang Amadeus Mozart. Both were popular and respected musicians in their time, and both remain among the best loved and most widely performed composers of our time. Haydn composed more than 100 symphonies and 68 string quartets, as well as sonatas, operas, masses, and other works. Although Mozart died just before he reached the age of 36, he composed more than 600 musical works, including over 40 symphonies and 20 concertos, which are considered among his greatest achievements.

A third major composer of the time, Ludwig van Beethoven, belongs both to the Classical period and to the next era, the Romantic period. Beethoven's compositions began in Classical style, but the texture, emotion, and new forms of his later music belong more to the Romantic period.

Check Your Understanding

Recall

1. To whom did artists of the Classical period look for standards and ideals?

2. What were the central attitudes of the Classical period?

3. What is chamber music?

4. For which instruments is a string quartet composed?

5. What is a symphony? Which four movements are usually included in a Classical symphony?

6. Who are the two major composers of the Classical period? What kinds of works did each compose?

Thinking It Through

1. Describe a Classical composition you have listened to. What characteristics mark the work as coming from the Classical period?

2. What do you think led Classical composers, other artists, and society in general to want less freedom and more structure?

Classical Period **157**

Networking with Your Community

Classical music is performed today frequently by vocal and instrumental groups. Large orchestras have many Classical pieces in their repertoire. Classical music is likewise performed in many church concerts, and by individuals in solo concert venues. Check with your local arts council, performing groups, and neighboring universities to discover locations and times of Classical performances for students to attend.

Notation in the Classical Period

Have students:
- Find copies of notation written by the hand of Mozart, Handel, or Telemann, and study the notation to get a feel for what had become standard by the time of the Classical period.
- Seek a local antique store, book store, or document gallery to find out how available or rare certain manuscripts are, and how much they might be worth.

Native, Asian, and African Cultures and the Classical Period

Have students:
- Explore the music that was being performed and created in other cultures from 1750 to 1820, using the following questions as guides: What music was occurring in the culture during this time period? What was the music like? Was there any influence from or to European Classical music? If so, how did these music types change each other, if at all?

CLASSICAL CONNECTIONS

Listening to . . .
Classical Music

This feature is designed to expand students' appreciation of choral and instrumental music of the Classical period.

CHORAL SELECTION: "Là Ci Darem la Mano" from *Don Giovanni* by Mozart
Have students:
- Read the information on this page to learn more about "Là Ci Darem la Mano."
- Watch as you follow a transparency of Blackline Master, Listening Map 5.

Using the Listening Map
Start at the upper left-hand corner and follow the words of the libretto and the melodic patterns of the instrumental interludes. Notice that each of the two singers is represented by a different heart. When they sing together, the hearts are entwined. Have students:
- Take notes as you define *opera, libretto, pianoforte, triplet, duet, tied notes, baritone, soprano,* and the musical controls used. (See Blackline Master, Listening Map 5 for definitions.)
- Note that the interplay between solo (one singer) or duet (two singers) changes the texture of the melody.
- Look at the translation of the Italian text to understand the story. (See the Blackline Master, Listening Map 5.)
- Listen to the music as you point to the transparency.

♪♩ CLASSICAL CONNECTIONS

Listening to . . .
Classical Music

CHORAL SELECTION

Mozart — *Don Giovanni,* Act I, "Là Ci Darem la Mano"

Don Giovanni is an opera in two acts. The characters are: Don Giovanni, a young nobleman; Leporello, his servant; the Commendatore Seville; Donna Anna, Seville's daughter; Don Ottavio, her fiancé; Donna Elvira, a lady of Burgos; Zerlina, a country girl; and Masetto, her fiancé.

In this aria, "Là Ci Darem la Mano," Don Giovanni sings to Zerlina, whom he meets at her engagement party. He is interrupted in his flirtatious overtures by the entrance of Donna Elvira, an old flame of his whom he had deserted. In the end of the opera, he receives just retribution for his actions when a supernatural flame destroys him and his palace. Zerlina marries Masetto.

INSTRUMENTAL SELECTION

Mozart — Symphony No. 40 in G Minor, First Movement

Symphony No. 40 was written in sonata form and is an excellent example of the form being followed exactly. This sonata form includes: exposition of a main theme in the tonic or home key, a bridge which modulates to a new key, and then a second theme in a new key. The closing section of this portion is in the key of the second theme. Development of the sonata includes a new treatment of the themes and various modulations, recapitulation with the first theme back in the tonic key, a bridge, a second theme closing in the tonic key, and finally a coda in the tonic key.

158 *Choral Connections   Level 3 Mixed Voices*

TEACHER'S RESOURCE BINDER
Blackline Master, Listening Map 5
Blackline Master, Listening Map 6
Optional Listening Selections:
Music: An Appreciation, 6th edition
"Là Ci Darem la Mano": CD 3, Track 61
Symphony No. 40 in G Minor, First Movement: CD 3, Track 5

National Standards
This lesson addresses the following National Standard:
6. Listening to, analyzing, and describing music. **(b)**

♪ CLASSICAL CONNECTIONS

Introducing . . .

"Sanctus"

Luigi Cherubini

Setting the Stage

Did you ever stop to consider what qualifies a radio favorite as a classic dance tune? Probably the tempo is steady and you feel a definite beat or pulse. (Can you imagine trying to dance to a piece that constantly changed meter? No way!) These same characteristics of deliberate pulsation and a definite feeling of meter were major traits of music from the Classical period. Certainly "Sanctus" is no exception. The piece is marked at ♩ = ca. 116, and the tempo is maintained throughout the piece with only a slight ritard at the end of the selection. The chordal texture is dominant throughout the piece, and we must remember when we sing this selection that the overall tone quality is light without vibrato.

Meeting the Composer

Luigi Cherubini (1760–1842)

Luigi Cherubini (1760–1842) was a famous Italian composer. He studied with his father as a young child, and was a student, subsequently, of Bartolomeo, Alessandro Felici, and Sarti. By the time he was 13 years old, he had already written a mass and a stage-intermezzo for a society theater. He settled in Paris, permanently, in 1788. He was one of the great modern masters of counterpoint, and his scores—especially his sacred music—bear witness to his skill. His works include 15 Italian and 14 French operas, a ballet, 17 cantatas, 14 choruses, 11 solemn masses, and 2 requiems.

Classical Connections **159**

INSTRUMENTAL SELECTION: Symphony No. 40 in G Minor, First Movement, by Mozart

Have students:

- Read the information on this page 158 to learn more about Mozart's Symphony No. 40 in G Minor.
- Watch as you follow a transparency of Blackline Master, Listening Map 6.

Using the Listening Map

Start at the upper left-hand corner. Each theme is indicated by a representative picture. Instruments that figure prominently are shown as well as rhythmic and melodic guides. The bridge is depicted in more detail where melodic direction and individual beats are indicated.

Have students:

- Share what they know about exposition, development, recapitulation, bridge, and coda. (See Blackline Master, Listening Map 6 for the definitions.)
- Look at the transparency and find the words that show the formal sonata-allegro structure. (Exposition, Development, etc.)
- Listen as you play theme A and theme B on the piano. (See your Blackline Master, Listening Map 6.)
- Listen to the recording as you point to the transparency.

INTRODUCING . . . "Sanctus"

This feature is designed to introduce students to the Classical Lesson on the following pages.

Have students:

- Read Setting the Stage on this page to learn more about "Sanctus."
- Read Meeting the Composer to learn more about Luigi Cherubini.
- Turn the page and begin the Classical Lesson.

Sanctus

Latin Text

COMPOSER: Luigi Cherubini
(1760–1842)

ARRANGER: Patrick Liebergen

Focus

OVERVIEW
Melodic steps and leaps; bright tone quality.

OBJECTIVES
After completing this lesson, students will be able to:
- Read and sing melodic leaps with supported tone.
- Sing with bright vocal tone quality.

CHORAL MUSIC TERMS
Define the Choral Music Terms for students, giving pronunciation, and answering any questions that may arise.

Warming Up

Vocal Warm-Up
This Vocal Warm-Up is designed to prepare students to:
- Relax and prepare to sing.
- Use good breath support while singing.
- Sing with light vocal tone quality.

Have students:
- Read through the Vocal Warm-Up directions.
- Sing, following your demonstration.

CLASSICAL LESSON

Sanctus

Latin Text

COMPOSER: Luigi Cherubini (1760–1842)

ARRANGER: Patrick Liebergen

CHORAL MUSIC TERMS
Classical
melodic leaps
melodic steps
vocal tone quality

VOICING
SATB

PERFORMANCE STYLE
Energetic and rhythmic
Accompanied by keyboard

FOCUS
- Read and sing melodic leaps with supported tone.
- Sing with bright vocal tone quality.

Warming Up

 Vocal Warm-Up
Before you begin singing, turn to a neighbor and give him or her a back rub, gently massaging the neck and shoulder areas. Finish with a light pounding on the back, up and down the spinal area. Reverse roles. Now, sing this exercise using *ha* and *hee*. Use plenty of breath support, and a light vocal tone quality. Move up by half steps as you repeat the exercise.

 Sight-Singing
Sight-sing this exercise using solfège and hand signs or numbers. Notice the 3/4 meter. Where are the broken chords? Where are the stepwise passages?

TEACHER'S RESOURCE BINDER
Blackline Master 18, *Translation and Pronunciation Guide for "Sanctus,"* page 96

National Standards
1. Singing, alone and with others, a varied repertoire of music. **(a, b, c)**
5. Reading and notating music. **(b)**
6. Listening to, analyzing, and describing music. **(e)**
8. Understanding relationships between music, the other arts, and disciplines outside the arts. **(a, c)**
9. Understanding music in relation to history and culture. **(d)**

Singing: "Sanctus"

Almost everyone has some idea of what "Classical" music sounds like. You have learned that this word describes music composed in the Classical period of music history, 1750–1820. What words would you use to describe music of the Classical period? What would the meter, rhythm, melody, tempo, and dynamics be? What mood would it evoke?

Listen to "Sanctus," then tell how it did and did not meet your predictions of music from the Classical period.

Now turn to the music for "Sanctus" on page 162.

HOW DID YOU DO?

? ?

Think about your preparation and performance of "Sanctus."

1. Describe your sight-singing ability. What can you do well? What is difficult or needs more work?

2. Describe the mood of "Sanctus," and the vocal tone quality you used. Demonstrate by singing in a quartet or double quartet, choosing part of "Sanctus" that you can do well.

3. How do you tell the difference between melodic steps and leaps visually and aurally? Does a performer do anything different for leaps than steps?

4. Explain why this piece is considered an exemplary model of vocal music of the Classical period. Give specific musical characteristics.

Sight-Singing

This Sight-Singing exercise is designed to prepare students to:

- Identify and sing skips and steps.
- Listen and tune triads by singing broken chords.
- Read and sing in 3/4 meter.

Have students:

- Read through the Sight-Singing exercise directions.
- Read through the exercise rhythmically, using rhythm syllables.
- Sight-sing through the exercise.
- Sing all parts together.

Singing: "Sanctus"

Predict characteristics of Classical music.

Have students:

- Read the text on page 161.
- Discuss the questions, predicting characteristics of music during the Classical period.
- Listen to "Sanctus," and then compare what they heard to their predictions.

Suggested Teaching Sequence

1. Review Vocal Warm-Up.
Prepare the body to sing. Sing steps and skips with good breath support and light vocal tone color.

Have students:
- Review the Vocal Warm-Up on page 160.
- Review good breathing techniques for singing.
- Identify and sing with a light vocal tone quality that is fully supported.

2. Review Sight-Singing.
Sight-sing using solfège and hand signs or numbers in 3/4 meter. Identify broken chords and stepwise melodic passages.

Have students:
- Review the Sight-Singing exercise on page 160 using solfège and hand signs or numbers.
- Identify 3/4 meter and clarify any problem areas.
- Identify the broken chords (first two measures of lines 1, 2, and 4) and stepwise passages (all other measures).
- Discuss the need to use good breath support at all times, especially when there are melodic skips and leaps.
- Look at the soprano part of "Sanctus," measures 5–7, and sing the leap of the 6th, followed by the leap of the 5th, increasing the air flow just prior to the "jump" and continue the increased air flow into the next phrase.
- Repeat, being sure the jaw is dropped.

Sanctus
From *Requiem* in C minor

Luigi Cherubini (1760–1842)
Edited and Arranged by Patrick M. Liebergen
English Setting by Patrick M. Liebergen

Four-part Chorus of Mixed Voices with Keyboard

162 *Choral Connections   Level 3 Mixed Voices*

MUSIC LITERACY

To help students expand their music literacy, have them:
- Review the notation for all editor's tempo, dynamics, and phrase markings.
- Sing, paying close attention to these expression markings.

3. **Sight-sing "Sanctus" using solfège and hand signs or numbers.**
Have students:
- Divide into voice sections (SATB) and read each part rhythmically, using rhythm syllables.
- Still in sections, sight-sing the pitches using solfège and hand signs or numbers, working on breath support on all leaps of more than a third.
- Divide into sections and recite the text rhythmically for each voice part.
- Sing the piece through with text as a full ensemble.

4. **Learn the Latin text.**
Have students:
- Using Blackline Master 18, *Translation and Pronunciation Guide for "Sanctus,"* say the words phonetically in a conversational manner.
- Speak the words rhythmically from the notation.
- Sing, using correct Latin pronunciation.

5. **Emphasize the light, Classical sound.**
Have students:
- Identify this piece as coming from the Classical period, where the sound is light, bouncy, and bright.
- Sing measures 24–31 of the music on *ee*, noticing the brighter sound.
- Sing through the piece using this light feeling.

Sanctus **163**

CURRICULUM CONNECTIONS
Creative Writing

Have students:
- Imagine that they are Cherubini, and have been assigned the task of writing this requiem for King Louis XVI of France.
- Research what type of king Louis XVI was, and how people might have felt about him at the time of his death.

- Write a journal entry of what Cherubini might have been thinking before and during the writing of this piece.

VOCAL DEVELOPMENT

To encourage vocal development, have students:

- Speak and sing the Latin text with tall, open vowels and stressed consonants.
- Use plenty of breath support to carry the *f* dynamics and sustained notes through the entire phrase.
- Identify the vertical and linear chord structures. Use solfège and hand signs or numbers to sing and tune the chords.
- Balance the chords by listening to each voice in the chords. Demonstrate the effect of balancing chords by giving more weight to one voice. Ask: How does it change the music?
- Articulate the rhythm by emphasizing any interesting rhythm patterns.
- Clap and speak the rhythm; conduct and speak the text in rhythm. Be precise on attacks and releases of phrases.
- Notice the musical road signs such as the slurs, dashes (*tenuto* means hold or press slightly), and dynamics.

Assessment

Informal Assessment
During this lesson, students showed the ability to:
- Read and sing with a light, supported vocal tone quality in the Vocal Warm-Up.
- Read and sing in 3/4 meter in the Sight-Singing exercise.
- Identify and sing melodic steps and skips in the Sight-Singing exercise.
- Read, identify, and sing in 3/4 meter with the appropriate breath support and vocal tone quality in "Sanctus."

Student Self-Assessment
Have students:
- Evaluate their performance with the How Did You Do? section on page 161.
- Answer the questions individually. Discuss them in pairs or small groups and/or write their responses on a sheet of paper.

Individual Performance Assessment
To further demonstrate accomplishment, have each student:
- In a double quartet, sing measures 23–31, demonstrating tuning and well-supported tones.
- In a double quartet, perform measures 13–23, demonstrating bright tone quality.

Sanctus **165**

Extension

Latin Pronunciation

When working with Latin, follow these guidelines: the single vowels are pronounced *ah, eh, ee, oh, ooh*; in double vowels, both are pronounced; consonant changes will be indicated.

Classical Characteristics

Have students:
- Describe the musical characteristics of "Sanctus."
- Recall characteristics of Classical music.
- Construct a Venn diagram, demonstrating the overlapping characteristics of the two that define the piece as an example of Classical music.

Evaluating the Piece and Performance

Have students:
- Discuss what evaluation criteria they would consider important when assessing a performance of "Sanctus."
- Construct a rubric, describing what characteristics would constitute an adequate, good, and excellent performance.
- Listen to a recording of their performance of "Sanctus," assessing the performance according to the rubric criteria.

Listening to a Classical Piece

Have students:
- Review the characteristics of Classical music, being specific about musical elements.
- Listen to the first movement of Mozart's Symphony No. 40.
- Identify the characteristics that place this piece in the Classical period.
- Discuss how the tone quality of the orchestral instruments compares with the vocal tone color worked on in this lesson.

National Standards

The following National Standards are addressed through the Extension and bottom-page activities:

1. Singing, alone and with others, a varied repertoire of music. **(a, b, c)**
5. Reading and notating music. **(a)**
6. Listening to, analyzing, and describing music. **(a, c, e, f)**
7. Evaluating music and music performances. **(a)**
8. Understanding relationships between music, the other arts, and disciplines outside the arts. **(c)**
9. Understanding music in relation to history and culture. **(a, c, d)**

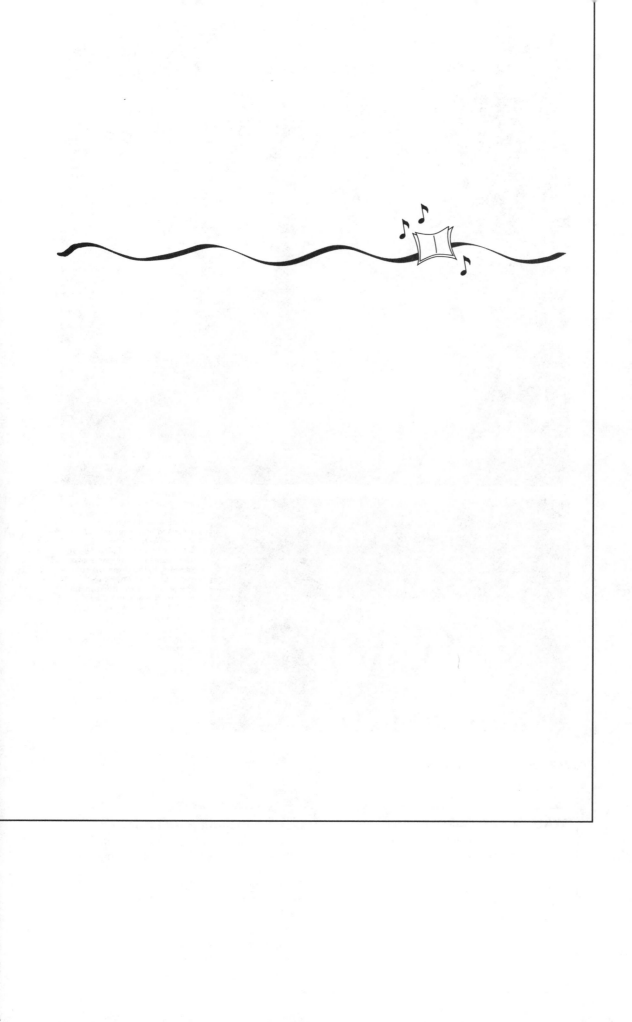

Romantic Period

Focus

OVERVIEW
Understanding the development of choral and instrumental music during the Romantic period.

OBJECTIVES
After completing this lesson, students will be able to:
- Describe characteristics of architecture, fine art, and music during the Romantic period.
- Identify several musical forms of the Romantic period.
- Define *art song, music critic,* and *nationalism;* explain how each of these terms is related to the Romantic period.
- Identify some of the key musical figures of the Romantic period.

CHORAL MUSIC TERMS
Define the Choral Music Terms for students, giving pronunciation, and answering any questions that may arise.

Introducing the Lesson

Introduce the Romantic period through visual art.
Analyze the artwork on pages 168 and 171.
Have students:
- Study the painting and architecture.
- Discuss the information about each artwork provided at the bottom of pages 169 and 170 in your Teacher's Wraparound Edition.

 An episode in the lives of the middle and lower classes of the nineteenth century is reflected in the realism of *Concert in the Tuileries* by Edouard Manet (1832–1883). The realistic treatment is also obvious in the dramatic subject matter that appeared in the operas of the Italian composers of the Romantic period, such as Rossini, Bellini, and Verdi.

1862. Edouard Manet. *Concert in the Tuileries.* (Detail.) Oil on canvas. 75 x 118 cm (30 x 46 ¹/₂″). National Gallery, London.

168   *Choral Connections   Level 3 Mixed Voices*

TEACHER'S RESOURCE BINDER
Fine Art Transparency 5, *Concert in the Tuileries,* by Edouard Manet

Optional Listening Selections:
Music: An Appreciation, 6th edition
"La donna è mobile": CD 6, Track 20
"March to the Scaffold": CD 5, Track 27

National Standards
This historical lesson addresses the following:
6. Listening to, analyzing, and describing music. **(a, b, c)**
7. Evaluating music and music performances. **(a)**
8. Understanding relationships between music, the other arts, and disciplines outside the arts. **(a, b, c, d, e)**
9. Understanding music in relation to history and culture. **(a, c, d, e)**

Romantic Period

After completing this lesson, you will be able to:

- Discuss the most important developments of the Romantic period.
- Identify the major musical forms of the Romantic period.
- Explain the importance of nationalism in Romantic music.
- Identify at least three major Romantic composers.

Emotion, imagination, and a concern for the individual returned to the arts with the Romantic period, which defined most of the nineteenth century, from about 1820 until around 1900. A new sense of political and artistic freedom emerged, as artists, including musicians, became impatient with established rules and tradition.

A Time of Freedom and Imagination

In many ways, the Romantic period was a reaction against the constraints of the Classical period. People became less interested in the balance and clarity of earlier times. Rather, their interests focused on adventure, a love of nature, and freedom of expression.

The Romantic period coincided with the Industrial Revolution, which created many new nonagricultural jobs and contributed to the growth of cities. The middle class grew in numbers, as well as in confidence and power. More and more people took an active part in their culture and their nation. A new sense of patriotism grew among citizens of individual European countries and of the United States.

Visual artists of the Romantic period reflected the era's attitudes with bolder, more colorful works. The enthusiasm for nature was reflected in the growing popularity of landscape paintings. The Romantic paintings of William Turner and John Constable express the movements and moods of nature. Later, Impressionist painters, including Edouard Manet, Claude Monet, and Pierre Auguste Renoir, developed new techniques to bring the sense and feeling of nature alive for the viewer.

Romantic Musical Developments

Romantic composers worked primarily with the same forms that had developed and become popular during the Classical period. However, Romantic composers treated these forms in ways that made new statements about music and about their own attitudes toward life. Romantic compositions, focused on both the heights and depths of human emotion, were characterized by complexity, exploration, and excitement. The interests of the period were expressed in larger, more complex vocal melodies and more colorful harmonies. In addition, instrumentation was expanded to enhance the overall possibilities of tone color in the music, and the rhythms became more free and more flexible.

COMPOSERS

Ludwig van Beethoven (1770–1827)
Franz Schubert (1797–1828)
Hector Berlioz (1803–1869)
Felix Mendelssohn (1809–1847)
Frédéric Chopin (1810–1849)
Robert Schumann (1810–1856)
Franz Liszt (1811–1886)
Richard Wagner (1813–1883)
Giuseppe Verdi (1813–1901)
Clara Schumann (1819–1896)
Johann Strauss (1825–1899)
Johannes Brahms (1833–1897)
Peter Ilyich Tschaikovsky (1840–1893)
Giacomo Puccini (1858–1924)

ARTISTS

Élisabeth Vigée-Lebrun (1755–1842)
Joseph Mallard William Turner (1775–1851)
John Constable (1776–1837)
Rosa Bonheur (1822–1899)
Edouard Manet (1832–1883)
James A. McNeill Whistler (1834–1903)
Edgar Degas (1834–1917)
Paul Cezanne (1839–1906)
Claude Monet (1840–1926)
Berthe Morisot (1841–1895)
Pierre Auguste Renoir (1841–1919)
Mary Cassatt (1845–1926)
Vincent van Gogh (1853–1890)
Georges Seurat (1859–1891)

AUTHORS

Noah Webster (1758–1843)
Sir Walter Scott (1771–1832)
Mary Wollstonecraft Shelley (1797–1851)
Ralph Waldo Emerson (1803–1882)
Elizabeth Barrett Browning (1806–1861)
Leo Tolstoy (1828–1910)

CHORAL MUSIC TERMS

art song

music critic

nationalism

Romantic Period **169**

Concert in the Tuileries

Manet's *Concert in the Tuileries* is an example of a new, reactionary type of art called Realism, which began to appear in the 1840s. Realists focused on everyday people and occurrences for their subjects, and tried to represent what they saw in an accurate, unsentimental way. Manet was the first artist in Western history to curve the hallowed horizon line, and he obscures the guiding verticals and camouflages the horizon. Every tree trunk is curved; every man's hat tilts. Just as Manet attempts to revise the viewer's notion of space, so composers of the Romantic period continually experimented with new forms, scales, harmonies, and styles—consistent with their search for new audiences.

Suggested Teaching Sequence

1. Examine the Romantic period.

Have students:

- Read the text on pages 169–171.
- Share what they know about the composers, artists, and authors listed on this page.
- Read, discuss, and answer the review questions individually, in pairs, or in small groups.
- Discuss their answers with the whole group, clarifying misunderstandings.

2. Examine the Romantic period in historical perspective.

Have students:

- Turn to the time line on pages 170–171 and read the citations.
- Discuss why these people and events are considered important dates during the Romantic period.
- Compare each of these events to what they know occurred before and after the Romantic period.
- Write a statement of one or two sentences in length that describes the Romantic period, based on one of the events of the time line. (President Abraham Lincoln abolished slavery, encouraging individuals to be in control of their own lives.)
- Write one additional sentence that tells how this Romantic period event is related to the student's world. (Today, some people suggest that there needs to be less government involvement in everyday life, and people need more freedom to make their own choices.)

3. Define the musical aspects of the Romantic period.

Have students:

- Review the changes in music during the Romantic period.
- Define *art song, music critic,* and *nationalism.*

Assessment

Informal Assessment

In this lesson, students showed the ability to:

- Identify characteristics of the Romantic period and music of the Romantic period.
- Compare music in the Romantic period to today's world.
- Define *art song, music critic,* and *nationalism,* and explain how each of these terms is related to the Romantic period.

Student Self-Assessment

Have students:

- Return to page 171 and answer the Check Your Understanding questions.
- Write a paragraph describing how much they understand about the development of music during the Romantic period.

Individual Performance Assessment

To further demonstrate accomplishment, have each student:

- Learn more about one aspect of music during the Romantic period.
- Share information with the class in a creative way, such as in a poster, demonstration, design for the cover of a CD or video, and so on.

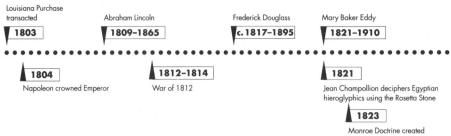

Louisiana Purchase transacted **1803**

Abraham Lincoln **1809–1865**

Frederick Douglass **c. 1817–1895**

Mary Baker Eddy **1821–1910**

1804 Napoleon crowned Emperor

1812–1814 War of 1812

1821 Jean Champollion deciphers Egyptian hieroglyphics using the Rosetta Stone

1823 Monroe Doctrine created

Many Romantic compositions reflect the period's spirit of **nationalism**, *pride in a country's historical and legendary past.* Composers used traditional legends, as well as nationalistic dramas and novels, as the basis for both vocal and instrumental works.

Nationalism is seen perhaps most clearly in the operas of Richard Wagner and Giuseppe Verdi. Wagner's works, including the series of four operas known as *The Ring of the Nibelung*, are based on epic sagas and are intended to preserve German legends and folk music. Verdi, who has become the most popular of all opera composers, emphasized the importance of following Italian historical and cultural traditions.

Other musical forms of the Romantic period also reflect the era's nationalism. There was an increased interest in the traditional folk tunes and folk dances of specific nations or regions; these folk tunes were often used or imitated in serious compositions. German folk songs can be heard in Robert Schumann's piano pieces and symphonies, for example. In the United States, the songs composed by Stephen Foster express his understanding of and special pride in the southern United States.

As the Romantic period progressed, the most important vocal form became the **art song**, *an expressive song about life, love, and human relationships for solo voice and piano.* Art songs are known in German as *lieder*, and the most famous composers of these Romantic works were German-speakers. Austrian Franz Schubert composed more than 600 songs, as well as symphonies, string quartets, and other works, before his death at the age of 31. German composers Robert Schumann and Johannes Brahms are also known for their *lieder*.

Instrumental music became more elaborate and expressive during the Romantic period. Symphonies gained in popularity. Symphony orchestras increased in size, and percussion held a new place of importance. The most famous symphonies of the period—and perhaps of all time—are those composed by Ludwig van Beethoven. Some symphonies, including Beethoven's *Ninth Symphony*, added a chorus to the instrumental music.

Dance music also grew in importance during this time. Great social occasions became popular and required new dance compositions. The waltzes of Johann Strauss were played throughout Europe; new polonaises and other dance forms were also composed.

Modern Innovations of the Romantic Period

During the Romantic period, musicians and other artists received less support from wealthy or aristocratic patrons. As a result, composers began to think about "selling" their music to an audience. For several Romantic musicians, a colorful and controversial private life was part of "the package"; it sparked public interest in the composer and his works.

Another innovation of the period was the emergence of the **music critic**, *a writer who explains composers and their music to the public and who helps set standards in musical taste.* As music became more diverse and as increasing numbers of people listened to and appreciated new compositions, critics often sought to guide the direction new music might take.

170 *Choral Connections   Level 3 Mixed Voices*

 Royal Pavilion

Romanticism was characterized by a heightened sense of the dramatic, but also strove for an idealized vision of the world through the arts. In John Nash's Royal Pavilion, characteristics of all architectural styles of the past are incorporated, but then idealized, embellished, and transformed into a fantasy vision of symmetrical beauty with great elaboration. An awareness of other cultures is evident in the domes and lattice work, as well as in the shapes of openings.

This idealized and elaborated style is represented in music by the increasingly elaborate operas and larger orchestral pieces, as well as the increased ranges, tone colors, harmonies, rhythms, and forms that allowed composers to explore the depths of emotion through music.

Mary Mason Lyon founds Mt. Holyoke Female Seminary

▼ 1837

American Civil War

▼ 1861–1865

Wireless telegraph developed by Guglielmo Marconi

▼ 1895

1835–1910
Mark Twain

1844–1900
Friedrich Nietzsche

1889
Jane Addams and Ellen Starr found Hull House

1898
Motion picture camera patented by Thomas Edison; sound recording developed

▲ John Nash (1752–1835) reaches for originality in his design of the Royal Pavilion in Brighton, England. The combination of Oriental onion domes and minarets with an interior in the Classical style is totally unique. Interest in the exotic was also a hallmark of Romantic composers who dealt with foreign lands as well as legends and mysticism in their works.

1815–23. John Nash. Royal Pavilion, Brighton, England.

Check Your Understanding

Recall

1. In what ways was the Romantic period a reaction against the Classical period?

2. What is nationalism? How is it important in Romantic music?

3. What are art songs? Which Romantic composers are especially noted for this kind of composition?

4. How did symphonies change during the Romantic period?

5. Why did composers of the Romantic period have to start thinking about "selling" their music to an audience?

6. What is a music critic?

Thinking It Through

1. Review what you know about the musical ideals of the Renaissance period, the Baroque period, the Classical period, and the Romantic period. What cycle or trend can you identify? What implications do you think that cycle or trend might have?

2. What relationship do you think might exist between the decline of the patronage system and the emergence of the music critic?

Romantic Period **171**

Extension

North America and the Romantic Period

What was going on in North America during the Romantic period?

Have students:

- Look at the time line and discover any citations that relate to North America.
- Research what music was being sung, played, and created in North America. Was there any contact between Europe and North America that affected music? Was Romantic music played in North America? Did the Romantic spirit foster any new musical inventions in North America?
- What non-European music was being performed and created in North America?

ANSWERS TO RECALL QUESTIONS

1. People became less interested in balance and clarity and focused on adventure, love of nature, and freedom of expression.

2. Pride in a country's historical and legendary past. Composers used traditional legends as the basis for both vocal and instrumental works.

3. Expressive songs about life, love, and human relationships for solo voice and piano. Franz Schubert, Robert Schumann, and Johannes Brahms.

4. They increased in size, and percussion held a new place of importance.

5. They received less support from wealthy or aristocratic patrons.

6. A writer who explains composers and their music to the public and who helps set standards in musical taste.

171

Listening to . . .
Romantic Music

This feature is designed to expand students' appreciation of choral and instrumental music of the Romantic period.

CHORAL SELECTION:
"La donna è mobile" from
Rigoletto by Verdi
Have students:
- Read the information on this page to learn more about "La donna è mobile."
- Watch as you follow a transparency of Blackline Master, Listening Map 7.

Using the Listening Map
Start at the introduction and follow the form: Intro A1, B1, Interlude, A2, B2, Coda.
Have students:
- Create a word list of descriptors from which to evaluate a tenor's performance of a romantic aria. (breath control, diction, pronunciation of Italian, range phrases, intonation, portamento) Students should also give reasons for their descriptors.
- Listen to the piece as you point to the transparency.

♪♪ ROMANTIC CONNECTIONS

Listening to . . .
Romantic Music

CHORAL SELECTION

Verdi — _Rigoletto_, Act III, "La donna è mobile"

Giuseppe Verdi (1813–1901) is considered the foremost Italian opera composer during the Romantic era. He is famous for expressive vocal melodies and many of his melodies are known throughout the world. In *Rigoletto*, Verdi chose a hunchbacked court jester as the main character. Rigoletto, the hunchback, is of questionable character but has a deep love for his daughter, Gilda. Rigoletto tries to protect her from the Duke of Mantua, a womanizer. Gilda eventually falls in love with the Duke and Rigoletto swears to avenge his daughter. In Act III, Rigoletto hires an assassin to kill the Duke. Gilda interferes in her father's plan and is killed instead. As Rigoletto is dragging the body bag that he thinks bears the dead body of his sworn enemy, he hears the Duke singing "La donna è mobile." He soon realizes that in the bag is actually his beloved daughter, Gilda.

INSTRUMENTAL SELECTION

Berlioz — _Symphonie fantastique_, Fourth Movement, "March to the Scaffold"

Hector Berlioz (1803–1869) is a famous French Romantic composer known for experimenting with orchestral sounds. During his time, the music establishment thought Berlioz was unconventional and sometimes irritating. In *Symphonie fantastique*, Berlioz uses an *idée fixe*, or fixed idea, throughout all five movements.

The recurrence of the same melody throughout five movements was a novel idea in Berlioz's day. In the fourth movement, "March to the Scaffold," the character dreams he is being led to his execution. The *fixed idea* returns before the guillotine's final blow as the character is thinking of his beloved.

TEACHER'S RESOURCE BINDER
Blackline Master, Listening Map 7
Blackline Master, Listening Map 8

Optional Listening Selections:
Music: An Appreciation, 6th edition
"La donna è mobile": CD 6, Track 20
"March to the Scaffold": CD 5, Track 27

National Standards

This lesson addresses the following National Standard:
7. Evaluating music and music performances. **(a)**

Introducing...

"If I Should See You All Alone"

Felix Mendelssohn

Setting the Stage

This German folk song setting is an example of the Nationalistic style that was popular during the Romantic period. The song has an idealized romantic text of undying and profound love, and is set in intimate 3/4 meter, with skipping rhythms like the leaping of the heart. The phrasing and repetition of text also enhances understanding of the piece. Through melodic line, dynamic contrast, and alternation of open and closed harmonies, the sense of protection and devotion is heightened.

Meeting the Composer

Felix Mendelssohn (1809–1847)

Felix Mendelssohn was born in Hamburg, Germany, in 1809. He was acclaimed as a fine pianist and conductor, and toured England. Although he died an early death at the age of 38, Mendelssohn's place in history is assured because of his compositions, his teaching at the Leipzig Conservatory, which he founded, and especially his rediscovery and performance of Bach's music.

Romantic Connections **173**

INSTRUMENTAL SELECTION: "March to the Scaffold" from *Symphony fantastique* by Berlioz
Have students:
- Read the information on page 172 to learn more about "March to the Scaffold."
- Watch as you follow a transparency of Blackline Master, Listening Map 8.

Using the Listening Map
Start in the upper left-hand corner where the Introduction is located. Follow the arrows.
Have students:
- Listen as you define program music. (symphonic music written to tell a story)
- Create a list of adjectives that might describe the fears and thoughts of a person who has been sentenced to death via the guillotine. (scared, fearful, panicked, remorseful, resolved, nervous, foreboding, eerie, calm)
- Relate the emotions listed above to music terms that predict how the composition might sound. (scared, fearful, and panicked—*forte*, nervous—*staccato*, remorseful—*pianissimo*)
- Listen to the piece as you point to the transparency.

INTRODUCING . . . "If I Should See You All Alone"
This feature is designed to introduce students to the Romantic Lesson on the following pages.
Have students:
- Read Setting the Stage on this page to learn more about "If I Should See You All Alone."
- Read Meeting the Composer to learn more about Felix Mendelssohn.
- Turn the page and begin the Romantic Lesson.

ASSESSMENT

Individual Performance Assessment

To further demonstrate understanding of Romantic music, have each student:
- Use the word list created in the activity above to evaluate the effectiveness of the tenor's performance in "La donna è mobile."
- Select specific sections of "March to the Scaffold" and evaluate how well Berlioz uses musical composition to convey the emotions in the story.

If I Should See You All Alone

German Folk Song

COMPOSER: Felix Mendelssohn (1809–1847)

ARRANGER: Richard Williamson

Focus

OVERVIEW

3/4 meter; dotted rhythms; major keys; key signature.

OBJECTIVES

After completing this lesson, students will be able to:

- Read and clap rhythms in 3/4 meter, including dotted rhythms.
- Sight-sing in a major key.
- Identify key signatures for major keys.

CHORAL MUSIC TERMS

Define the Choral Music Terms for students, giving pronunciation, and answering any questions that may arise.

Warming Up

Vocal Warm-Up

This Vocal Warm-Up is designed to prepare students to:

- Read and clap in 3/4 meter.
- Read and clap dotted rhythms.
- Loosen the upper torso by conducting with both arms.
- Articulate rhythms.

Have students:

- Read through the Vocal Warm-Up directions.
- Sing, following your demonstration.

If I Should See You All Alone

CHORAL MUSIC TERMS

dotted rhythm

key

key signature

3/4 meter

tonal center

German Folk Song

COMPOSER: Felix Mendelssohn (1809–1847)

ARRANGER: Richard Williamson

VOICING

SAB

PERFORMANCE STYLE

Tenderly

Accompanied by piano

FOCUS

- Read and clap rhythms in 3/4 meter including dotted rhythms.
- Sight-sing in a major key.
- Identify key signatures for major keys.

Warming Up

 Vocal Warm-Up

First clap the rhythm of this exercise. Notice the dotted rhythms. Next sing the exercise using solfège and hand signs or numbers. Keep the rhythm and pitches accurate. Move up or down by half steps.

Finally, conduct in 3/4 meter as you sing, using both arms mirroring each other. This will help loosen your upper body.

What key does this exercise begin in? How do you know?

Sight-Singing

Review this exercise in your head before singing it. Look for trouble spots. Now sight-sing using solfège and hand signs or numbers, repeating if necessary. Advanced readers are encouraged to conduct while reading.

TEACHER'S RESOURCE BINDER

Blackline Master 19, *Translation and Pronunciation Guide for "If I Should See You All Alone,"* page 97

Skill Master 19, *Conducting Patterns,* page 42

Skill Master 20, *Key Signatures,* page 43

National Standards

1. Singing a varied repertoire of music. **(a, b, c)**
5. Reading and notating music. **(a, b)**
6. Listening to, analyzing, and describing music. **(e)**
8. Understanding relationships between music and other disciplines. **(a, c)**
9. Understanding music in relation to history and culture. **(a)**

Singing: "If I Should See You All Alone"

Do you have any recordings or tapes in your collection that are "typically romantic"? Many songs like this have a very singable melody, one that sticks in your mind all day.

Mendelssohn wrote "If I Should See You All Alone" over a hundred years ago, but it is one of those typically romantic catchy tunes. Its music is bonded with the words to express the meaning as the words alone cannot do. There are soaring dynamics and soft delicate sounds which contrast to intensify the expression—again typically romantic, and an excellent example of vocal music of the Romantic period.

Now turn to the music for "If I Should See You All Alone" on page 176.

HOW DID YOU DO?

? ?

Even a good tune requires skill to be performed effectively. Think about your preparation and performance of "If I Should See You All Alone."
1. Tell how 3/4 meter works, and then sing and conduct the Sight-Singing exercise to demonstrate your skill.
2. How do dotted rhythms work? Sing the phrase beginning at measure 25 to demonstrate your skill at performing dotted rhythms.

3. Describe the key in which this piece is written. How do you know what key it is in?
4. Describe why this piece is considered an exemplary model of Romantic vocal music. Give specific musical characteristics.

This Sight-Singing exercise is designed to prepare students to:
- Analyze notation before sight-singing to identify potential problems.
- Sight-sing in a major key using solfège and hand signs or numbers.
- Sight-sing dotted quarter-eighth rhythms.
- Identify key signatures in major keys.

Have students:
- Read through the Sight-Singing exercise directions.
- Read through the exercise rhythmically, using rhythm syllables.
- Sight-sing through the exercise.
- Sing all parts together.

Singing: "If I Should See You All Alone"

Identify characteristics of a "typically romantic" tune.
Have students:
- Read the text on page 175.
- Identify their favorite "typically romantic" popular tunes.
- Listen to the melody "If I Should See You All Alone" as you sing it.

Suggested Teaching Sequence

1. Review Vocal Warm-Up.

Read and clap dotted rhythms. Conduct in 3/4 meter.

Have students:

- Review the Vocal Warm-Up on page 174.
- Read and clap the rhythm.
- Sing the pitches accurately.
- Learn and use the 3/4 meter conducting pattern. (See Skill Master 19, *Conducting Patterns,* in the TRB.)

2. Review Sight-Singing.

Sight-sing in 3/4 meter in A major using solfège and hand signs or numbers. Read dotted rhythms. Conduct in 3/4 meter.

Have students:

- Review the Sight-Singing exercise on page 174 using solfège and hand signs or numbers.
- Discuss any problems with dotted rhythms.
- Identify the key as A major, noticing the key signature.
- Use Skill Master 20, *Key Signatures,* in the TRB, to identify how key signatures work in major keys.

If I Should See You All Alone

(Folk Song)

Felix Mendelssohn
Arranged by Richard Williamson

Three-part Chorus of Mixed Voices
with Piano Accompaniment

Lyrics (Soprano, Alto):

If I should see you all a-lone out in the storm, out in the storm, Then with my coat I'd cov-er you and keep you warm, and keep you warm. And if the storms of sad-ness come to

O säh' ich auf der Hai-de dort im Stur-me dich, im Stur-me dich! Mit mei-nem Man-tel vor dem Sturm be-schützt' ich dich, be-schützt' ich dich. Und kommt mit sei-nem Stur-me je dir

176 *Choral Connections   Level 3 Mixed Voices*

TEACHING STRATEGY

Evaluating the Piece and Performance

Have students:

- Discuss what evaluation criteria they would consider important when assessing a performance of "If I Should See You All Alone."
- Construct a rubric, describing what characteristics would constitute an adequate, good, and excellent performance.
- Listen to a recording of their performance of "If I Should See You All Alone," assessing the performance according to the rubric criteria.

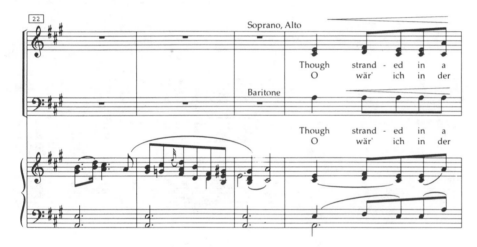

15
sfz

trouble you, to trouble you, My heart will then your
Un - glück nah', dir Un - glück nah', Dann wär' dies Herz dein

18

shel - ter be and com - fort you, and com - fort you.
Zu - fluchts-ort, gern theilt' ich's ja, gern theilt ich's ja!

22
Soprano, Alto

Though strand - ed in a
O wär' ich in der

Baritone

Though strand - ed in a
O wär' ich in der

If I Should See You All Alone **177**

3. Sight-sing "If I Should See You All Alone" using solfège and hand signs or numbers.

Have students:
- Establish the key of the piece, using the key signature.
- Divide into voice sections (SAB) and read each part rhythmically, using rhythm syllables.
- Still in sections, sight-sing with solfège and hand signs or numbers, identifying and working on problem areas.
- Sing the piece through, using solfège and hand signs or numbers, with full ensemble.

4. Learn the German text.

Have students:
- Using Blackline Master 19, *Translation and Pronunciation Guide for "If I Should See You All Alone,"* say the words phonetically in a conversational manner.
- Speak the words rhythmically from the notation.
- Sing, using correct German pronunciation.

 MUSIC LITERACY

To help students expand their music literacy, have them:
- Review the notation for all editor's tempo, dynamics, and phrase markings.
- Sing, paying close attention to these expression markings.
- Review the characteristics of Romantic music in the piece, being specific about its musical elements.

- Listen to a recording of the Second Movement of Beethoven's Symphony No. 5. Identify the characteristics that place this piece in the Romantic period. Discuss how the tone quality of the orchestral instruments compares with the vocal tone color studied in this lesson.

Assessment

Informal Assessment

During this lesson, students showed the ability to:

- Read, sing, and conduct in 3/4 meter in the Vocal Warm-Up and Sight-Singing exercises.
- Read and sing dotted rhythms in the Vocal Warm-Up and Sight-Singing exercises.
- Identify key signatures of major keys in the Sight-Singing exercise.
- Sing, demonstrating 3/4 meter, dotted rhythms, and reading in a major key in "If I Should See You All Alone."

Student Self-Assessment

Have students:

- Evaluate their performance with the How Did You Do? section on page 175.
- Answer the questions individually. Discuss them in pairs or small groups and/or write their responses on a sheet of paper.

Individual Performance Assessment

To further demonstrate accomplishment, have each student:

- In a small group, read and clap an assigned rhythm, including dotted rhythms.
- Identify the key and sing an assigned phrase from any piece of your choosing, using correct pitches based on the key signature.

CONNECTING THE ARTS
Dance

Have students:

- Create a dance that matches the phrases and mood of this piece.
- The dance may be in a modern dance style, as opposed to a folk dance, and may only be for two individuals, or a small group, reflecting the intimacy of the piece.

German Pronunciation

When working with the German text, several letters and combinations of letters give particular problems. When two dots appear over a vowel, they alter its sound; the dots are called an "umlaut" (oohm'-lout). Certain consonants change sounds, as well; pay close attention to the phonetic spellings of the words.

Extra Practice with Dotted Rhythms

Have students:
- Review the rhythm challenge in 4/4 meter on page ix to review dotted rhythms.
- Construct two- or four-measure patterns in 3/4 meter that include dotted rhythms, then share them with one another to practice reading.
- Combine some of these shorter patterns to use as rhythm drills at the beginning of class. Students can direct these drills themselves.

Romantic Characteristics

Have students:
- Describe the musical characteristics of "If I Should See You All Alone."
- Recall characteristics of Romantic music.
- Construct a Venn diagram, demonstrating the overlapping characteristics of the two that define the piece as an example of Romantic music.

If I Should See You All Alone **179**

National Standards

The following National Standards are addressed through the Extension and bottom-page activities:

1. Singing, alone and with others, a varied repertoire of music. **(a, b, c)**
5. Reading and notating music. **(a)**
6. Listening to, analyzing, and describing music. **(a, c, e, f)**

7. Evaluating music and music performances. **(a)**
8. Understanding relationships between music, the other arts, and disciplines outside the arts. **(c)**
9. Understanding music in relation to history and culture. **(a, c, d)**

Contemporary Period

Focus

OVERVIEW
Understanding the development of choral and instrumental music during the Contemporary period.

OBJECTIVES
After completing this lesson, students will be able to:

- Describe characteristics of architecture, fine art, and music during the Contemporary period.
- Identify several musical forms of the Contemporary period.
- Define *abstract, aleatoric music, dissonance, fusion,* and *Impressionism,* identifying what motivated the creation of these styles.
- Identify some of the key musical figures of the Contemporary period.

CHORAL MUSIC TERMS
Define the Choral Music Terms for students, giving pronunciation, and answering any questions that may arise.

Introducing the Lesson

Introduce the Contemporary period through visual art.
Analyze the artwork on pages 180 and 183.
Have students:

- Study the painting and architecture.
- Discuss the information about each artwork provided at the bottom of pages 181 and 183 in your Teacher's Wraparound Edition.

Individuals in contemporary society are increasingly interested in expressing their ethnic backgrounds. Palmer Hayden shows this interest by juxtaposing the comedy, tragedy, and pleasures of the African-American painter who works during the day as a janitor, yet aspires to be a great artist. Music of the twentieth century is influenced by many different cultures as well as by technology and experimentation.

1937. Palmer Hayden. *The Janitor Who Paints.* Oil on canvas. 99.4 x 83.5 cm (39 ¹/₈ x 32 ⁷/₈"). National Museum of American Art, Washington, D.C.

180 *Choral Connections   Level 3 Mixed Voices*

TEACHER'S RESOURCE BINDER
Fine Art Transparency 5, *The Janitor Who Paints,* by Palmer Hayden

Optional Listening Selections:
Music: An Appreciation, 6th edition
"Tonight": CD 8, Track 42
Theme and Variations on "Simple Gifts": CD 8, Track 6

National Standards

5. Reading and notating music. **(d)**
6. Listening to, analyzing, and describing music. **(a, b, c)**
7. Evaluating music and music performances. **(a)**
8. Understanding relationships between music, the other arts, and disciplines outside the arts. **(a, b, c, d, e)**
9. Understanding music in relation to history and culture. **(a, c, d, e)**

Contemporary Period

After completing this lesson, you will be able to:

- Identify technological advancements that have affected the involvement of the general public in the music of the Contemporary period.
- Discuss at least five musical developments of the Contemporary period.
- Identify at least four Contemporary composers.
- Explain the importance of fusion in Contemporary music.

The twentieth century has been a period of rapid change. The developments in transportation may typify the rate at which change has taken place in all aspects of modern life. In 1900, the first automobiles were coming into use, and the first successful airplane was yet to be built. Today, highways are jammed with automobiles, commercial flights take off regularly from large and small airports, and unmanned spaceflights explore the farthest reaches of the solar system.

Political events have brought repeated and often radical changes in the lives and ideas of people around the world. Among the major political events of the twentieth century have been two world wars, many localized wars, revolutions in Russia and China, the Great Depression, the Cold War, and the rise and fall of communism in many countries. All these changes and more have been part of the Contemporary period, the time from 1900 to right now.

Technology and Contemporary Music

Technological advancements have affected many aspects of twentieth-century life, including the musical interests and involvement of the general public. First, phonographs and records made music readily available to everyone who wanted to hear it. Then, radio brought live musical performances and a wide variety of musical recordings into people's homes. By now, television has replaced radio as a source of news and entertainment—including news about music and musical entertainment—in most homes. Audiotapes, CDs, and computers with interactive software have also become popular, bringing higher quality sounds and images to the public. In addition, synthesizers now make it easier and less expensive for everyone to become involved in making and listening to music.

During the Contemporary period, music and musicians have had to rely much more on the general public for support than during any past time. Composers or musicians may still be employed by reli-

COMPOSERS

Richard Strauss (1864–1949)
Ralph Vaughan Williams (1872–1958)
Arnold Schoenberg (1874–1951)
Charles Ives (1874–1954)
Béla Bartók (1881–1945)
Igor Stravinsky (1882–1971)
Sergei Prokofiev (1891–1953)
Paul Hindemith (1895–1963)
George Gershwin (1898–1937)
Aaron Copland (1900–1990)
Samuel Barber (1910–1981)
Gian Carlo Menotti (1911–)
Benjamin Britten (1913–1976)
Leonard Bernstein (1918–1990)
Philip Glass (1937–)
John Rutter (1945–)

ARTISTS

Henri Rousseau (1844–1910)
Edvard Munch (1863–1944)
Wassily Kandinsky (1866–1944)
Henri Matisse (1869–1954)
Pablo Picasso (1881–1973)
Georgia O'Keeffe (1887–1986)
Palmer Hayden (1890–1973)
Jackson Pollock (1912–1956)
Andrew Wyeth (1917–)
Andy Warhol (1930–1987)

AUTHORS

George Bernard Shaw (1856–1950)
Sir Arthur Conan Doyle (1859–1930)
Edith Wharton (1862–1937)
William Faulkner (1897–1962)
Maya Angelou (1928–)

CHORAL MUSIC TERMS
abstract
aleatoric music
dissonance
Expressionism
fusion
Impressionism
twelve-tone music

Contemporary Period **181**

Suggested Teaching Sequence

1. Examine the Contemporary period.
Have students:
- Read the text on pages 181–185.
- Share what they know about the composers, artists, and authors listed on this page.
- Read, discuss, and answer the review questions individually, in pairs, or in small groups.
- Discuss their answers with the whole group, clarifying misunderstandings.

2. Examine the Contemporary period in historical perspective.
Have students:
- Turn to the time line on pages 182–185 and read the citations.
- Discuss why these people and events are significant to the Contemporary period.
- Compare each of these events to those they know occurred before.
- Write a statement of one or two sentences in length that describes the Contemporary period, based on one of the events in the time line.
- Devise one additional sentence which tells how this Contemporary event is related to the student's world.

The Janitor Who Paints

The Contemporary period is indeed a period with a style for everyone, where form, function, and art are sometimes inextricably bound together. Old ideas are often used, but are many times abandoned for a new way of looking at the world. Palmer Hayden's *The Janitor Who Paints,* a self-portrait, is symbolic rather than realistic, and communicates that the self is intertwined with the world, not separate from it. Hayden communicates what he feels like and thinks, rather than what he looks like. The painting finds its parallel in the natural musical forms that come out of the African-American tradition—jazz, blues, and soul music.

3. Define the musical aspects of the Contemporary period.

Have students:

- Review the changes in music during the Contemporary period.
- Define *abstract, aleatoric music, dissonance, fusion,* and *Impressionism,* and explain what motivated the creation of these styles.

Wright Brothers' flight **1903**

Model-T Ford introduced **1908**

Leopold Stokowski named conductor of the Philadelphia Symphony Orchestra **1912**

1905 First motion picture theater opens

1909 Sergei Diaghilev presents "Ballet Russe" for the first time in Paris

1914–1918 World War I

1919 Observations of the total eclipse of the sun confirm Albert Einstein's theory of relativity

gious organizations, city orchestras, or schools, but most support themselves through the sale of concert tickets, published music, and professional recordings. Music also receives some support from nonprofit organizations, but the era of the patronage system is clearly over.

Musical Developments of the Contemporary Period

The twentieth century has been a time of musical changes. Many composers have continued to use forms from the Romantic period, such as the opera, symphony, and art song, but they have adapted these forms to express new musical ideas. Many compositions from the early part of the century are considered **Impressionism**, *works that create a musical picture with a dreamy quality through chromaticism.* Many later works are considered examples of **Expressionism**, *bold and dynamic musical expression of mood with great dissonance.*

Composers of the Contemporary period have experimented with many different approaches to music. Some have worked in an objective style, creating works that stress music for its own sake. Their compositions are **abstract**, *focusing on lines, rows, angles, clusters, textures, and form.*

Many composers have also experimented with music that lacks a tonal center and a scale-oriented organization of pitch. Rather than using traditional chords built on intervals of a third, these modern compositions feature **dissonance**, *chords using seconds, fourths, fifths, and sevenths.*

Another new development is **twelve-tone music**. In this organization, *the twelve tones of the chromatic scale are arranged in a tone row, then the piece is composed by arranging and rearranging the "row" in different ways—backward, forward, in clusters of three or four pitches, and so on.* Twelve-tone compositions can be approached mathematically, and the possible combinations are nearly limitless, especially when arrangements are layered, instrument over instrument. Although this approach to composition fascinates some composers, not all listeners find the resulting works satisfying.

Some Contemporary composers have also created **aleatoric**—or chance—**music**, *works that have only a beginning and an end, with the rest left to chance.* An aleatoric work usually does have a score, but each performer is given the freedom to make many choices, including which pitch to begin on, how long to hold each pitch, how fast to play, and when to stop playing.

Other compositional elements of the Contemporary period include more angular contour of the melody, different concepts of harmony, which may emphasize dissonance, complex rhythms, and specific performance markings. These musical innovations are most evident in the secular music of the twentieth century, but they can be seen in many sacred works as well. The number of sacred compositions has decreased

First complete talking film
1928

1927
Lindbergh's solo flight
across the Atlantic

1929
New York stock market collapses;
Great Depression begins

**Television begins under
commercial license**
1939

1939–1945
World War II

First atomic bomb exploded
1945

1950–1953
Korean War

▲ **Just as new compositional techniques in various formats are prevalent in Contemporary music, the architecture in the Opera House in Sydney, Australia, incorporated new materials and construction techniques. Award-winning Danish architect Jørn Utzon (1918–) called for segmented, precast concrete in the construction of the white tiled shells that form the roof of this imaginative and poetic building.**

1959–72. Jørn Utzon. Opera House, Sydney, Australia.

during this century. However, important Contemporary musicians, including Leonard Bernstein, Paul Hindemith, Benjamin Britten, Charles Ives, and Gian Carlo Menotti, have composed masses, sacred cantatas, chorales, and othe religious works.

A New Mix

Rapid improvements in communication and transportation have brought people from all parts of the world into closer touch with one another. Individuals and groups have shared many aspects of their cultures, including traditional musical techniques and new musical developments. One of the results of this sharing is **fusion**, *a blending*

Contemporary Period **183**

The Sydney Opera House

The Sydney Opera House is an imposing structure, designed to fit into its harbor home. The white shells represent sails of the boats in the harbor, and the large glass windows allow the concertgoers to experience the environment as a natural setting open to the water. This structure stands out in the landscape, beckoning all to partake and participate in the arts.

The Opera House is an experiment in design drawn from nature. It is also an experimental exploration of form, symmetry, elaboration and simplicity, grandeur, and function. Likewise, Contemporary composers may also be composing pieces that experiment with traditional musical elements.

Assessment

Informal Assessment
During this lesson, students showed the ability to:
- Identify characteristics of the Contemporary period and music of the Contemporary period.
- Explore the role of music in today's world.
- Define *abstract, aleatoric music, dissonance, fusion,* and *Impressionism,* and explain what motivated the creation of these styles.

Student Self-Assessment
Have students:
- Return to page 184 and answer the Check Your Understanding questions.
- Write a paragraph describing how much they understand about the development of music during the Contemporary period.
- Answer the questions individually. Discuss them in pairs or small groups and/or write their responses on a sheet of paper.

Individual Performance Assessment
To further demonstrate accomplishment, have each student:
- Learn more about one aspect of music during the Contemporary period.
- Share their findings with the class in a creative way, such as in a poster, demonstration, CD or video design contest, and so on.

183

Extension

Notation in the Contemporary Period
Have students:
- Explore scores of Contemporary vocal and instrumental pieces to see the range of styles, and also the new complexities brought about by the larger pieces of work. Find copies of a magazine called *Score* to see the graphic types of representations being explored.

Using Graphic Notation
Graphic notation can be anything that graphically represents sound. It could be pictures on index cards which are arranged in a specific way. It could be the environment viewed object by object. It could be the contour of a juice bottle. Anything goes.
Have students:
- Choose a graphic representation to play in sound.
- Choose sound sources for the visual images.
- Decide how to play the "piece."
- Perform it for the ensemble.
- Discuss the result in terms of its musical elements—rhythm, melody, dynamics, form, etc. Then tell whether they liked it or not.

U.S. satellite put into orbit
1958

U.S. astronaut John Glenn orbits the Earth
1962

Voting age lowered from 21 to 18
1971

1957
First Earth satellite put into orbit by USSR

1961
Soviet cosmonaut orbits the Earth

1969
U.S. astronauts land on the moon

1972
Robert Moog patents the Moog synthesizer

of musical styles. Tejano music, for example, is a blending of Mexican and Country styles; zydeco is a blending of African-American, Cajun, and French Canadian styles.

The Contemporary period has also been a time of fusion between popular music styles and art music. Pop singers occasionally perform with professional orchestras and choirs, and opera singers record popular songs and traditional folk music.

Many new kinds of popular music have emerged during the Contemporary period. Some, including blues, jazz, country, rock, and reggae, continue to thrive and to blend with other kinds of popular music. Other styles, such as ragtime, seem to have become part of history rather than popular culture. Popular music styles are part of the change characteristic of the period, and new styles will continue to develop.

The Future of Music

The changes of the Contemporary period are ongoing, and the music of the period continues to evolve. Which trends will prove most significant? When will a new direction emerge that will mark the end of this period? What name will future historians give to the time we call Contemporary? As a consumer of music—and perhaps even as a music maker—you may help determine the answers to these questions.

Check Your Understanding

Recall
1. What is Impressionism?
2. What is abstract music?
3. What is dissonance?
4. List at least three choices that are left up to performers of aleatoric music.
5. What is the status of sacred music in the Contemporary period?
6. What is fusion? Give at least two examples of fusion.

184 *Choral Connections   Level 3 Mixed Voices*

Little League accepts girls
1975

Fall of the Berlin Wall
1989

1975
U.S. withdraws from Vietnam

1991
Dissolution of the Union
of Soviet Socialist Republics

1976
U.S. celebrates its 200th birthday

Thinking It Through

1. How do you think the change from a patronage system to a reliance on public support has affected the development of music? Explain your ideas.

2. What forms of Contemporary music do you like best? Why? Be specific.

3. Which previous period—Renaissance, Baroque, Classical, or Romantic—do you consider most like the Contemporary period? What similarities can you identify? What do you consider the most important differences?

Abstract Art Styles of the Contemporary Period

Abstract art can be represented in sound, visual images, or dance. Have students:

- Choose a piece of abstract art, for example a work by: Jackson Pollock, Joan Miro, Alexander Calder, Louise Nevelson, or Mondrian.
- Using the work as a model, create their own painting, sculpture, or mobile in the style of the artist.
- Using their art as a graphic notation, create a sound composition that follows the notation provided by the painting, mobile, or sculpture.
- Using their music as a guide, create a dance that shows the elements of color and sound through movement.
- Perform the sound composition and dance as the art is exhibited on a large screen behind the performers.

Contemporary Period **185**

ANSWERS TO RECALL QUESTIONS

1. Works that create a musical picture with a dreamy quality through chromaticism.
2. Musical works that focus on lines, rows, angles, clusters, textures, and form.
3. Chords using seconds, fourths, fifths, and sevenths.
4. Any three: which pitch to begin on; how long to hold each pitch; how fast to play; and when to stop playing.
5. It has decreased during this century; however, important Contemporary musicians have composed masses, sacred cantatas, chorales, and other religious works.
6. A blending of musical styles. Tejano and zydeco.

CONTEMPORARY CONNECTIONS

Listening to...
Contemporary Music

This feature is designed to expand students' appreciation of choral and instrumental music of the Contemporary period.

CHORAL SELECTION: "Tonight" from *West Side Story* by Bernstein

Have students:

- Read the information on this page to learn more about *West Side Story*.
- Watch as you follow a transparency of Blackline Master, Listening Map 9.

Using the Listening Map

Follow the words sung by the different characters and groups— Riff, the Jets, Bernardo, the Sharks, Anita, Tony, and Maria. The last box at the bottom is sung by all characters together and simultaneously.

Have students:

- Share what they know about Shakespeare's *Romeo and Juliet* and compare story lines.
- Look at the listening map as you identify the characters that will be heard as Riff and the Jets, Bernardo and the Sharks, Anita, Tony, and Maria.
- Listen to the recording as you point to the transparency.

Listening to...
Contemporary Music

CHORAL SELECTION

Bernstein—"Tonight" from *West Side Story*

West Side Story is a modern-day version of Shakespeare's *Romeo and Juliet*, set in the slums of New York. It deals with the conflict between gang rivalry and youthful love. The plot revolves around a fight ("rumble") between two gangs and the doomed love of its principal characters, Tony and Maria. Tony is shot and dies in Maria's arms.

INSTRUMENTAL SELECTION

Copland—Theme and Variations on "Simple Gifts" from *Appalachian Spring*, Section 7

Aaron Copland (1900–1990), a leading American composer, was born in Brooklyn, New York, to Russian-Jewish immigrant parents. He wanted to write music that would be specifically American in character, so he often drew on American folklore. *Appalachian Spring* originated as a ballet score for the dance choreographer Martha Graham. It is a story about a pioneer celebration in spring around a newly built farmhouse in the Pennsylvania hills. Copland used the Shaker melody, "Simple Gifts," as a folk tune in the score. Section 7 accompanies "scenes of daily activity for the husband and wife."

TEACHER'S RESOURCE BINDER
Blackline Master, Listening Map 9
Blackline Master, Listening Map 10

Optional Listening Selections:
Music: An Appreciation, 6th edition
"Tonight": CD 8, Track 42
Theme and Variations on "Simple Gifts":
   CD 8, Track 6

National Standards

This lesson addresses the following National Standard:

8. Understanding relationships between music, the other arts, and disciplines outside the arts. **(a)**

CONTEMPORARY CONNECTIONS

Introducing...
"Still, Still, Still"

John Rutter

Meeting the Arranger
John Rutter

John Rutter was born in 1945 in London, where he first learned music as part of a boys' chorus. He and his fellow choristers performed the first recording of Benjamin Britten's *War Requiem*, conducted by Britten and featuring famous soloists of the time. The experience proved to be inspirational for the young Rutter. Pursuing his music studies at Cambridge, he conducted his first recording while still an undergraduate student. Soon after, a large-scale choral and orchestral piece of Rutter's was premiered at the university.

Following these auspicious beginnings, Rutter's compositional career has been broad and far-reaching—he has composed both large- and small-scale choral works, various orchestral and instrumental pieces, a piano concerto, two children's operas, and music for BBC television. Three of his works—*Christmas Night-Carols of the Nativity*, *Requiem*, and *Gloria*—have sold over 100,000 copies.

Currently, Rutter runs his own record label, *Collegium*, one of the most successful independent music companies in Britain. *Collegium* has produced several albums by the Cambridge Singers, a popular mixed-voice choir that Rutter directs. In addition to these involvements in his native country, Rutter spends much of his time in the United States, where he has become something of a TV personality, and a requested speaker and conductor at universities, churches, music festivals, and conferences.

Contemporary Connections **187**

INSTRUMENTAL SELECTION: Theme and Variations on "Simple Gifts" from *Appalachian Spring* by Copland
Have students:
- Read the information on page 186 to learn more about Copland's Theme and Variations on "Simple Gifts."
- Watch as you follow a transparency of Blackline Master, Listening Map 10.

Using the Listening Map
Start by following the theme as the clarinet plays. Tap with the steady beat four times on each chair, pair of horseshoes, broom, and house. Point to the needle and caning material, the bowl, and the bridge during transitions. On Variation 2, tap the steady beat on the water drops in the pitchers.
Have students:
- Share what they know about the Shaker community.
- Look at the listening map as you point out the icons representing elements of the Shaker lifestyle which correspond to the sections of the music. (the chair made with cane, the water pitcher and bowl, the horseshoes made by a blacksmith, the handmade brooms, the Shaker-design house)
- Listen as you sing the theme "Simple Gifts."
- Listen to the recording as you point to the transparency.

INTRODUCING...
"Still, Still, Still"

This feature is designed to introduce students to the Contemporary Lesson on the following pages.
Have students:
- Read Setting the Stage on this page to learn more about "Still, Still, Still."
- Read Meeting the Arranger to learn more about John Rutter.
- Turn the page and begin the Contemporary Lesson.

Still, Still, Still

German Folk Song
ARRANGER: John Rutter

Focus

OVERVIEW
Humming with energy; dynamic contrast.

OBJECTIVES
After completing this lesson, students will be able to:
- Hum with energy and accurate intonation.
- Sing with dynamic contrast.

CHORAL MUSIC TERMS
Define the Choral Music Terms for students, giving pronunciation, and answering any questions that may arise.

Warming Up

Vocal Warm-Up
This Vocal Warm-Up is designed to prepare students to:
- Increase breath support.
- Sing long, smooth phrases.
- Sing using buzzing lips, or lip trills.

Have students:
- Read through the Vocal Warm-Up directions.
- Sing, following your demonstration.

CONTEMPORARY LESSON — *Still, Still, Still*

German Folk Song
ARRANGER: John Rutter

VOICING
SATB

PERFORMANCE STYLE
Sweetly
A cappella

FOCUS
- Hum with energy and accurate intonation.
- Sing with dynamic contrast.

CHORAL MUSIC TERMS
contemporary
dynamic contrast
intonation

Warming Up

Vocal Warm-Up
Sing this Vocal Warm-Up with buzzing lips—lip trills. Keep the pitches accurate. Continue up by half steps.

Continue up by half steps.

Sight-Singing
Sight-sing these pitches using solfège and hand signs or numbers. Can you read it correctly the first time? Listen to the chords and tune them carefully. Repeat this exercise *ppp, pp, p, mp, mf, f,* and *ff* (but don't yell).

TEACHER'S RESOURCE BINDER

National Standards
This lesson addresses the following National Standards:
1. Singing, alone and with others, a varied repertoire of music. **(a, b, c)**
5. Reading and notating music. **(a, b)**
6. Listening to, analyzing, and describing music. **(e)**

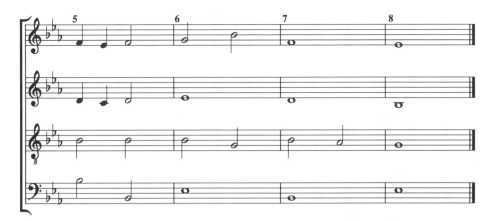

Sight-Singing
This Sight-Singing exercise is designed to prepare students to:
- Sing close harmonies.
- Sing skips of a perfect 4th and octave.
- Sing at different dynamic levels.

Have students:
- Read through each voice part rhythmically, using rhythm syllables.
- Sight-sing through each part separately.
- Sing all parts together.

Singing: "Still, Still, Still"

How well can you hum? Here are the steps to better humming:

- Pinch the bridge of your nose and hum—feel the resonant tones. How do you think you can get maximum amount of energy and sound out of your hum?

- Sing a series of vowels (*oh* or *ah*) into your rounded hands, and feel the buzzing sensation.

- Keep this sensation as you withdraw your hands from your mouth.

- Continue singing, but gradually close your lips until they are barely touching, and sing the following:

M-mah _____ m-moh _____ m-moo.

- Sight-sing measures 5–16 of "Still, Still, Still" on the vowel *o*, remembering the buzzing.

- Repeat, but gently close the lips, remembering to sing *oh* behind closed lips.

- Use lots of breath support to keep in tune.

  Now turn to the music for "Still, Still, Still" on page 190.

Singing: "Still, Still, Still"

Learn how to hum with maximum sound.
Have students:
- Read the text on page 189.
- Do the suggested activities in sequence, building a resonant humming sound. (See the Teaching Strategy at the bottom of page 191 for further hints.)
- Sing the humming part of "Still, Still, Still" from measures 5 to 8.

HOW DID YOU DO?

Think about your preparation and performance of "Still, Still, Still."
1. Describe how to get the maximum sound from your hum, and then demonstrate.
2. Describe the dynamics in "Still, Still, Still." Perform the piece with a small group, demonstrating your skill at using dynamic contrast.

3. Is this piece a good example of contemporary vocal music? Why? Why not? Can any piece be a good example of contemporary vocal music?

Still, Still, Still **189**

Suggested Teaching Sequence

1. Review Vocal Warm-Up.
Sing with buzzing lips.
Have students:
- Review the Vocal Warm-Up on page 188.
- Work to keep the pitches accurate.
- Keep the phrase flowing.

2. Review Sight-Singing.
Sight-sing in four close parts. Practice dynamic contrasts.
Have students:
- Review the Sight-Singing exercise on page 188 using solfège and hand signs or numbers.
- Identify any problems in singing the pitches accurately.
- Sing at each of the suggested dynamic levels.

3. Sight-sing "Still, Still, Still" using solfège and hand signs or numbers.
Have students:
- Divide into voice sections (SATB) and read each part rhythmically, using rhythm syllables.
- Still in sections, sing with solfège and hand signs or numbers, identifying and working on problem areas.
- Sing the piece through, using solfège and hand signs or numbers, with full ensemble.
- Divide into sections and recite the text rhythmically for each voice part.
- Sing the piece through with text as a full ensemble.

4. Add dynamics.
Have students:
- Review the notation of "Still, Still, Still," noticing dynamic markings.
- Sing, attending carefully to the dynamic contrasts.
- Sing the entire selection with soloists, noting the effectiveness of the hum in measures 5–16 and the definition of dynamics in measures 17–end.

Still, Still, Still

German Carol
Arranged by John Rutter
Words translated from the German
by John Rutter

Mixed Voices, SATB (div.), A cappella

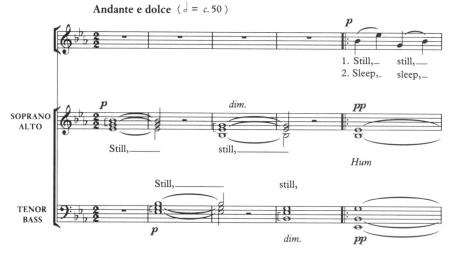

*These solos may instead be sung by a semi-chorus.

crib lies— sleep- ing, An - gels— round him watch are— keep- ing.
gen - tly— holds you, Safe- ly— in her arms en - folds you.

Still,— still,— still: The night is— calm and— still.
Sleep,— sleep,— sleep: Sweet Je - sus,— soft - ly— sleep.

3. Joy,— joy,— joy;— Glad— ti - dings of great— joy! For,
Glad ti - dings of joy!

Assessment

Informal Assessment
During this lesson, students showed the ability to:
- Hum properly in the preparatory activities.
- Buzz lips and sing long phrases in the Vocal Warm-Up.
- Sight-sing in four parts and sing dynamic contrasts in the Sight-Singing exercise.
- Sing, demonstrating in tune, strong humming, and dynamic contrast in "Still, Still, Still."

Student Self-Assessment
- Evaluate their performance with the How Did You Do? section on page 189.
- Answer the questions individually. Discuss them in pairs or small groups and/or write their responses on a sheet of paper.

Individual Performance Assessment
To further demonstrate accomplishment, have each student:
- In a small group hum the Sight-Singing exercise, demonstrating an energized tone.
- In a small ensemble, sing measures 17–end, demonstrating the written dynamic contrasts.

TEACHING STRATEGY
More Strategies for Good Humming

Have students:
- Push air toward their lips.
- Keep their whole jaw relaxed, especially the lips.
- Keep ample vertical space inside the mouth.
- Observe the breath marks that are written in the music.

Extension

Contemporary Characteristics

Have students:
- Describe the musical characteristics of "Still, Still, Still."
- Recall characteristics of Contemporary music.
- Construct a Venn diagram, demonstrating the overlapping characteristics of the two that define the piece as an example of Contemporary music.

Listening to a Contemporary Piece

Have students:
- Review the characteristics of Contemporary music, being specific about musical elements.
- Listen to Moses Hogan's "Elijah Rock."
- Identify the characteristics that place this piece in the Contemporary period.

TEACHING STRATEGY

Evaluating the Piece and Performance

Have students:
- Discuss what evaluation criteria they would consider important when assessing a performance of "Still, Still, Still."
- Construct a rubric, describing what characteristics would constitute an adequate, good, and excellent performance.
- Listen to a recording of their performance of "Still, Still, Still," assessing the performance according to the rubric criteria.

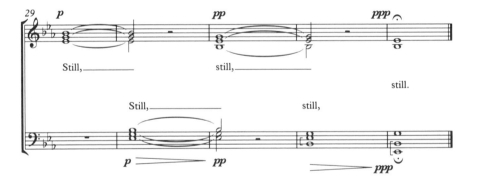

National Standards

The following National Standards are addressed through the Extension and bottom-page activities:

1. Singing, alone and with others, a varied repertoire of music. **(a, b, c)**
5. Reading and notating music. **(a)**
6. Listening to, analyzing, and describing music. **(a, c, e, f)**
7. Evaluating music and music performances. **(a)**
8. Understanding relationships between music, the other arts, and disciplines outside the arts. **(c)**

Additional Performance Selections

WARM-UPS FOR PERFORMANCE SELECTIONS

Shut De Dō

COMPOSER: Randy Stonehill

ARRANGER: Mark Hayes

Warming Up

Vocal Warm-Up

Have students:
- Read the Vocal Warm-Up directions.
- Sing the pattern on *ho*.
- Clap the rhythm of the exercise, then find it in "Shut De Dō," beginning on page 197.
- Move up by half steps on each repeat of the exercise.

Now turn to page **197**.

The River

COMPOSERS: Garth Brooks and Victoria Shaw

ARRANGER: Carl Strommen

Warming Up

Vocal Warm-Up

Have students:
- Read the Vocal Warm-Up directions.
- Warm-up the body and voice together using *bluh*.
- Keep the tempo quick to get the jaw moving.
- Move up or down a half step on each repeat.

Now turn to page **204**.

VOICING

| SATB

PERFORMANCE STYLE

| Moderately, Latin feel
Accompanied by claves, drum, and temple blocks

Shut De Dō

Warming Up

Vocal Warm-Up

Sing this exercise on *ho*. Notice the syncopation, and sing in a percussive style. Move up by half steps on each repeat.

Continue up by half steps.

Ho ho ho   ho. _____ Ho ho ho   ho. _____

Now turn to page **197**.

VOICING

| SATB

PERFORMANCE STYLE

| Moderate, gospel style.
Accompanied by piano, optional guitar, bass, and drums

The River

Warming Up

Vocal Warm-Up

As you sing this exercise on *bluh*, loosen up the upper part of your body (shoulders, neck, arms, wrist, hands, and jaw). Move up or down a half step on each repeat.

Bluh, bluh, bluh, etc.

etc.

Now turn to page **204**.

VOICING
SATB

PERFORMANCE STYLE
Brightly
A cappella

Look-A That Star

Warming Up

Vocal Warm-Up
Sing these chord progressions on *doo*. Notice the syncopation in the second measure, and sing the rhythm crisply. Move up by half steps on each repeat.

Continue up by half steps.

Doo doo doo doo   doo doo doo doo.

Now turn to page **210.**

VOICING
SATB

PERFORMANCE STYLE
Gently
Accompanied by piano

A Holiday Wish

Warming Up

Vocal Warm-Up
Sing the exercise using the cheerful holiday text. Move a half step up on each repetition. Notice the tonic leap from *so* to high *do*, then the descending stepwise scale pattern. Think of another seasonal text to use that incorporates different vowels on each syllable.

etc.

Hap - py — hol - i - days.

Now turn to page **217.**

Look-A That Star

COMPOSER: Jay Althouse

TEXT: Jay Althouse

Warming Up

Vocal Warm-Up
Have students:
- Read the Vocal Warm-Up directions.
- Sing the pattern on *doo.*
- Move up by half steps on each repeat of the exercise.
- Clap the rhythm of the exercise, and then find it in "Look-A That Star" on page 210.

Now turn to page **210.**

A Holiday Wish

COMPOSER: Jay Althouse

TEXT: Jay Althouse

Warming Up

Vocal Warm-Up
Have students:
- Read the Vocal Warm-Up directions.
- Sing the pattern with the text.
- Move up a half step on each repetition of the exercise.
- Identify and tune the leap upward, and the stepwise scale tones downward.
- Create their own text to practice different vowel sounds.

Now turn to page **217.**

El Progreso Honduras

COMPOSER: Elliot Z. Levine
TEXT: Sheila Maldonado

Warming Up

Vocal Warm-Up

Have students:
- Read the Vocal Warm-Up directions.
- Read the pattern slowly, using solfège and hand signs or numbers and tuning the intervals carefully.
- Repeat the pattern until it is comfortable.
- Look through "El Progreso Honduras" (page 223) to find these patterns in their own parts.

Now turn to page **223**.

El Progreso Honduras

Warming Up

Vocal Warm-Up

Sing this pattern using solfège and hand signs or numbers until the intervals and rhythms are comfortable. Notice that the tonal center is *so*, giving the melody a modal feeling.

Now turn to page **223**.

Shut De Dō

Words and Music by
Randy Stonehill
Arranged by Mark Hayes

© 1983 by Stonehillian Music (adm, by WORD, INC.)
All Rights Reserved. Used by Permission.

Shut De Dō **197**

Performance Tips

Rhythmic Focus
Explain to students:
- The Latin feel of the piece, maintained by syncopation, occurs throughout the selection.

Melodic Focus
Tell students:
- The melody, confined within the range of a sixth, is very singable.
- The melody appears in the soprano and tenor voices.

More Ideas
- Claves, temple blocks, and low drum have written ostinato patterns that continue throughout the piece.
- Other than the percussion, this piece is sung a cappella.
- If there are students who are familiar with gospel-style improvisation, they may find places to add their own personal touch to this piece.

"Shut De Dō"

This piece has characteristics of both African-American and Caribbean music. The text is similar to spirituals that call upon God as a source of protection from evil. The image of the candle is symbolic of protection provided by light. This symbolism is found in most cultures. The syncopated rhythm and Latin percussion give an island feel to the piece. The stylized language is derived from the African slave adaptation of English, resulting from the lack of the *th* and final *r* sound in the mother-tongue African languages. The inconsistent usage is one clue that this is a composed song in the style, rather than an authentic folk song.

Hot Spots

- In sections C and E, the bass rhythm is different from the SAT pattern. Care must be taken to maintain precision and steady tempo.

Program Ideas

- This lively piece would make a fine closing number, or liven things up for a change of pace after a quiet ballad.

"Jesu Dulcis Memoria"—
de Victoria
"Werfet Panier Auf Im Lande"—
Telemann
"It Was a Lover and His Lass"—
Larkin
"Flow Gently, Sweet Afton"—
Leavitt
"Shut De Dō"—Stonehill

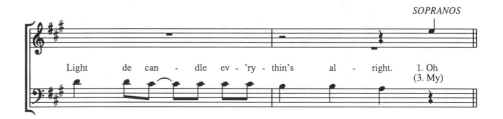

proved to me ___ they're not the same. ___
so I sing ___ this song for you. ___

I say

Shut de dō, ___ keep de dev - il in the night. ___

Shut de-dō, keep ___ out de dev-il. Shut de dō, ___ keep de

de dō de dev - il

dev - il in the night. ___ Shut de dō, ___ keep ___ out de dev-il.

de dō de dev - il

3rd time to ⊕

Light de can - dle, ev - 'ry-thin's al - right. Light de can - dle, ev - 'ry-

Shut De Dō **199**

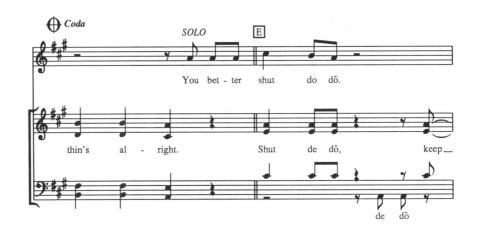

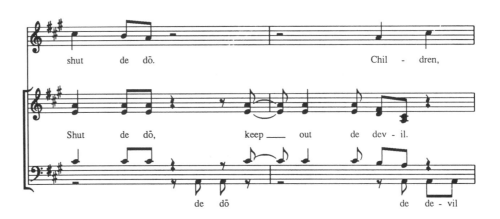

Shut De Dò **203**

The River

Performance Tips

Rhythmic Focus
Explain to students:
- The rhythm of this piece is very tricky. It was written as a solo, and a solo voice can play around the rhythm, but an ensemble must perform it together.
- The rhythm must be accurately learned, either by echo or reading.
- After it is well learned, allow the choir to "round off" some of the rhythms to give it more of a pop-country style.

Melodic Focus
Tell students:
- The form is AB, with verses and refrain.
- Two-part harmony is predominant.
- The chorus section is in four distinct parts, all moving rhythmically together.

More Ideas
- The optional guitar, bass, and drums will add to performance authenticity and intrigue.
- If there are not enough students to play these parts, perhaps this is an opportunity to make connections with musicians in the community.
- A step-touch and the clap at measures 31–35 should be very effective.
- Try this piece as an amplified quartet, with one confident student on a part, each with a microphone. Keep the accompaniment in balance.

The River

Words and Music by
Garth Brooks and Victoria Shaw
Arranged by Carl Strommen

SATB, Accompanied with Optional Guitar, Bass, and Drums

*Guitar: Play ad lib. from chord symbols in piano part.
Bass: Double bottom notes in left hand of piano part, adjusting octaves whenever necessary.

204 *Choral Connections   Level 3 Mixed Voices*

TEACHING STRATEGY
Understanding the Text
Be sure to take time to go over the text with students so they understand the message of the piece. The composers' message is that you should take risks and get into living life, rather than stand at the edge and watch life pass you by.

dream-er's just___ a ves-sel___ that must fol-low where it goes.___ Try - ing to
put off 'til___ to - mor - row___ has___ now be - come to - day.___ So, don't you

G   D/F#   Em7   A

learn from what's_ be - hind you___ and nev - er know-ing what's_ in store makes each
sit up - on___ the shore - line_____ and___ say you're sat - is - fied.

unis.

E   D   Bm   G

day a con - stant bat - tle___ just to stay be - tween_ the shores.___
Choose to chance_ the rap - ids___ and___ dare to dance_ the tide.___

D   G/D   D   F#m/A   D

Hot Spots
- Measures 31–35 should be sung a cappella. Precise tuning is of extreme importance.

Program Ideas
- This easy, pop-ballad style makes it a good selection for later in a program, after a lively and challenging selection.

"Sanctus"—Cherubini/ Liebergen
"Music, When Soft Voices Die"—Young
"I Hear a Sky-Born Music"— Land
"The River"—Brooks and Shaw/ Strommen
"Dream a Dream"—Robertson

And I will sail my ves-sel 'til the riv-er runs____ dry.____ Like a

bird up-on____ the wind,____ these wa-ters are my sky. I'll nev-er

reach my des-ti-na-tion if I nev-er try. I will

sail my ves-sel____ 'til the riv-er runs____ dry. Too man-y

dry. And there's **bound to be**____ rough wa-ters____ and I

know I'll take_ some falls. But with the *man____ as____ my cap-tain____ I can

* Original text: Good Lord.

Look-A That Star

Performance Tips

Rhythmic Focus
Explain to students:
- The rhythm of the piece is repetitive and simple.
- The syncopation gives the piece a little "spunk."
- The key to this piece is to all feel the rhythm together.

Melodic Focus
Tell students:
- The melody is predictable, as are the voice leadings in the homophonic refrain.
- There are some male and female solo parts during the verses, with the chorus providing responses.
- These solos can be elaborated upon with passing tone improvisations once they are secure.

Words and Music by
Jay Althouse

SATB Voices, A cappella

*Also available for 3-part mixed voices (4732).

 TEACHING STRATEGY

Accompaniment

This piece has characteristics of the African-American spiritual style, and also a little Caribbean feeling. If there are students who play the conga drum or in a steel drum group, add them to the arrangement in some way. These instruments will give two totally different feelings to the piece, depending upon which you use. It is also possible to do a recorder or symphonic wind arrangement with some Latin percussion.

shine in the night. Look-a that star   shine in the night. Look-a that star

shine in the night,   show-in' the way to   Beth-e-le-hem.

1st VERSE: female solo

1. Mar-y and Jo-seph saw that star.

2nd VERSE: male solo

2. Mar-y had a lit-tle ba-by boy.

S.

A.   Show-in' the way to

T.

B.

More Ideas

- This selection is unaccompanied.
- Care should be taken to observe the specific tempo markings, especially on measures 45–56, which call for a "free" style.

Hot Spots

- The sections are repetitive, so the performers must observe all expression marks, especially at chorus entrances, so their part will remain vibrant and full of contrast.

Program Ideas

- This would make an unusual closing piece for a holiday concert, because of the spicy syncopated rhythm.

"Alleluia"—James
"Four Spanish Carols"— Sanchez
"Still, Still, Still"—Rutter
"A Holiday Wish"—Althouse
"Look-A That Star"—Althouse

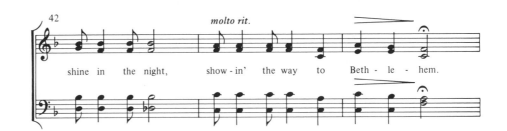

shine in the night, show-in' the way to Beth - le - hem.

Look-a that star in the East-ern sky. ___

Look-a that star and won-der why.

Ba - by came down from heav'n on high, ___ show-in' the way to glo - ry. Oh, ___

look-a that star, look-a that star, show-in' the way ___ home.

Look at the star _____ show-in' the way to Beth-e-le-hem.

Look-a that star shine in the night, show-in' the way to Beth-e-le-hem.

Look-a that star shine in the night, _____

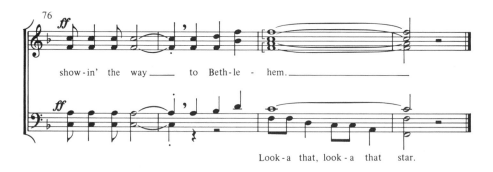

show-in' the way ____ to Beth-le - hem. _____

Look-a that, look-a that star.

A Holiday Wish

Words and Music by
Jay Althouse

SATB Voices and Piano

> What I want most of all this Christ-mas____ is a

* Also available for S.A.B., Level Three (11313), and 2-part, Level Two (11314).
SoundTrax Cassette available (3896).

A Holiday Wish **217**

A Holiday Wish

Performance Tips

Rhythmic Focus
Explain to students:
- The rhythm of the piece is straightforward.
- Use correct word stress to make these simple rhythms work.

Melodic Focus
Tell students:
- The melody is pleasing and sure to appeal to a holiday audience.
- The piece is centered in C major, later modulating to D♭ major.
- There are no unusual demands.

More Ideas

- The form is fairly standard: verse-bridge-verse (related to Classical ABA form).
- Discuss and work on phrasing and dynamics, so all are breathing at the same point and singing through each phrase.
- Work for a smooth, blended, unforced vocal tone.

Hot Spots

- There are no specific problem areas in this piece. Just convey the message of the text—a wish for peace and love for all.

Program Ideas

- This would make a nice closing piece for a holiday concert, perhaps with all choirs combined.
- If you perform with your feeder school choirs, they would enjoy singing this with you, maybe alternating sections of the piece between choirs.

"O Domine Jesu Christe"—
    Palestrina
"In Memoria Aeterna"—Vivaldi
"If I Should See You All
    Alone"—Mendelssohn
"Dream a Dream"—Robertson
"El Progreso Honduras"—
    Levine
"A Holiday Wish"—Althouse

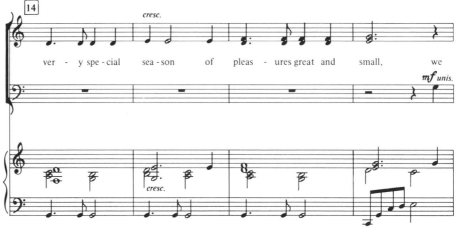

CONNECTING THE ARTS
Visual Art/Video

If there are students who have artistic talent, have them:

- Make a mural or banner that has images inspired by this song, or
- Choose an image to draw for each phrase, and then transfer those images

to either color transparencies or slides to be shown as the piece is performed.

- Create a music video with students from the school as actors, and show it as the piece is performed.

sing of hope and prom - ise and of peace, good-will to

all. _____ What I want most of all this Christ - mas _____ is a

world where all are free, _____ with a great mul - ti - tude of

A Holiday Wish **219**

col - ors_____ who live in har - mo - ny._____

mp unis.

In this

cresc.

ver - y spe - cial sea - son of pleas - ures great and

unis. mp

oo_____   oo_____   oo_____

cresc.

ha - tred and fear have end - ed and war and strife shall

ev - er cease: a world of faith and love and

Slower
peace.

For the Mark Twain J.H.S. Chorus and
The Western Wind Vocal Ensemble
Commissioned by "Meet the Composer"

El Progreso Honduras

Elliot Z. Levine

Sheila Maldonado

Two-part Mixed Choruses (SAB and SATB) A cappella

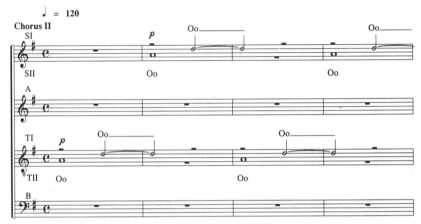

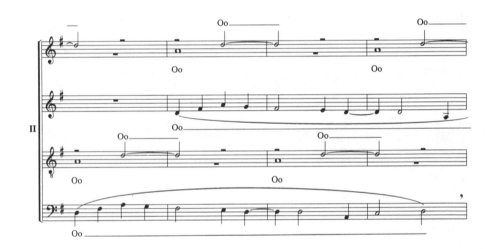

El Progreso Honduras **223**

El Progreso Honduras

Performance Tips

This piece is written for two mixed choruses, SAB and SATB, to be sung a cappella.

Rhythmic Focus

Explain to students:

- The rhythm of this piece is very tricky in places. The rhythms need to be clapped or spoken with the text until they are secure.
- The rhythm follows the plot of the text, setting the pastoral scene: preparing for rain, experiencing the rainstorm, playing in the wet streets, and then fading away.
- There is a lot of syncopation.
- There are triplet patterns against four eighth patterns from measures 25–31. The easier triplet patterns occur later, and may be learned first.

Melodic Focus

Tell students:

- The tonal center of the piece is around D (*so*), giving a modal feeling.
- There are many intervals of a third and quite a few leaps in each part.
- Chordal harmonies are often in thirds or triads.
- There are staggered entrances and some imitative melodic lines.

TEACHER'S RESOURCE BINDER

Blackline Master 20, Translation for *"El Progreso Honduras,"* page 99

More Ideas

- The poem is in four sections, and the music is written in four sections, with an introduction leading into the first section, and an ending which returns to the first section and fades out.
- The four sections are measures 9–19, measures 23–32, measures 33–44, and measures 44–55. There is a bridge between sections 1 and 2.
- As the piece comes together, pay careful attention to dynamics and articulation marks.

Hot Spots

- The slides at measures 19 and 20 are fun but tricky.
- The melodic leaps must be accurately tuned, for example at measures 43 and 44.
- The triplets need to be practiced.
- Watch for altered tones from measures 29–40.
- The rhythm at measure 54 should be practiced in isolation.
- Entrances that begin on upbeats should be crisp.
- The transitions from one section to the next should be practiced until smooth.

TEACHING STRATEGY

- Use Blackline Master 20, *Translation for "El Progreso Honduras"* to review the text of the poem.
- Find each section of the poem in the music.
- Identify the musical elements which reflect the mood of each section of the text.

- This piece is perfect for a time when the high school group is giving a performance and the feeder group is invited as motivation to continue. As an alternative, the high school group could join the lower grade chorus for their concert, contributing to this piece. Perhaps the two groups would perform several numbers for each other, then this piece together.

"I Hear a Sky-Born Music"—Land
"Werfet Panier Auf Im Lande"—Telemann
"It Was a Lover and His Lass"—Larkin
"El Progreso Honduras"—Levine
"Pål På Haugen"—Ellingboe
"May the Road Rise to Meet You"—Hamilton

"El Progreso Honduras"

"El Progreso Honduras" was written in 1989 for the Mark Twain Junior High School Chorus and The Western Wind vocal ensemble. The text, written by Sheila Maldonado when she was a junior high student at Mark Twain, describes her native village of Progreso in the country of Honduras. Elliot Levine, baritone with The Western Wind, is a composer, performer, and teacher. This piece was published first as a collaborative effort of The Western Wind, an internationally acclaimed vocal sextet, and the Indianapolis Children's Choir, conducted by Henry Leck.

31

Chorus I

tacet

doo   doo   doo   doo

Chorus II

y   de - sa - ma - rra - mos____   la   *ha-ma - ca   de   los   ár - bo - les

y   de - sa - ma - rra - mos____   la   *ha-ma - ca   de   los   ár - bo - les

Chorus II

legato

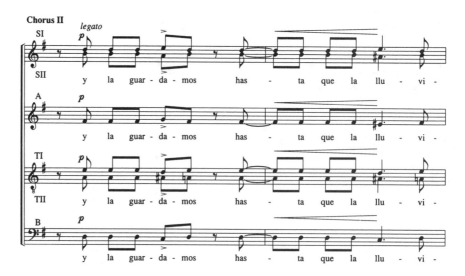

y   la   guar - da - mos   has - ta   que   la   llu - vi -

y   la   guar - da - mos   has - ta   que   la   llu - vi -

y   la   guar - da - mos   has - ta   que   la   llu - vi -

y   la   guar - da - mos   has - ta   que   la   llu - vi -

Pronounced mah-kah

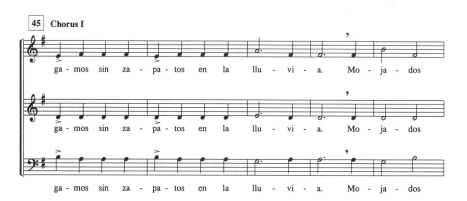

Glossary

Choral Music Terms

A

a cappella (ah-kah-PEH-lah) [It.] Unaccompanied vocal music.

accelerando (*accel.*) (ah-chel-leh-RAHN-doh) [It.] Gradually increasing the tempo.

accent Indicates the note is to be sung with extra force or stress. (𝄐)

accidentals Signs used to indicate the raising or lowering of a pitch. A sharp (♯) alters a pitch by raising it one-half step; a flat (♭) alters a pitch by lowering it one-half step; a natural (♮) cancels a sharp or a flat.

accompaniment Musical material that supports another; for example, a piano or orchestra accompanying a choir or soloist.

adagio (ah-DAH-jee-oh) [It.] Slow tempo, but not as slow as largo.

ad libitum (ad. lib.) [Lt.] An indication that the performer may vary the tempo, add or delete a vocal or instrumental part. Synonymous with a *piacere*.

al fine (ahl FEE-neh) [It.] To the end.

alla breve Indicates cut time; duple meter in which there are two beats per measure, the half note getting one beat. (¢)

allargando (*allarg.*) (ahl-ahr-GAHN-doh) [It.] To broaden, become slower.

aleatoric or chance music Music in which chance is deliberately used as a compositional component.

allegro (ah-LEH-groh) [It.] Brisk tempo; faster than moderato, slower than *vivace*.

allegro assai (ah-LEH-groh ah-SAH-ee) [It.] Very fast; in seventeenth-century music, the term can also mean "sufficiently fast."

altered pitch A note that does not belong to the scale of the work being performed.

alto The lower female voice; sometimes called contralto or mezzo-soprano.

anacrusis (a-nuh-KROO-suhs) [Gk.] *See* upbeat.

andante (ahn-DAHN-teh) [It.] Moderately slow; a walking tempo.

andante con moto (ahn-DAHN-teh kohn MOH-toh) [It.] A slightly faster tempo, "with motion."

animato Quick, lively; "animated."

anthem A choral composition in English using a sacred text. *See also* motet.

antiphonal Music performed by alternating ensembles, positioned in opposing locations, as in choirs or brass; first brought to prominence by Giovanni Gabrielli at St. Mark's Cathedral, Venice, in the Baroque period.

appassionato (uh-pah-shun-NAHT-oh) [It.] With deep feeling, passionately.

appoggiatura (uh-pah-zhuh-TOOR-uh) [It.] A nonharmonic tone, usually a half or whole step above the harmonic tone, performed on the beat, resolving downward to the harmonic tone.

aria (AHR-ee-uh) [It.] A song for a solo singer and orchestra, usually in an opera, oratorio, or cantata.

arpeggio (ahr-PEH-jee-oh) [It.] A chord in which the pitches are sounded successively, usually from lowest to highest; in broken style.

art song Expressive songs about life, love, and human relationships for solo voice and piano.

articulation Clarity in performance of notes and diction.

a tempo (ah TEM-poh) [It.] Return to the established tempo after a change.

atonality Music not organized around a key center.

augmentation A technique used in composition by which the melody line is repeated in doubled note values; opposite of *diminution*.

augmented The term indicating that a major or perfect interval has been enlarged by one-half step; as in C-F♯ (augmented fourth) or C-G♯ (augmented fifth).

B

balance and symmetry Even and equal.

baritone The male voice between tenor and bass.

bar line (measure bar) A vertical line drawn through the staff to show the end of a measure. Double bar lines show the end of a section or a piece of music.

Bar Line   Double Bar Line

Baroque period (buh-ROHK) [Fr.] Historic period between c. 1600 and c. 1750 that reflected highly embellished styles in art, architecture, fashion, manners, and music. The period of elaboration.

bass The lowest male voice, below tenor and baritone.

bass clef Symbol at the beginning of the staff for lower voices and instruments, or the piano left hand; usually referring to pitches lower than middle C. The two dots lie on either side of the fourth-line F, thus the term, F clef. 𝄢

beat A steady pulse.

bel canto (bell KAHN-toh) [It.] Italian vocal technique of the eighteenth century with emphasis on beauty of sound and brilliance of performance.

binary form Defines a form having two sections (A and B), each of which may be repeated.

bitonality The designation of music written in two different keys at the same time.

breath mark A mark placed within a phrase or melody showing where the singer or musician should breathe. (⸴)

C

cadence Punctuation or termination of a musical phrase; a breathing break.

caesura (si-ZHUR-uh) [Lt.] A break or pause between two musical phrases. (//)

call and response A song style that follows a simple question-and-answer pattern in which a soloist leads and a group responds.

calypso style Folk-style music from the Caribbean Islands with bright, syncopated rhythm.

cambiata The young male voice that is still developing.

canon A compositional form in which the subject is begun in one group and then is continually and exactly repeated by other groups. Unlike the round, the canon closes with all voices ending together on a common chord.

cantata (kan-TAH-tuh) [It.] A collection of vocal compositions with instrumental accompaniment consisting of several movements based on related secular or sacred text segments.

cantabile In a lyrical, singing style.

cantor A solo singer in the Jewish and Roman Catholic traditions who leads the congregation in worship by introducing responses and other musical portions of the services.

cantus firmus (KAHN-tuhs FUHR-muhs) [Lt.] A previously-composed melody which is used as a basis for a new composition.

chance music See aleatoric music.

chantey (SHAN-tee) [Fr.] A song sung by sailors in rhythm with their work.

chant, plainsong Music from the liturgy of the early church, characterized by free rhythms, monophonic texture, and sung *a cappella*.

chorale (kuh-RAL) [Gr.] Congregational song or hymn of the German Protestant (Evangelical) Church.

chord Three or more pitches sounded simultaneously.

chord, block Three or more pitches sounded simultaneously.

chord, broken Three or more pitches sounded in succession; see also arpeggio.

chromatic (kroh-MAT-ik) [Gr.] Moving up or down by half steps. Also the name of a scale composed entirely of half steps.

Classical period The period in Western history beginning around 1750 and lasting until around 1820 that reflected a time when society began looking to the ancient Greeks and Romans for examples of order and ways of looking at life.

clef The symbol at the beginning of the staff that identifies a set of pitches; see also bass clef and treble clef.

coda Ending section; a concluding portion of a composition. (⊕)

common time Another name for 4/4 meter; see also cut time. (𝐜)

composer The creator of musical works.

compound meter Meter whose beat can be subdivided into threes and/or sixes.

con (kohn) [It.] With.

con brio (kohn BREE-oh) [It.] With spirit; vigorously.

concerto Composition for solo instrument and an orchestra, usually with three movements.

con moto (kohn MOH-toh) [It.] With motion.

consonance A musical interval or chord that sounds pleasing; opposite of dissonance.

Contemporary period The time from 1900 to right now.

continuo A Baroque tradition in which the bass line is played "continuously," by a cello, double bass, and/or bassoon while a keyboard instrument (harpsichord, organ) plays the bass line and indicated harmonies.

contrapuntal See counterpoint.

counterpoint The combination of simultaneous parts; see polyphony.

crescendo (*cresc.*) (kreh-SHEN-doh) [It.] To gradually become louder.

cued notes Smaller notes indicating either optional harmony or notes from another voice part.

cut time 2/2 time with the half note getting the beat. (¢)

D

da capo (*D.C.*) (dah KAH-poh) [It.] Go back to the beginning and repeat; see also dal segno and al fine.

dal segno (*D.S.*) (dahl SAYN-yoh) [It.] Go back to the sign and repeat. (𝄋)

D. C. al fine (dah KAH-poh ahl FEE-neh) [It.] Repeat back to the beginning and end at the "fine."

decrescendo (*decresc.*) (deh-kreh-SHEN-doh) [It.] To gradually become softer.

delicato Delicate; to play or sing delicately.

descant A high, ornamental voice part often lying above the melody.

diaphragm The muscle that separates the chest cavity (thorax) from the abdomen. The primary muscle in the inhalation/exhalation cycle.

diction Clear and correct enunciation.

diminished The term describing an interval that has been descreased by half steps; for example, the *perfect fourth* (3 whole and one half steps) becomes a *diminished fourth* (3 whole steps). Also used for a triad which has a minor third (R, 3) and a diminished fifth (R, 5); for example, C, E♭, G♭.

diminuendo (*dim.*) (duh-min-yoo-WEN-doh) [It.] Gradually getting softer; *see also* decrescendo.

diminution The halving of values; that is, halves become quarters, quarters become eighths, etc. Opposite of *augmentation*.

diphthong A combination of two vowel sounds consisting of a primary vowel sound and a secondary vowel sound. The secondary vowel sound is (usually) at the very end of the diphthong; for example, in the word *toy*, the diphthong starts with the sound of "o," then moves on to "y," in this case pronounced "ee."

dissonance Discord in music, suggesting a state of tension or "seeking"; chords using seconds, fourths, fifths, and sevenths; the opposite of consonance.

divisi (*div.*) (dih-VEE-see) [It.] Divide; the parts divide.

dolce (DOHL-chay) [It.] Sweet; *dolcissimo*, very sweet; *dolcemente*, sweetly.

dominant The fifth degree of a major or minor scale; the triad built on the fifth degree; indicated as V in harmonic analysis.

Dorian mode A scale with the pattern of whole-step, half, whole, whole, whole, half, and whole. For example, D to D on the keyboard.

dotted rhythm A note written with a dot increases its value again by half.

double bar Two vertical lines placed on the staff indicating the end of a section or a composition; used with two dots to enclose repeated sections.

double flat (♭♭) Symbol showing the lowering of a pitch one whole step (two half steps).

double sharp (𝄪) Symbol showing the raising of a pitch one whole step (two half steps).

doubling The performance of the same note by two parts, either at the same pitch or an octave apart.

downbeat The accented first beat in a measure.

D. S. al coda (dahl SAYN-yoh ahl KOH-dah) [It.] Repeat from the symbol (𝄋) and skip to the coda when you see the sign. (⊕)

D. S. al fine (dahl SAYN-yoh ahl FEE-neh) [It.] Repeat from the symbol (𝄋) and sing to fine or the end.

duple Any time signature or group of beats that is a multiple of two.

duet Composition for two performers.

dynamics The volume of sound, the loudness or softness of a musical passage; intensity, power.

E

enharmonic Identical tones that are named and written differently; for example, C sharp and D flat.

ensemble A group of musicians or singers who perform together.

enunciation Speaking and singing words with distinct vowels and consonants.

espressivo (*espress.*) (es-preh-SEE-vo) [It.] For expression; *con espressione*, with feeling.

ethnomusicology The musical study of specific world cultures.

expressive singing To sing with feeling.

exuberance Joyously unrestrained and enthusiastic.

F

fermata (fur-MAH-tah) [It.] A hold; to hold the note longer. (⌢)

fine (FEE-neh) Ending; to finish.

flat Symbol (accidental) that lowers a pitch by one half step. (♭)

folk music Uncomplicated music that speaks directly of everyday matters; the first popular music; usually passed down through the oral tradition.

form The structure of a musical composition.

forte (*f*) (FOR-teh) [It.] Loud.

fortissimo (*ff*) (for-TEE-suh-moh) [It.] Very loud.

freely A direction that permits liberties with tempo, dynamics, and style.

fugue (FYOOG) [It.] A polyphonic composition consisting of a series of successive melody imitations; *see also* imitative style.

fusion A combination or blending of different genres of music.

G

gapped scale A scale resulting from leaving out certain tones (the pentatonic scale is an example).

grandioso [It.] Stately, majestic.

grand staff Two staves usually linked together by a long bar line and a bracket.

grave (GRAH-veh) [It.] Slow, solemn.

grazioso (grah-tsee-OH-soh) [It.] Graceful.

H

half step The smallest distance (interval) between two notes on a keyboard; the chromatic scale is composed entirely of half steps, shown as (˅).

half time *See* cut time.

harmonic interval Intervals that are sung or played simultaneously; *see also* melodic interval.

harmony Vertical blocks of different tones sounded simultaneously.

hemiola (hee-mee-OH-lah) [Gk.] A metric flow of two against a metric flow of three.

homophonic (hah-muh-FAH-nik) [Gk.] A texture where all parts sing similar rhythm in unison or harmony.

homophony (hah-MAH-fuh-nee) [Gk.] Music that consists of two or more voice parts with similar or identical rhythms. From the Greek words meaning "same sounds," homophony could be described as "hymn-style."

hushed A style marking indicating a soft, whispered tone.

I

imitation, imitative style Restating identical or nearly identical musical material in two or more parts.

improvised Invented on the spur of the moment.

improvisation Spontaneous musical invention, commonly associated with jazz.

interval The distance from one note to another; intervals are measured by the total steps and half steps between the two notes.

intonation The degree to which pitch is accurately produced in tune.

introduction An opening section at the beginning of a movement or work, preparatory to the main body of the form.

inversion May be applied to melody and harmony: *melodic inversion* occurs in an exchange of ascending and descending movement (for instance, a third becomes a sixth, a fourth becomes a fifth, etc.); *harmonic inversion* occurs in the position of the chord tones (that is, root position with the root as lowest tone, first inversion with the third as lowest tone, and second inversion with the fifth as the lowest tone).

K

key The way tonality is organized around a tonal center; *see also* key signature.

key change Changing an initial key signature in the body of a composition.

key signature Designation of sharps or flats at the beginning of a composition to indicate its basic scale and tonality.

L

leading tone The seventh degree of a scale, so called because of its strong tendency to resolve upward to the tonic.

legato (leh-GAH-toh) [It.] Smooth, connected style.

ledger lines Short lines that appear above, between treble and bass clefs, or below the bass clef, used to expand the notation.

leggiero (leh-JEH-roh) [It.] Articulate lightly; sometimes nonlegato.

lento Slow; a little faster than *largo*, a little slower than *adagio*.

linear flow, line Singing/playing notes in a flowing (smooth) manner, as if in a horizontal line.

liturgical Pertaining to prescribed forms of worship or ritual in various religious services. Western music contains much literature written for the liturgy of the early Roman Catholic Church.

lullaby A cradle song; in Western music, usually sung with a gentle and regular rhythm.

M

madrigal   A secular vocal form in several parts, popular in the Renaissance.

maestoso   (mah-eh-STOH-soh) [It.] Perform majestically.

major (key, scale, mode)   Scale built on the formula of two whole steps, one half step, three whole steps, one half step.

Letter Names:	G	A	B	C	D	E	F#	G
Movable Do:	do	re	mi	fa	so	la	ti	do
Numbers:	1	2	3	4	5	6	7	1

Major 2nd   The name for an interval of one whole step or two half steps. For example, from C to D.

Major 6th   The name for an interval of four whole steps and one-half step. For example, from C to A.

Major 3rd   The name for an interval of two whole steps or four half steps. For example, from C to E.

major triad   Three tones that form a major third *do* to *mi* and a minor third *mi* to *so* as in C E G.

marcato   (mahr-KAH-toh) [It.] Long but separated pitches; translated as marked.

mass   The main religious service of the Roman Catholic Church. There are two divisions of mass: the Proper of the Mass in which the text changes for each day, and the Ordinary of the Mass in which the text remains the same for every mass. Music for the mass includes the Kyrie, Gloria, Credo, Sanctus, and Agnus Dei as well as other chants, hymns, and psalms. For special mass occasions composers through the centuries have created large musical works for choruses, soloists, instrumentalists, and orchestras.

measure   The space from one bar line to the next; also called bars.

One Measure   One Measure

medieval   Historical period prior to the Renaissance, c. 500-1450.

medley   A group of tunes, linked together and sung consecutively.

melisma (n.) or melismatic (adj.)   (muh-LIZ-mah or muh-liz-MAT-ik) [Gk.] A term describing the setting of one syllable of text to several pitches.

son, e - le - - i - son.
us, On - us - mer - cy.

melodic interval   Intervals that are performed in succession; *see also* harmonic interval.

melody   A logical succession of musical tones; also called tune.

meter   The pattern into which a steady succession of rhythmic pulses (beats) is organized.

meter signature   The divided number at the beginning of a clef; 4/4, 3/4, and so forth; *see also* time signature.

metronome marking   A sign that appears over the top line of the treble clef staff at the beginning of a piece indicating the tempo. It shows the kind of note that will get the beat and the numbers of beats per minute as measured by a metronome; for example, ♪ = 100.

mezzo forte   (*mf*) (MEHT-soh FOR-teh) [It.] Medium loud.

mezzo piano   (*mp*) (MEHT-soh pee-AH-noh) [It.] Medium soft.

mezzo voce   (MET-soh VOH-cheh) [It.] With half voice; reduced volume and tone.

middle C   The note that is located nearest the center of the piano keyboard; middle C can be written in either the treble or bass clef.

minor (key, scale)   Scale built on the formula of one whole step, one half step, two whole steps, one half step, two whole steps.

Letter Names:	D	E	F	G	A	B♭	C	D
Movable Do:	la	ti	do	re	mi	fa	so	la
Numbers:	6	7	1	2	3	4	5	6

minor mode   One of two modes upon which the basic scales of Western music are based, the other being major; using W for a whole step and H for a half step, a minor scale has the pattern W H W W H W W.

minor triad   Three tones that form a minor third (bottom) and a major third (top), such as A C E.

minor third   The name for an interval of three half steps. For example, from A to C.

mixed meter   Frequently changing time signatures or meters.

moderato   Moderate.

modulation   Adjusting to a change of keys within a song.

molto   Very or much; for example, *molto rit.* means "much slower."

monophonic   (mah-nuh-FAH-nik) [Gk.] A musical texture having a single melodic line with no accompaniment; monophony.

monophony (muh-NAH-fuh-nee) [Gk.] One sound; music that has a single melody. Gregorian chants or plainsongs exhibit monophony.

motet Originating as a Medieval and Renaissance polyphonic song, this choral form of composition became an unaccompanied work, often in contrapuntal style.

motive A shortened expression, sometimes contained within a phrase.

musical variations Changes in rhythm, pitch, dynamics, style, and tempo to create new statements of the established theme.

mysterioso Perform in a mysterious or haunting way; to create a haunting mood.

N

nationalism Patriotism; pride of country. This feeling influenced many Romantic composers such as Wagner, Tchaikovsky, Dvořák, Chopin, and Brahms.

natural (♮) Cancels a previous sharp (♯) lowering the pitch a half step, or a previous flat (♭), raising the pitch a half step.

no breath mark A direction not to take a breath at a specific place in the composition. (⌐ ⌐ or **N.B.**)

non-harmonic tones Identifies those pitches outside the harmonic structure of the chord; for example, the *passing tone* and the *appoggiatura*.

non troppo (nahn TROH-poh) [It.] Not too much; for example, allegro non troppo, not too fast.

notation Written notes, symbols, and directions used to represent music within a composition.

nuance Subtle variations in tempo, phrasing, dynamics, etc., to enhance the musical performance.

O

octave An interval of twelve half steps; 8 or 8va = an octave above; 8vb = an octave below.

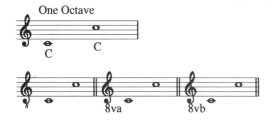
One Octave

opera A combination of singing, instrumental music, dancing, and drama that tells a story.

operetta A lighter, "popular" style of operatic form, including sung and spoken dialogue, solo, chorus, and dance.

optional divisi (*opt. div.*) Indicating a split in the music into optional harmony, shown by the smaller cued note.

opus, Op. The term, meaning "work," used by composers to show the chronological order of their works; for example, Opus 1, Op. 2.

oratorio A piece for solo voices, chorus, and orchestra, that is an expanded dramatic work on a literary or religious theme presented without theatrical action.

ostinato (ahs-tuh-NAH-toh) [It.] A rhythmic or melodic passage that is repeated continuously.

overtones The almost inaudible higher pitches which occur over the fundamental tone, resulting from the division of the vibrating cycle into smaller segments; compare to partials, harmonics.

P

palate The roof of the mouth; the *hard palate* is forward, the *soft palate* (*velum*) is at the back.

parallel major and minor keys Major and minor keys having the same tonic, such as A major and A minor (A major being the parallel major of A minor and A minor the parallel minor of A major).

parallel motion The movement of two or more voice parts in the same direction, at the same interval from each other.

peak The high point in the course of a development; for example, the high point of a musical phrase or the high point in a movement of instrumental music.

pentatonic scale A five-tone scale constructed of *do, re, mi, so, la* (degrees 1, 2, 3, 5, 6) of a corresponding major scale.

Perfect 5th The name for an interval of three whole steps and one half step. For example, C to G.

Perfect 4th The name for an interval of two whole steps and one half step. For example, C to F.

phrase A musical sentence containing a beginning, middle, and end.

phrase mark In music, an indicator of the length of a phrase in a melody; this mark may also mean that the singer or musician should not take a breath for the duration of the phrase. (⌒)

phrasing The realization of the phrase structure of a work; largely a function of a performer's articulation and breathing.

pianissimo (*pp*) (pee-uh-NEE-suh-moh) [It.] Very soft.

piano (*p*) (pee-ANN-noh) [It.] Soft.

Picardy third An interval of a major third used in the final, tonic chord of a piece written in a minor key.

pick-up *See* upbeat.

pitch Sound, the result of vibration; the highness or lowness of a tone, determined by the number of vibrations per second.

piu (pew) [It.] More; for example, *piu forte* means "more loudly."

poco (POH-koh) [It.] Little; for example, *poco dim.* means "a little softer."

poco a poco (POH-koh ah POH-koh) [It.] Little by little; for example, *poco a poco cresc.* means "little by little increase in volume."

polyphony (n.) or polyphonic (adj.) (pah-LIH-fuh-nee or pah-lee-FAH-nik) [Gk.] The term that means that each voice part begins at a different place, is independent and important, and that sections often repeat in contrasting dynamic levels. Poly = many, phony = sounds.

polyrhythmic The simultaneous use of contrasting rhythmic figures.

presto (PREH-stoh) [It.] Very fast.

program music A descriptive style of music composed to relate or illustrate a specific incident, situation, or drama; the form of the piece is often dictated or influenced by the nonmusical program. This style commonly occurs in music composed during the Romantic period. For example, "The Moldau" from *Má Vlast*, by Bedřich Smetana.

progression A succession of two or more pitches or chords; also melodic or harmonic progression.

R

rallentando (*rall.*) (rahl-en-TAHN-doh) [It.] Meaning to "perform more and more slowly." *See also* ritardando.

recitative (res-uh-TAY-teev) [It.] A speechlike style of singing used in opera, oratorio, and cantata.

register, vocal A term used for different parts of a singer's range, such as head register (high notes) and chest register (low notes).

relative major and minor keys The relative minor of any major key or scale, while sharing its key signature and pitches, takes for its tonic the sixth scale degree of that major key or scale. For example, in D major the sixth scale degree is B (or *la* in solfège), *la* then becomes the tonic for A minor.

D major　　B minor

Renaissance period The historic period in Western Europe from c. 1430 to 1600; the term means "rebirth" or "renewal"; it indicates a period of rapid development in exploration, science, art, and music.

repeat sign A direction to repeat the section of music (‖:‖); if the first half of this sign is omitted, it means to "go back to the beginning" (:‖).

repetition The restatement of a musical idea; repeated pitches; repeated "A" section in ABA form.

resolution (*res.*) A progression from a dissonant tone or harmony to a consonant harmony; a sense of completion.

resonance Reinforcement and intensification of sound by vibrations.

rest Symbols used to indicated silence.

rhythm The pattern of sounds and silences.

rhythmic motif A rhythmic pattern that is repeated throughout a movement or composition.

ritardando (*rit.*) The gradual slowing of tempo; also called "ritard."

Rococo Music of the Baroque period so elaborate it was named after a certain type of fancy rock work.

Romantic period A historic period starting c. 1820 and ending c. 1900 in which artists and composers attempted to break with classical music ideas.

rondo form An instrumental form based on an alternation between a repeated (or recurring) section and contrasting episodes (ABACADA).

root The bottom note of a triad in its original position; the note on which the chord is built.

round A composition in which the perpetual theme (sometimes with harmonic parts) begins in one group and is strictly imitated in other groups in an overlapping fashion. Usually the last voice to enter becomes the final voice to complete the song.

rubato (roo-BAH-toh) [It.] Freely; allows the conductor or the performer to vary the tempo.

S

sacred music Of or dealing with religious music; hymns, chorales, early masses; *see* secular music.

scale A pattern of pitches arranged by whole steps and half steps.

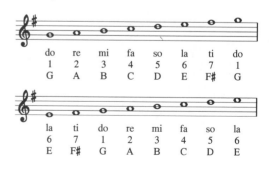

	do	re	mi	fa	so	la	ti	do
	1	2	3	4	5	6	7	1
	G	A	B	C	D	E	F#	G

	la	ti	do	re	mi	fa	so	la
	6	7	1	2	3	4	5	6
	E	F#	G	A	B	C	D	E

score   The arrangement of instrumental and vocal staffs that all sound at the same time.

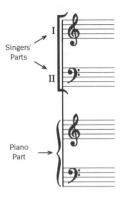

secular music   Music without religious content; *see* sacred music.

sempre   (SEHM-preh) [It.] Always, continually.

seventh chord   By adding a seventh above the root of a triad (R, 3, 5), the result is a four-tone chord (R, 3, 5, 7).

sforzando   (*sfz*) (sfohr-TSAHN-doh) [It.] A sudden strong accent on a note or chord.

sharp   A symbol (accidental) that raises a pitch by one half step. (♯)

sight-sing   Reading and singing of music at first sight.

simile   (*sim.*) (SIM-ee-leh) [It.] To continue in the same way.

simple meter   Meter in which each beat is divisible by 2.

skip   Melodic movement in intervals larger than a whole step.

slur   Curved line placed over or under a group of notes to indicate that they are to be performed without a break. (   )

solfège   (SOHL-fehj) [Fr.] A method of sight-singing, using the syllables *do, re, mi, fa, so, la, ti*, etc. for pitches of the scale.

solo   Composition for one featured performer.

sonata-allegro form   (suh-NAH-tuh ah-LEH-groh) [It.] Large A B A form consisting of three sections: exposition, development, and recapitulation.

soprano   The higher female voice.

sostenuto   (SAHS-tuh-noot-oh) [It.] The sustaining of a tone or the slackening of tempo; the right pedal of a piano, which, when depressed, allows the strings to vibrate.

sotto voce   In a quiet, subdued manner; "under" the voice.

spirito   (SPEE-ree-toh) [It.] Spirited; for example, *con spirito*, with spirit.

spiritual   A type of song created by African Americans who combined African rhythms with melodies they created and heard in America.

staccato   (stah-KAH-toh) [It.] Performed in a short, detached manner, as opposed to legato.

staff   Series of five horizontal lines and four spaces on which music is written to show pitch.

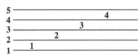

staggered entrances   Voice parts or instruments begin singing or playing at different points within the composition.

steady beat   A metrical pulse; *see also* beat, meter, rhythm.

step   Melodic movement from one note to the next adjacent note, either higher or lower.

stepwise melodic movement   Motion from one note to an adjacent one.

stress   Emphasis on certain notes or rhythmic elements.

strong beat   Naturally accented beats; beats 1 and 3 in 4/4 meter, beat 1 in 3/4 meter.

strophic   Description of a song in which all the stanzas of the text are sung to the same music; opposite of *through-composed*.

style   The particular character of a musical work; often indicated by words at the beginning of a composition, telling the performer the general manner in which the piece is to be performed.

subito   (sub.) (SOO-bee-toh) [It.] Suddenly; for example, *sub. piano* means "suddenly soft."

suspension or suspended tone   The tone or tones in a chord that are held as the remainder of the notes change to a new chord. The sustained tones often form a *dissonance* with the new chord, into which they then resolve.

sustained tone   A tone sustained in duration; sometimes implying a slowing of tempo; *sostenuto* or *sostenendo*, abbreviated *sost.*

swing   This is a performance style in which a pair of eighth notes ( ) are no longer performed evenly, but instead like a triplet ( ), yet they are still written ( ); usually indicated at the beginning of a song or a section.

symphony   An extended work in several movements, for orchestra; also an orchestra configured to perform symphonic music.

syncopation   Deliberate shifts of accent so that a rhythm goes against the steady beat; sometimes referred to as the "offbeat."

T

tactus   (TAKT-us) [Lt.] The musical term for "beat" in the fifteenth and sixteenth century; generally related to the speed of the human heart.

tempo   A pace with which music moves, based on the speed of the underlying beat.

tempo I or tempo primo   Return to the first tempo.

tenor   A high male voice, lower than the alto, but higher than bass.

tenuto   (teh-NOO-toh) [It.] Stress and extend the marked note. (ē)

text   Words, usually set in a poetic style, that express a central thought, idea, moral, or narrative.

texture   The thickness of the different layers of horizontal and vertical sounds.

theme and variation form   A musical form in which variations of the basic theme comprise the composition.

tie   A curved line connecting two successive notes of the same pitch, indicating that the second note is not to be articulated. ( )

timbre   Tone color; the unique quality produced by a voice or instrument.

time signature   The sign placed at the beginning and within a composition to indicate the meter; for example, 4/4, 3/4; *see also* cut time, meter signature.

to coda   Skip to the ⊕ or CODA.

tonality   The organized relationships of pitches with reference to a definite key center. In Western music, most tonalities are organized by the major and minor scales.

tone   A sound quality of a definite pitch.

tone color, quality, or timbre   That which distinguishes the voice or tone of one singer or instrument from another; for example, a soprano from an alto or a flute from a clarinet.

tonic chord   (TAH-nik kord) [Gk.] The name of a chord built on the tonal center of a scale; for example, C E G or *do, mi, so* for C major.

tonic or tonal center   The most important pitch in a scale; *do*; the home tone; the tonal center or root of a key or scale.

tonic triad   A three-note chord comprising root, third, and fifth; for example, C E G.

transposition   The process of changing the key of a composition.

treble clef   The symbol that appears at the beginning of the staff used for higher voices, instruments, or the piano right hand; generally referring to pitches above middle C, it wraps around the line for G, therefore it is also called the G-clef.

triad   A three-note chord built in thirds above a root tone.

trill   A rapid change between the marked note and the one above it within the same key. (*tr*⌇⌇)

triplet   A group of notes in which three notes of equal duration are sung in the time normally given to two notes of equal duration.

troppo   (TROHP-oh) [It.] Too much; for example, *allegro non troppo*, not too fast.

troubadour   A wandering minstrel of noble birth in southern France, Spain, and Italy during the eleventh to thirteenth centuries.

tuning   The process of adjusting the tones of voices or instruments so they will sound the proper pitches.

tutti   (TOO-tee) [It.] Meaning "all" or "together."

twelve-tone music   Twentieth-century system of writing music in which the twelve tones of the chromatic scale are arranged into a tone row (numbered 1 to 12), and then the piece is composed by arranging and rearranging the "row" in different ways; for example, backward, forward, or in clusters of three or four pitches.

U

unison   Voice parts or instruments sounding the same pitches in the same rhythm simultaneously.

upbeat   A weak beat preceding the downbeat.

V

variation   *See* theme and variation form, musical variations.

vivace   (vee-VAH-chay) [It.] Very fast; lively.

voice crossing (or voice exchange)   When one voice "crosses" above or below another voice part.

W

whole step   The combination of two successive half steps. (⌐⌐)

whole tone scale   A scale consisting only of whole steps.

For use with Sight-Singing exercises. Use the keyboard and notation on this page to identify and perform the notes in your voice part.

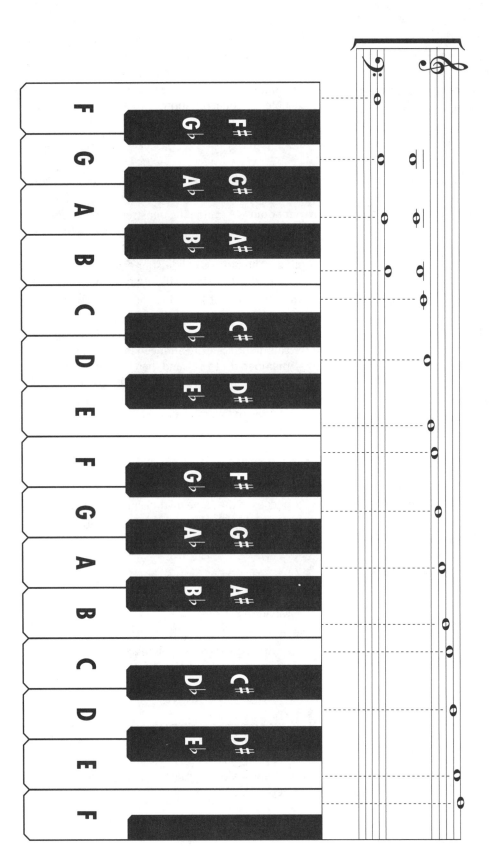